INTRODUCTION

to the

U.S. LEGAL SYSTEM

for

FOREIGN-TRAINED LAWYERS

INTRODUCTION
to the
U.S. LEGAL SYSTEM
for
FOREIGN-TRAINED LAWYERS

MARY L. PERRY

Carolina Academic Press
Durham, North Carolina

LIBRARY OF CONGRESS CATALOGING-IN-PUBLICATION DATA

Names: Perry, Mary L., author.
Title: Introduction to the U.S. legal system for foreign-trained
lawyers / by Mary L. Perry.
Other titles: Introduction to the US legal system for
foreign-trained lawyers
Description: Durham, North Carolina : Carolina Academic Press, 2021.
Identifiers: LCCN 2021017640 (print) | LCCN 2021017641 (ebook) |
ISBN 9781531022846 (paperback) | ISBN 9781531022853 (ebook)
Subjects: LCSH: Law--Study and teaching--United States. |
Lawyers, Foreign--United States. | Practice of law--United States |
Law students--United States
Classification: LCC KF283 .P47 2021 (print) | LCC KF283 (ebook) |
DDC 349.73--dc23
LC record available at https://lccn.loc.gov/2021017640
LC ebook record available at https://lccn.loc.gov/2021017641

Carolina Academic Press
700 Kent Street
Durham, North Carolina 27701
Telephone (919) 489-7486
Fax (919) 493-5668
www.cap-press.com

Printed in the United States of America

To Mike

Thank you for your love and support through the decades.

— ★ —

CONTENTS

THREE

SOME BACKGROUND ON U.S. HISTORY AND GOVERNMENTAL STRUCTURE ★ 21

FOUR

CHOOSING A COURT ★ 31

FIVE

WHAT LAW APPLIES? ★ 95

SIX

THE ANATOMY OF A LAWSUIT: TRIAL COURT ★ 121

TABLES OF AUTHORITIES ★ 229

INDEX ★ 237

— ★ —

PREFACE

To the Foreign-Trained Law Student:

For more than a decade, I had the privilege of teaching an introductory course on U.S. law to foreign-trained lawyers as part of Washington University Law's LL.M. program. Early in my teaching of that course, I noticed that many students were struggling despite being talented and diligent. They were struggling to keep up with their coursework, to answer questions in class, and to synthesize the materials so that they could present effective answers to exam questions. After using an existing casebook and examining other possible book options, I decided to create my own materials that would address the particular sources of the challenges that I observed. Those materials, which I used and refined over seven years, are the basis for this casebook.

Studying U.S. law as a foreign-trained lawyer presents unique challenges. On one hand, your knowledge of the U.S. legal system is less than that of your U.S. peers who have been taught or have absorbed background information about the U.S. legal system simply by having spent their lives in the United States. And in any upper-level class, the J.D. students will have acquired further legal knowledge because they will have completed the entire first-year curriculum, whereas you may be taking your first 1L course while also taking upper-level courses.

On the other hand, your knowledge of *a* legal system—albeit your own legal system, not the U.S. system—is superior to your J.D. peers' knowledge of *any* legal system. You already have completed your study of one legal system and may have even practiced in that legal system. In contrast, many of your J.D. peers are still learning a *first* legal system. But this advantage over your peers can also be a detriment in that the assumptions you bring based on your prior education can get in the way of learning U.S. law, particularly if you let that prior information fill in any gaps in your understanding of U.S. law.

These are challenges you can overcome, though. In fact, these challenges may be why you have chosen to study U.S. law: you understand that U.S. law is very different from what you have studied before, and you are curious to learn more about it.

The materials that I have selected for this textbook were chosen to ease your transition to the study of U.S. law. Fundamental concepts regarding the U.S. legal system are introduced throughout the book and presented in contexts that help to show their significance. The book also focuses on concepts or issues that will appear in the cases that you read for other classes. For instance, you may read a case in a torts class where a federal court applies state law or a case in a class on corporate law where the appellate court reviews the trial court's grant of a motion to dismiss. The application of state law in federal court or the procedural device of a motion to dismiss is not the point of reading those cases for your torts or corporate-law classes. Students who have completed the 1L curriculum will realize that and not be distracted by those concepts. This text will give you a concise introduction to common concepts and ideas so that they will not be distractions for you as well. And, whenever possible, the text specifically addresses potential differences between other legal systems in general and the U.S. legal system in particular.

Even the way of learning in a U.S. law school can be shockingly different for some foreign-trained lawyers. For that reason, this book uses cases, rather than exposition, to illustrate important concepts. By using cases to teach these preliminary concepts, you will begin immediately to experience learning in a typical U.S. law school classroom. The book also prepares you for this manner of learning by addressing how to prepare for class and how to synthesize law that has developed through a string of judicial decisions, for example.

I hope that this book is as helpful for you as the materials have been for the hundreds of students who have used them over the years at Washington University Law. I have confidence in your ability to excel in your new educational environment with the assistance provided by an introductory course such as the one you are about to take using this book as its text.

A final note: To allow you to focus on key issues, the cases reproduced in this book do not contain all of the citations included in the published cases. The omission of citations is not indicated by ellipses or any other notation. Any removal of text is, however, indicated by ellipses.

Mary L. Perry
St. Louis, Missouri
March 2021

INTRODUCTION

to the

U.S. LEGAL SYSTEM

for

FOREIGN-TRAINED LAWYERS

— ★ —

ONE

THE IMPORTANCE OF READING

A. INTRODUCTION

Do you have an image in your mind of what attending a U.S. law school will be like? If you do, and if that image has you poring over a textbook, then you have a realistic view of law school. Yes, law school will involve writing, particularly if you take a seminar or a legal writing class. And, yes, there will be simulations if you take courses such as negotiations or participate in moot court. You will also attend interesting lectures and observe lively discussions in the classroom. But there is no escaping the truth that you will spend the majority of your time reading class assignments.

Reading will not only take much of your time but also be essential to your learning. In the American system of legal education, in-class instruction is not intended or designed to teach you everything that you need to know. Classroom instruction merely introduces you to the relevant rules and concepts. The details are left for you to learn outside of class through your reading.

Considering the large amount of time that you will spend reading and the importance of that reading to your legal education, it makes sense to examine how to read legal textbooks effectively and efficiently.

B. GENERAL READING STRATEGIES FOR NON-NATIVE ENGLISH SPEAKERS

One of the greatest challenges for non-native speakers of English is developing a reading speed comparable to that of native speakers. All students — whether or not they are native-English speakers — initially find that reading legal textbooks takes considerable time. Native speakers, however, typically become considerably faster and more effective at reading assignments as the semester progresses. Eventually, they will often increase their reading speed to 250 (or more) words per minute because that speed will be necessary to complete all of the assignments. *See* Ruth Ann McKinney, Reading Like a Lawyer: Time-Saving Strategies for Reading Law Like an Expert 268 (Carolina Academic Press 2d ed. 2014). But that reading speed will not come naturally to most non-native English speakers. The good news, though, is that while it may take some work, you can increase your reading speed if you focus on the following reading techniques.

1. Read in Meaningful Chunks

One way to increase reading speed is to put words together that represent a unit of meaning and read these words almost as one single word. Native-English speakers often read in this way. In contrast, many non-native speakers read a passage word by word, sometimes even sub-vocalizing the words (speaking them in their minds). This approach can slow a reader down dramatically.

Take the following sentence, for example: "This appeal arises from a final judgment entered on a jury verdict for damages incurred by [the plaintiffs] as a result of the discovery that their bedroom and bathroom contained 'two-way' mirrors...." *Mas v. Perry*, 489 F.2d 1396, 1398 (1974).

Word by word reading will treat each word as a separate item:

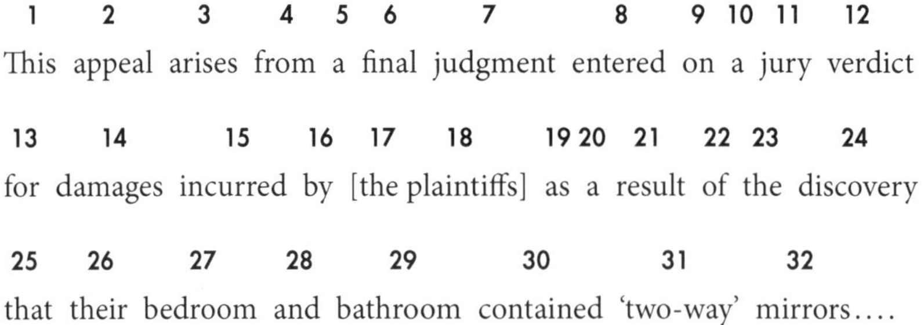

The time required to read a passage in this manner is as long as the time it would take to read it aloud. It will take much less time if you instead read in meaningful "chunks." For example, the passage above, which contains 32 words, can be read as 5 meaningful "chunks:"

1 This appeal arises from a final judgment 2 entered on a jury verdict

3 for damages incurred by [the plaintiffs] 4 as a result of the discovery

5 that their bedroom and bathroom contained 'two-way' mirrors....

Rather than reading, "This – appeal – arises – from – a – final – judgment," a reader who reads in meaningful units would read "Thisappealarisesfromafinaljudgment," almost as if it were a single word.

You may have been exposed to this chunking-method of reading in your English language studies. And, if not, there exists much material on the internet about this reading approach if you want to read more about it. Switching to this method will require some adjustments to your reading style, adjustments that will not happen overnight. Just like growing a muscle, you have to develop this reading "muscle." To do this, designate a time every day to practice reading using the chunking method. Keep track of your reading speed, but also write down how much of the reading you understand. Initially, it will not be much, but with consistent training, you will see a steady improvement.

Keep in mind that the chunking method will not work for all legal reading, but it will work well as a method of reading cases for your classes. For a contract, though, the method may not work as well, because the specific meaning of certain words, phrases, and sentences may be so important that you will have to use the word-by-word method. However, even then, a first reading using the chunking method will make it easier to return to the document and look for specific words.

★ EXERCISE 1 ★

How would you read the following excerpts from judicial decisions if you were using the chunking method? How would you group the words into meaningful chunks? As you read, circle each group of words that represents a unit of meaning.

a. "[T]he railroad is not liable for injuries to undiscovered trespassers resulting from its negligence, unless it be wanton or willful." *Erie R.R. Co. v. Tompkins*, 304 U.S. 64, 70 (1938).

b. "There, Brown & Yellow, a Kentucky corporation..., and the Louisville & Nashville Railroad, also a Kentucky corporation, wished that the former should have the exclusive privilege of soliciting passenger and baggage transportation at the Bowling Green, Ky., Railroad station." *Erie R.R. Co. v. Tompkins*, 304 U.S. 64, 73 (1938).

c. "During closing argument, plaintiff suggested that the jury think about plaintiff's injury in terms of daily pain and suffering, and then determine what amount of damages would be appropriate compensation for each day of suffering. An average daily figure was suggested to the jury, which it could then multiply by the number of days plaintiff would live, counting from the day of the accident until the end of her life expectancy, some thirty-five years." *Debus v. Grand Union Stores*, 621 A.2d 1288, 1290 (Vt. 1993).

d. "The jury brought in a verdict of $30,000; and the judgment entered thereon was affirmed by the Circuit Court of Appeals, which held that it was unnecessary to consider whether the law of Pennsylvania was as contended, because the question was one not of local, but of general, law, and that 'upon questions of general law the federal courts are free, in absence of a local statute, to exercise their independent judgment as to what the law is; and it is well settled that the question of the responsibility of a railroad for injuries caused by its servants is one of general law." *Erie R.R. Co. v. Tompkins*, 304 U.S. 64, 70 (1938).

2. Use the Entire Passage to Help Understand Unknown Words

To improve reading speed, you will want to avoid consulting a dictionary every time you encounter a word that you do not know. If the word is a legal term, you may indeed need to consult a dictionary. But if the word is just an English word with which you are not familiar, the reading will often contain enough background or contextual information to help you understand the word's meaning without ever consulting a dictionary. Deriving the meaning of the word in this manner will save you considerable time.

How does the context help you understand words whose meaning you otherwise did not know? As an example, let's consider the very first paragraph in this chapter:

> Do you have an image in your mind of what attending a U.S. law school will be like? If you do, and if that image has you poring over a textbook, then you

> have a realistic view of law school. Yes, law school will involve writing, particularly if you take a seminar or a legal writing class. And, yes, there will be simulations if you take courses such as negotiations or participate in moot court. You will also attend interesting lectures and observe lively discussions in the classroom. But there is no escaping the truth that you will spend the vast majority of your time reading class assignments.

Even if you were uncertain as to the meaning of the word "poring," the paragraph contained numerous clues as to the word's meaning. For one, you knew immediately that "poring" was something that a person does with a book. From that hint alone, "reading" may have jumped into your mind as a possible meaning for the word. That potential meaning was reinforced as you read the remainder of the paragraph. The last sentence starts with the word "but," signaling a contrast from "writing" or "simulations," the topics of the prior two sentences. Then, the last sentence reveals the meaning of "poring," as it explains that most of your time will be spent "reading." Thus, if you had read the entire paragraph (quickly using chunking), you would have learned the meaning of "poring" without ever interrupting your reading to consult a dictionary.

"Simulations" may have been another challenging word in that passage, but you did not need to consult a dictionary for the meaning of this word, either. Unlike "poring," whose meaning could be determined from the passage, the passage does not clearly reveal the meaning of "simulations." Nevertheless, the paragraph contains numerous hints that the meaning of that word was not important. The paragraph's focus is "reading." The third through fifth sentences (which include the word "simulations") explain that law school will involve more than reading, although those other activities will not be as important as reading. Indeed, the title of the chapter—The Importance of Reading—reaffirms that anything unrelated to "reading" is not the chapter's focus. "Simulations" (whatever they may be) are not "reading," and hence it is not necessary to understand precisely what they are.

Now let's look at a more challenging passage from a case in Chapter 6 of this book—*Sioux City & Pacific Railroad Co. v. Stout*. The words that might cause you to stop and get the dictionary are highlighted below in gray.

> That the turntable was a dangerous machine, which would be likely to cause injury to children who resorted to it, might fairly be inferred from the injury which actually occurred to the plaintiff....
>
> So, in looking at the remoteness of the machine from inhabited dwellings, when it was proved to the jury that several boys from the hamlet were

> at play there on this occasion, and that they had been at play upon the turntable on other occasions, and within the observation and to the knowledge of the employees of the defendant, the jury were justified in believing that children would probably resort to it, and that the defendant should have anticipated that such would be the case.

The first word that may be challenging is "remoteness." The machine is remote "*from* inhabited dwellings." "From" indicates a separation between "the machine" and the "inhabited dwellings," and that is exactly what "remoteness" means here.

But what does "inhabited dwellings" mean? As you read further into the passage, you learn that there were "several boys from the hamlet." So a "hamlet," whatever it means precisely, is a place where a number of families live or congregate because "several boys" are "from" that place. You might begin to realize that the passage is saying that boys from a nearby town play on the machine even though the machine is not near their town. Thus, "inhabited dwellings" mean homes.

Next, consider the meaning of the word "observation." The sentence refers to "observation" and "knowledge." The use of the word "knowledge" indicates the defendant's employees knew that the children play on the machine. How might they know that children play on the machine? Because they have seen children play on the machine. That is the meaning of observation—the employees have seen the children playing on the machine.

Next the passage indicates that "children would probably resort to it." The first ambiguity to resolve is the meaning of "it" in this phrase. If you realized that "it" refers to the "machine," i.e., the turntable, you already knew that the children liked playing on the machine. In other words, "resort" in this context means "the children would probably" play on the machine. The sentence is building to the point that the children playing on the machine should not have been a surprise. And that brings us to the final word of uncertainty—"anticipated." "Anticipated" means that there should be no surprise as to what happened. Reading the paragraph as a whole, hopefully without turning to a dictionary, you can gather enough of the meaning of the passage to continue with your reading.

★ EXERCISE 2 ★

Without consulting a dictionary, read the following excerpts from judicial decisions. In each passage, what is the meaning of the words or phrases highlighted in gray? What contextual clues helped you understand those words or phrases?

a. "The trial court, unwilling to accept this testimony, adopted instead Brian Dailey's version of what happened, and made the following findings:

> '...Brian Dailey, picked up a lightly built wood and canvas lawn chair..., moved it sideways a few feet and seated himself therein, at which time he discovered the plaintiff, Ruth Garratt, about to sit down at the place where the lawn chair had formerly been, at which time he hurriedly got up from the chair and attempted to move it toward Ruth Garratt to aid her in sitting down in the chair;...due to the defendant's small size and lack of dexterity he was unable to get the lawn chair under the plaintiff in time to prevent her from falling to the ground. That plaintiff fell to the ground and sustained a fracture of her hip, and other injuries and damages as hereinafter set forth.'

...

"We have here the conceded volitional act of Brian, i.e., the moving of a chair. Had the plaintiff proved to the satisfaction of the trial court that Brian moved the chair while she was in the act of sitting down, Brian's action would patently have been for the purpose or with the intent of causing the plaintiff's bodily contact with the ground, and she would be entitled to a judgment against him for the resulting damages." *Garratt v. Dailey*, 46 Wash. 2d 197, 199, 201 (1955).

b. "On April 19, 1932, the defendant, while locked in her room, had a violent attack. The plaintiff heard a crashing of furniture and then knew that the defendant was ugly, violent and dangerous. The defendant told the plaintiff and a Miss Maroney, 'the maid,' who was with the plaintiff in the adjoining room, that if they came into the defendant's room, she would kill them. The plaintiff and Miss Maroney looked into the defendant's room, 'saw what the defendant had done,' and 'thought it best to take the broken stuff away before she did any harm to herself with it.' They sent for a Mr. Emerton, the defendant's brother-in-law. When he arrived the defendant was in the middle of her room about ten feet from the door, holding upraised the leg of a low-boy as if she were going to strike. The plaintiff stepped into the room and walked toward the defendant, while Mr. Emerton and Miss Maroney remained in the doorway. As the plaintiff approached the defendant and tried to take hold of the defendant's hand which held the leg, the defendant struck the plaintiff's

Ana Maria Bettin.

head with it, causing the injuries for which the action was brought." *McGuire v. Almy*, 297 Mass. 323, 324–25 (1937).

c. "The defendants then introduced evidence tending to show that at the time of the alleged sale it was believed by both the plaintiff and themselves that the cow was barren and would not breed; that she cost $850, and if not barren would be worth from $750 to $1,000; that after the date of the letter, and the order to Graham, the defendants were informed by said Graham that in his judgment the cow was with calf, and therefore they instructed him not to deliver her to plaintiff, and on the twentieth of May, 1886, telegraphed plaintiff what Graham thought about the cow being with calf, and that consequently they could not sell her. The cow had a calf in the month of October following." *Sherwood v. Walker*, 66 Mich. 568, 570–71 (1887).

d. "Unless otherwise indicated, an offer may be accepted in any manner reasonable under the circumstances. RESTATEMENT (SECOND) OF CONTRACTS § 30 (1981). Generally, '[t]he mode of expressing assent is inconsequential so long as it effectively makes known to the offeror that his offer has been accepted.' *Fujimoto v. Rio Grande Pickle Co.*, 414 F.2d 648, 652 (5th Cir.1969); *Embree, Inc. v. Sw. Bell Media, Inc.*, 772 S.W.2d 209, 211 (Tex.App.-Dallas 1989, writ denied). It is well established that acceptance may be shown by conduct. *Patrick v. Smith*, 90 Tex. 267, 38 S.W. 17, 19 (1896); *In re Citgo Petroleum Corp.*, 248 S.W.3d 769, 774 (Tex. App.-Beaumont 2008, no pet.); *see* RESTATEMENT (SECOND) OF CONTRACTS § 50 (1981). Horton's act in tendering the first installment of $500.00 was a clear, unequivocal act indicating acceptance. The act effectively informed [defendants] that the offer had been accepted and was within the time specified for acceptance of the offer. The contract was formed when Horton tendered the first installment." *Horton v. DaimlerChrysler Fin. Services Americas, LLC*, 262 S.W.3d 1, 6 (Tex. App. 2008).

3. Read the Edited Version of the Decision in Your Textbook, Not the Full Decision

Legal textbooks are often called casebooks. That nomenclature has developed precisely because these books primarily contain decisions from real cases. But the decisions (also sometimes called opinions) reported in your textbooks will not necessarily be the court's full decision. Indeed, most of what you will read for your classes will be edited versions of judicial decisions. For example, when a plaintiff files suit, the plaintiff might include a tort claim and a contract claim in that single lawsuit. If the resulting judicial decision is included in a textbook for a contracts class, the textbook's author will likely not include the decision's discussion of the tort claim. On the other hand, if the decision were included in a textbook for a torts class, the author would likely omit the contract-law discussion but include the discussion of the tort claim.

The editing of the cases may be even more nuanced. If a judicial opinion analyzes the existence of both an offer and an acceptance, an author who chooses to include that opinion in a contracts textbook might conclude that only the discussion of offer is significant. The edited version of the opinion that the author includes in the textbook might then omit the analysis of acceptance. By this editing, the author has indicated the portion of the opinion that you should know and understand — the portion discussing offer. You do not need to know anything about the portion of the opinion that analyzes the issue of acceptance.

Students sometimes think it will be helpful to read the full version of the case rather than, or in addition to, the edited version in their textbook, but that is rarely true. Reading the full version of the decision is unlikely to resolve any confusion that you may have after reading the edited version in your casebook, because your confusion is not due to the editing, but to the complex nature of the issue or to the court's writing style.

Not only does reading the full decision fail to solve problems, but also it can actually create them. It takes time — time that you will need to complete your assignments — to find the decision and read the portions that the author of your textbook has already deemed irrelevant as indicated by the author's choice not to include those portions of the decision in the textbook. Worse yet, reading the full case might make it more difficult for you to understand the aspect of the case that the author — and hence, your instructor as well — considers important for your studies. Thus, as a general rule, you should focus on the abbreviated versions of the decisions in your textbook. The textbook's author has tried to save you time by omitting irrelevant portions of the decision. Take advantage of that assistance and focus on the materials as presented in the textbook.

Lastly, in your country, legal education might have rewarded external, additional research and reading. But the U.S. legal system does not work in that way. You can excel in a U.S. law school by having command of the material that you have been assigned to read and an understanding of the discussions in class. Discussing law review articles, cases, or portions of cases not included in your textbook will not earn you additional points on your final exam.

— ★ —

TWO

UNDERSTANDING JUDICIAL DECISIONS IN A LEGAL TEXTBOOK

In a common law system, attorneys read cases to distill principles, and those principles often depend on the facts of the particular case. In contrast, in a civil law system, a student might be taught the legal principles detached from any factual context. This is a key and important distinction between your prior learning, if you studied in a civil law country, and the way of learning that you will experience in an LL.M. program in the United States. If you find yourself asking, "what is *the* rule that I should get from this case?", you are likely asking the wrong question, because most cases will give multiple rules or principles, and those rules or principles may need factual context to have any value. This way of learning will be one of our primary focuses during this course.

So, if during this class or any other, you read a case simply to identify a rule, you will have fallen far short of your mission. You must know the facts and reasoning of the case as well. Your instructors will therefore expect you to know the case in great detail, the kind of detail that can only be acquired through careful reading. The following are some strategies for reading that will best prepare you to understand a case at the required level.

A. IDENTIFY THE COURT AND DATE OF THE DECISION

Before reading even a single word of the court's decision, identify the court authoring the decision and determine whether the court is within a state or the federal judicial system. Federal courts will generally have the phrase "United States" in their names, such as "United States Court of Appeals" or "United States District Court." State courts will include the name of a state, such as New York Court of Appeals or Missouri Supreme Court. Next identify the level of the court within that judicial system. In the federal judicial system and most state judicial systems, there are three primary levels of courts: trial courts, intermediate appellate courts, and a single supreme court.

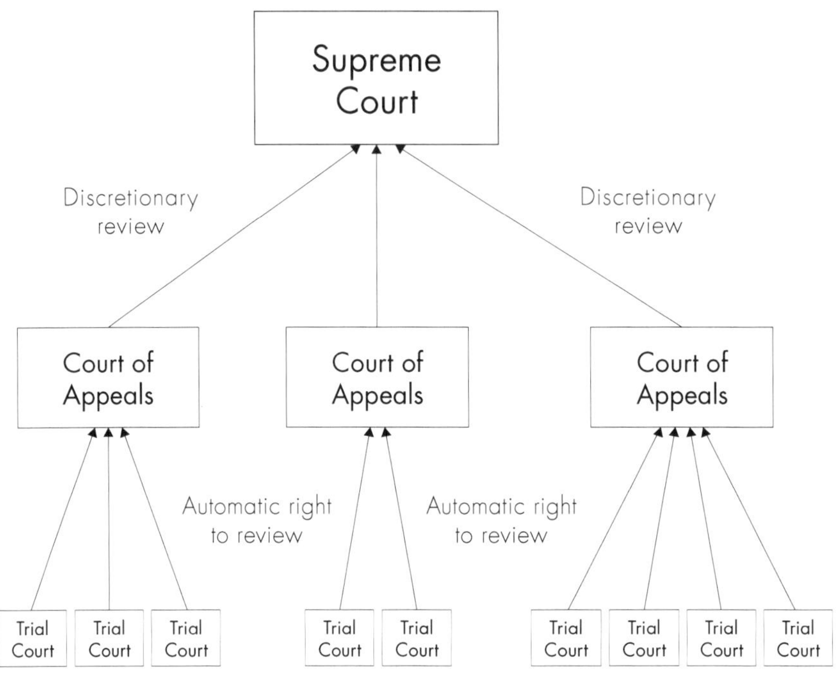

If a party is dissatisfied with the outcome in the trial court, there is commonly an automatic right to appeal to an intermediate appellate court. In other words, if the losing party timely and properly requests it, the intermediate appellate court must review that party's challenges to the trial court's decision and render an opinion on those challenges.

Any party dissatisfied with the decision of the intermediate appellate court may then request review by that judicial system's supreme court, typically by filing a petition for writ of certiorari. Unlike review by the intermediate appellate court, which is required if timely requested, the supreme court is not required to review most cases. Supreme courts tend to limit their review to cases that present new issues that are likely to recur or issues over which the lower courts have reached inconsistent conclusions. *See, e.g.,* S. Ct. R. 10. Because supreme courts accept review of a small percentage of cases that request it, an intermediate appellate court is generally the highest court to review most cases.

While most states describe their courts with the nomenclature used above, it is helpful to know that not all do. New York, for example, calls its highest court the Court of Appeals, its intermediate courts are called appellate divisions, and its civil trial courts are called Supreme Courts. *See* http://ww2.nycourts.gov/courts/8jd/structure.shtml. Be sure to pay attention to all of the signals in your reading to notice if you are reading a case from a jurisdiction that does not use the standard titles for its courts.

Lastly, identify the year of the decision. The information about the court, as well as the date of the decision, can be found after the case name before the text of the opinion even begins. The date of the decision is easy to identify, and so there is no reason not to know it. And sometimes the date can provide important context. Is the case very old or recent? Was the decision rendered during a significant time in history, such as during the Great Depression, or while the United States was involved in a war or while it was experiencing particular social upheaval? As you pay attention to the dates, you will begin to identify key times in U.S. history that may provide additional context to the decision you are about to read.

B. IDENTIFY THE PARTIES

Identifying the parties to the action is also a critical task to complete before reading the entire opinion. The case name, sometimes called the case caption, is a starting point, but certainly not an ending point, in identifying the parties. The case name or caption usually consists of one name for each of the opposing parties separated by a "v.". In the trial court, the first name in the caption is the name of one plaintiff (a party who filed the lawsuit). The second name in the caption will belong to one defendant (a party against whom the plaintiff has brought the action and seeks relief). Even if there are multiple plaintiffs and multiple defendants, only one name will appear on each side of the "v." Typically, the first plaintiff listed in the complaint appears as the plaintiff in the case caption (on the left side of the "v."), and the first-listed defendant in the complaint appears as the defendant in the case caption (on the right side of the "v.").

If a party is an individual (rather than a company or corporation), the name in the caption will typically be that party's last name. Thus, if the text of the complaint listed three plaintiffs in this order—Carol Chan, Jose Rodriguez, and Mary Smith — the plaintiff's portion of the trial court caption would be "Chan." The same will be true if there are multiple businesses or corporate parties on one side of the litigation. Only one of those names will be listed in the case caption. Thus, if Carol Chan were the first name listed in the complaint as a plaintiff and Waterworld, Incorporated, is the first of five defendants listed in the complaint, the case caption in the trial court would be *Chan v. Waterworld, Inc.* — the first-listed plaintiff versus the first-listed defendant.

On appeal, the parties pick up additional titles. The party who seeks review is called either an "appellant" or a "petitioner," depending on the terminology used in that court. The other party is known as the "appellee" (in courts using the term "appellant") or "respondent" (in courts using the term "petitioner").

In addition, the order of the parties' names in the caption may change in the case caption of a decision from an appellate court. In some appellate courts, the names of the plaintiff and the defendant remain in the same place in the caption regardless of which party is seeking review. But in other appellate courts, the order of the names in the caption reflects which party is seeking review. In those courts, the caption will list first the party seeking review; in other words, that party's name will appear before the "v." So, if the defendant seeks review, the names in the appellate caption would appear in different places from their places in the trial court caption. In other words, if Waterworld, Inc. lost in the trial court and sought review, the case caption in such a court would be *Waterworld, Inc. v. Chan*. Thus, when identifying the parties, you cannot assume the first-listed name in the caption is that of the plaintiff. Nor can you assume that the first-listed party is the party seeking review.

If the caption only identifies one plaintiff and one defendant, and not even necessarily their roles in the trial court, how does one identify the parties and their role in the litigation? That information is typically found within the text or body of the opinion, usually near the beginning. Because it is common for an important party not to be listed in the caption, you must be aware of the party-status of any individual or entity who is central to the decision, not just those names that appear in the case caption.

C. UNDERSTAND THE PROCEDURAL HISTORY

Legal textbooks mainly contain appellate decisions. As a result, the opinions in a legal textbook do not represent the first judicial decision concerning that case. Judicial proceedings in a lower court will have already occurred, and the opinion in your textbook will present the authoring court's review of the lower court's decision. This prior procedure in the lower court, often recited or described in the reviewing court's decision, is called the procedural history or procedural posture of the case. Because such procedure will be discussed in nearly every case that you read, we will study some of the most common and fundamental areas of procedure. By gaining some familiarity with those concepts, you should be able to understand those sections of your reading with greater ease, thereby allowing more time to focus on other aspects of the law presented by the opinion.

Because the other chapters will provide more specifics on procedure, at this point, you need only know that each case will describe the procedures that preceded the court's decision.

D. IDENTIFY THE DISPOSITION

Before reading the entire opinion, identify the court's result or ruling. That result might be that the court reversed the lower court's decision. Or the court may have vacated the lower court's ruling and sent the case back to the lower court for more proceedings. Alternatively, the court may have affirmed the lower court's ruling. Each of these results, and any other result that the court may create, is often called the "disposition," in other words, the manner in which the court disposed of the case.

If the court "**affirms**" the lower court, it leaves the *result* of the lower court in place; in other words, it does not change the result reached by the lower court. An appellate opinion that affirms the lower court, however, may not agree with the reasons given by that lower court. Indeed, the reviewing court may believe that the lower court's reasoning was completely wrong and yet affirm the lower court's decision. In that situation, the appellate court will give different reasoning for the result.

The meaning of the term "**reverse**" is not as uniform. One might think that a reversal should change the conclusion of the lower court, in other words, compel entry of a judgment opposite to that which the lower court had entered. However, this disposition — "reverse" — will also be used when the court vacates the lower court's ruling without directing a particular result. Instead, the reviewing court will direct the lower court to conduct further proceedings, often with the idea that the lower court should now proceed with the benefit of the insight as to the law provided by the reviewing court's opinion. Another characterization of this result is that the judgment is "**vacated and remanded**," that is, the lower court decision is set aside (vacated) and the case is returned to that court (remanded) for further proceedings. While these are the most commonly used phrases, courts are by no means limited to using them, although the use of others can create uncertainty for the lower court, the parties, and the reader.

As you read case decisions in this class and others, use your knowledge of the disposition of the case to help you understand the court's opinion and speed your ability to clarify areas of confusion.

E. USE EXTERNAL CUES

Before reading the entire case, it is also important to orient yourself to the instructor's purpose in having you read the case as well as the case's relationship to the larger subject matter that you are studying. Using available external cues, you can quickly achieve this orientation. Start first with the most general source of information: the table of contents in your textbook. Look at the title of the subsection in which the case is located in the book and the titles of the surrounding subsections. Look also at the title of the section in which these subsections are located. These titles will help you understand, at a very broad level, the author's purpose in including the case and the author's perception of the relationship of that case to the other cases that you will read or will have previously read.

Next, always read the material — usually quite brief — before the case. These passages will add to the knowledge that you gained from looking at the Table of Contents by providing more specifics about the law.

And finally, before reading the case, skim the Notes that follow the case. (After reading the case, reread the Notes in more detail.) The Notes will indicate what aspects of the case are important or unique. For example, the second note after the case *Garrett v. Dailey* in one torts textbook alerts the reader: "Note that the trial judge was the finder of fact at both trials." Beginning law students may not realize that it is unusual for the judge to be the factfinder in a torts case; usually, a jury fills that role. But the author tries to help beginning law students by alerting them to an aspect of the case that is both unusual and that might be relevant to class discussion. Paying attention to a note like this one will make you better prepared for class discussion.

F. STAY ENGAGED WITH THE READING

Once you begin reading the case, you will probably find, like most law students, that it is difficult to remain at a high level of engagement and interest when the reading is of any considerable length. Nevertheless, it is essential to success that you remain engaged with your reading. Legal reading requires so much more than simply reading to understand the words on the page.

To stay engaged with the reading, keep your body, not just your mind, involved in the reading process by writing as you read. Every time you pick up your pen to write a note you ensure that you are absorbing the content of the reading by summarizing the significance of what you have just read. The ideal place for these notes is the margin of your textbook—the white spaces on every page that surround the text. Many students are reluctant to write in their books because they plan to resell them, but the cost in time wasted by not notating in this manner far outweighs the cost of the books.

The key to good margin notes is brevity. For example, writing the simple word "policy" in the margin next to a paragraph discussing why the court's decision makes good sense will both ensure that you understand the purpose of the paragraph and also help you quickly orient to that portion of the opinion when the in-class discussion turns to justifications for the court's result. If, within that policy paragraph, the court offered three policy reasons, write 1, 2, and 3 in the text just before the start of the discussion of each. Now you can glance at that paragraph and know that it sets forth 3 policy reasons for the court's decision.

Writing does not need to involve words, either. The old saying, "A picture is worth a thousand words," is true even in law school. Non-verbal writing can convey much information but takes only a moment to put on paper. For example, don't be afraid to draw pictures or make simple line sketches depicting the factual situation. If this helps you visualize the facts, do it! You might also draw an arrow from the discussion of a statute to the actual language of the statute, which may have appeared paragraphs earlier.

Note, though, that margin notes are a supplement to, not a substitute for, any other preparation requirements that a professor may have. A "case brief" is a common class-preparation device that some professors may require. Professors requiring such briefs may even have a particular format that they suggest or require. Your preparation should include such a brief, if required, in addition to margin notes.

— ★ —

THREE

SOME BACKGROUND ON U.S. HISTORY AND GOVERNMENTAL STRUCTURE

A. CONSTITUTIONAL HISTORY

Even before the first days of the United States as a country, tension already existed over how much power should be held locally and how much should be held at a national level. Indeed, the very inception of the country—its revolution and breaking away from England—stemmed from the colonies' feelings that the far-away national government (England) had too much control and the local (colonial) level had too little. The colonies' lack of representation in the British Parliament, along with growing loss of autonomy as the British government imposed more taxes and regulations, sparked the American Revolution.

An interim governing body—the First Continental Congress—was established in 1774 shortly before the start of the Revolutionary War in April 1775. In May 1775, the Second Continental Congress was assembled. It issued a Declaration of Independence on July 4, 1776, and adopted the Articles of Confederation in 1777. In 1781, the Articles received the final needed state ratification. When the Revolutionary War ended just two years later in 1783, it quickly became apparent that the Articles suffered from a serious shortcoming: the federal government was too weak. The weakness of the federal government under the Articles was not surprising given that fears of a central authority had driven the colonies to revolt from Britain in the first place. And, even though the new country consisted of only 13 states (much less than the 50 states that currently comprise the United States), those states already viewed their country as large and found it difficult to believe that legislators at a national level could adequately know and defend the interests of the people they represented.

In response to these concerns, the country's founders designed the Articles to create a weak federal government and only a loose relationship between the states. Concerning the federal government, the Articles created a congress only. The Articles did not provide for an executive or judicial branch. And the congress that the Articles had created was not even strong enough to raise taxes. See U.S. Art. of Confed. art. VIII (giving taxing power to states). Nor were congressional powers exclusive to congress: during periods of its recess, a Committee of the States could execute its functions. U.S. Art. of Confed. art. IX, para. 5 & art. X. The relationship between the states was not particularly strong either. The Articles described the states as forming a "firm league of friendship" and ensured that each state retained its "sovereignty, freedom, and independence." U.S. Art. of Confed. art. III & II.

By 1787, the Confederation was on the brink of failure. The solution, in 1788, was the ratification of the Constitution of the United States. The Constitution consists in part of seven Articles. The first three are the most cited. Article I creates and defines the powers of the Legislative Branch. Article II recognizes and describes the powers of the Executive Branch, and Article III provides for the Judicial Branch.

Courts mention these first three articles with the assumption that the reader will understand them as shorthand references to the legislative, executive, and judicial powers created in the Constitution. For example, in *Wellness Intern. Network, Ltd. v. Sharif*, 575 U.S. 665, 668 (2015), the Supreme Court referenced Article III: "Congress has also authorized the appointment of bankruptcy and magistrate judges, who do not enjoy the protections of Article III, to assist Article III courts in their work." In *Seila Law LLC v. Consumer Financial Protection Bureau*, 140 S. Ct. 2183, 2205 (2020), the Court's opinion references Article II: "As we have explained many times before, the President's removal power stems from Article II's vesting of the 'executive Power' in the President."

Articles IV and VI, two other important Articles in the Constitution, establish key aspects of the U.S. system of federalism. Article IV creates requirements for the relationships between the states. For example, no state can discriminate against another state's citizens with respect to "privileges and immunities," and each state must respect the judicial decisions of the other states. U.S. Const. art. IV, §§ 1 & 2. If an individual flees from one state to another in an attempt to avoid justice, the receiving state cannot shelter that individual and, upon request, must return the individual to the state from which he or she fled. U.S. Const. art. IV, § 2, cl. 2. Article VI remedies some of the problems of the earlier

Articles of Confederation in that it establishes the supremacy of federal law. U.S. Const. art. VI, § 2.

In addition to the seven Articles, the U.S. Constitution includes 27 Amendments. In 1791, three years after ratification of the Constitution, the first ten amendments — known as the Bill of Rights — were adopted and ratified. The First Amendment ensures the right to freedom of religion and freedom of speech and of the press, the separation of church and state, and the right to assemble and petition. The Second Amendment guarantees the right to "bear arms," and the Fourth Amendment ensures freedom from unreasonable search or seizure. The Sixth Amendment creates procedural protections in criminal proceedings, including the right to a "speedy and public trial, by an impartial jury," to be informed of the charges, to be "confronted with the witnesses against" the defendant, to compel the testimony of witnesses, and to have the assistance of counsel. Other amendments ensure the right to a jury trial and prohibit cruel, unusual, or excessive punishment. U.S. Const. amend. VII & VIII. The Tenth Amendment sets up a key aspect of the relationship between the federal government and the states: "The powers not delegated to the United States by the Constitution, nor prohibited by it to the States, are reserved to the States respectively, or to the people." In other words, the federal government has only the powers granted to it by the Constitution, and all other powers remain with the states.

Since 1791, 17 additional amendments have been added to the Constitution, the last being ratified in 1992. The Thirteenth Amendment abolished slavery. The Eighteenth Amendment gave rise to Prohibition, and the Twenty-First Amendment ended it. Voting rights were assured for all races in the Fifteenth Amendment, but it was not until 1920 with the ratification of the Nineteenth Amendment that voting rights were extended to women. The Fourteenth Amendment requires the states to provide due process. The Twenty-Second Amendment limits the President to two terms in office. These are just some highlights of the amendments, but neither the Constitution nor its 27 amendments are particularly long and are well worth a casual read to have a fuller understanding of some of the basics of the U.S. federal government.

B. THE THREE BRANCHES OF GOVERNMENT

The U.S. Constitution creates three branches of government: a legislative, an executive, and a judicial branch. The three branches create a system of checks and balances on each other. For example, the Legislative Branch enacts laws, but the Executive Branch (via the President) can veto those laws. And the Judicial Branch assesses the constitutionality of those laws. If the Legislative Branch disagrees with the Executive-Branch veto or the Judicial-Branch interpretation of a statute, the Legislative Branch can gather more votes to override the veto or draft new legislation to address the Judicial Branch's concerns about the existing statute. This design was intended to prevent one branch from having more power than another.

1. Legislative Branch

The Legislative Branch consists of a House of Representatives and a Senate, collectively called Congress. U.S. Const. art. I, § 1. To qualify to serve as a member of the House of Representatives, an individual must be at least 25 years old, a U.S. citizen for at least seven years, and an inhabitant of the state he or she represents. U.S. Const. art. I, § 2, cl. 2. Each representative must run for election every two years to retain his or her position. U.S. Const. art. I, § 2, cl. 1. The number of representatives for each state is calculated based on state population as a percentage of U.S. population. U.S. Const. art. I, § 2, cl. 3. Each state is divided into districts, and each House member represents a specific district within that state.

In contrast, the Senate consists of two senators from each state, regardless of the size or population of the state. U.S. Const. art. I, § 3, cl. 1. And the senators represent the entire state, not a portion of the state, as with representatives. Additionally, a senator's term is six years, U.S. Const. art. I, § 3, three times longer than that of a representative. The qualifications for serving as a senator are also more stringent. In addition to being an inhabitant of the state (a requirement for representatives as well), a senator must be at least 30 years old and a U.S. citizen for at least nine years. U.S. Const. art. I, § 3, cl. 3.

The job of Congress is to enact laws. Before a law can go into effect, the law must be passed by both the House and the Senate. The subjects on which Congress can legislate are quite varied. It can enact statutes to "lay and collect Taxes;" "establish a uniform Rule of Naturalization, and uniform Laws on the subject of Bankruptcies throughout the United States;" and "establish Post Offices," to name a few. *See* U.S. Const. art. I, § 8. But the provision that gives Congress the most power may be the commerce clause. That clause gives Congress the power to "regulate Commerce ... among the several States" and has been interpreted as granting Congress the power to regulate almost anything that passes through interstate commerce. U.S. Const. art. I, § 8, cl. 3.

2. Executive Branch

At the head of the Executive Branch is the President of the United States. U.S. Const. art. II, § 1, cl. 1. The President is elected to serve a term of four years and is limited to two terms. U.S. Const. art. II, § 1, cl. 1; U.S. Const. amend. XXII. Only a "natural born Citizen" can serve as President, and that individual must be at least 35 years old. U.S. Const. art. II, § 1, cl. 5.

The manner of electing the President is different from the election of any other elected federal official. While representatives and senators are elected based on the majority of the votes cast within their district or state, respectively, the President is not elected based on a majority of the votes cast nationally. Instead, a candidate wins the presidential election by winning a majority of the votes of the electoral college as described in Article II of the Constitution. U.S. Const. art. II, § 1, cl. 2 & 3. Each state is granted a number of electoral college votes equal to "the whole Number of Senators and Representatives to which the State may be entitled in the Congress." U.S. Const. art. II, § 1, cl. 2. In 2020, the total number of electoral college votes was 538.

The candidate receiving the majority of electoral college votes is the candidate who becomes President, even if that candidate did not receive a majority of the votes cast in the country. This situation occurred in 2000 when Al Gore received more votes nationally than George W. Bush, but Bush became President. In 2016, the same thing occurred in the election between Donald J. Trump and Hillary R. Clinton.

In addition to addressing how Presidents are elected, Article II addresses how they can be removed from office during their term. U.S. Const. art. II, § 4.

The responsibilities of the President are also identified in Article II. The President is the Commander in Chief of the Army and Navy of the United States and, with the "advice and consent of senate," has the powers to make treaties. U.S. Const., art. II, § 2, cl. 1 & 2. The President "by and with the advice and consent of the Senate shall appoint Ambassadors, other public Ministers and Consuls, Judges of the supreme Court, and all other Officers of the United States, whose Appointments are not herein otherwise provided for." U.S. Const. art. II, § 2, cl. 2. One key responsibility of the President is to "take Care that the Laws be faithfully executed." U.S. Const. art. II, § 3. This broad grant of authority is the basis for much of the work of the Executive Branch.

The President also has the power to approve or veto legislation. U.S. Const. art. I, § 7, cl. 2. If the President vetoes legislation, Congress must repass the legislation by two-thirds majority vote of the Senate and of the House of Representatives to override the President's veto and enact the legislation as a law. *Id.*

3. Judicial Branch

The Constitution creates a Supreme Court but does not set the Court's size. U.S. Const. art. III, § 1. However, since 1869, the Supreme Court has consisted of nine justices. *See* Judiciary Act of 1869, ch. 22, 16 Stat. 44 (available at https://www.loc.gov/law/help/statutes-at-large/41st-congress/session-1/c41s1ch22.pdf). The Constitution also gives Congress the power to "ordain and establish" lower courts. U.S. Const. art. III, § 1; *see also* Art. I, § 8, cl. 9. Although Congress did not initially use that power, it has since created many lower courts. The judges, both of the Supreme Court and of these lower courts, hold their offices so long as they exercise "good behaviour," U.S. Const. art. III, § 1, which has effectively created life tenure for federal judges, as failing the "good behaviour" standard is extremely difficult

The jurisdictional potential of the lower federal courts is set out in section 2 of Article III:

> The judicial power shall extend to all cases, in law and equity, arising under this Constitution, the laws of the United States, and treaties made, or which shall be made, under their authority; — to all cases affecting ambassadors, other public ministers and consuls; — to all cases of admiralty and maritime jurisdiction; — to controversies to which the United States shall be a party; — to controversies between two or more states; — between a state and citizens of another state; — between citizens of different states; — between citizens of the same state claiming lands under grants of different states, and between a state, or the citizens thereof, and foreign states, citizens or subjects."

This language describes the *potential* jurisdiction of the lower courts because Congress's power to create or not create lower courts implicitly includes the power to set the jurisdiction of those courts within the limits set by the Constitution. For example, the Constitution grants jurisdiction, without limit, over cases "between citizens of different states." U.S. Const. art. III, § 2. Nevertheless, Congress has limited that jurisdiction to cases in which the value of the case exceeds a certain monetary minimum. *See* 28 U.S.C. § 1332(a).

The lower courts in the federal system as it exists today include trial courts (called "district courts"). Smaller states might have only one district. Larger states will have multiple districts. Missouri, for example, has *two* districts within the state — the western district (on the left in shades of gray) and the eastern district (on the right in white).

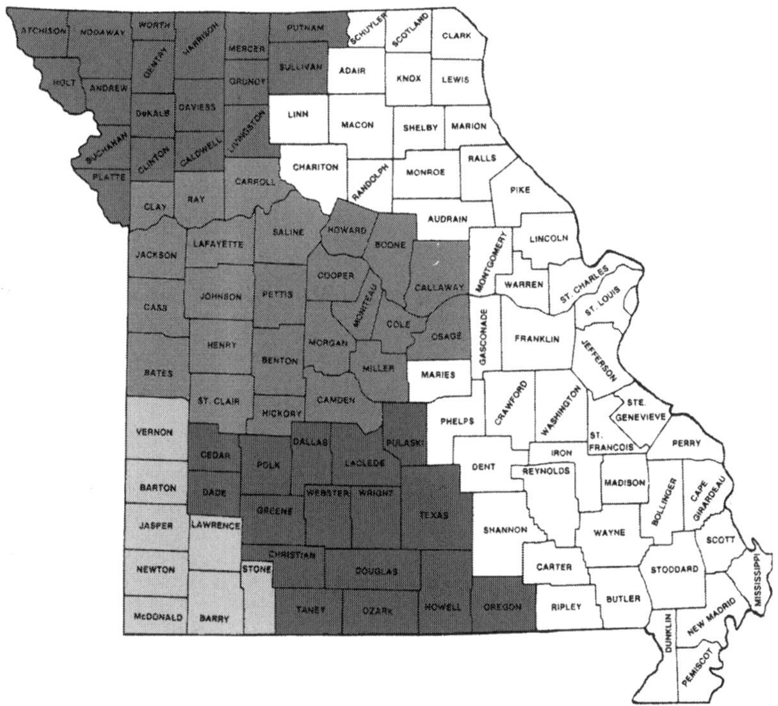

Above the trial courts are intermediate appellate courts, called Courts of Appeals and sometimes "circuit courts." The circuit courts are numbered from one to eleven, and there is one additional circuit court for the District of Columbia, the location of the nation's capital. As the graphic below shows, each circuit (other than District of Columbia) covers a number of states, meaning that it hears appeals from any district court in those states. The appellate courts for any particular circuit have offices in numerous locations within the circuit.

The Federal Circuit court is another appellate court within the federal system. It is a little different in that it has jurisdiction over specific types of claims only, such as patents and trademarks, among others. If a case involves a subject-matter within the Federal Circuit's jurisdiction, the parties can take an appeal from any federal district court in the country to the Federal Circuit.

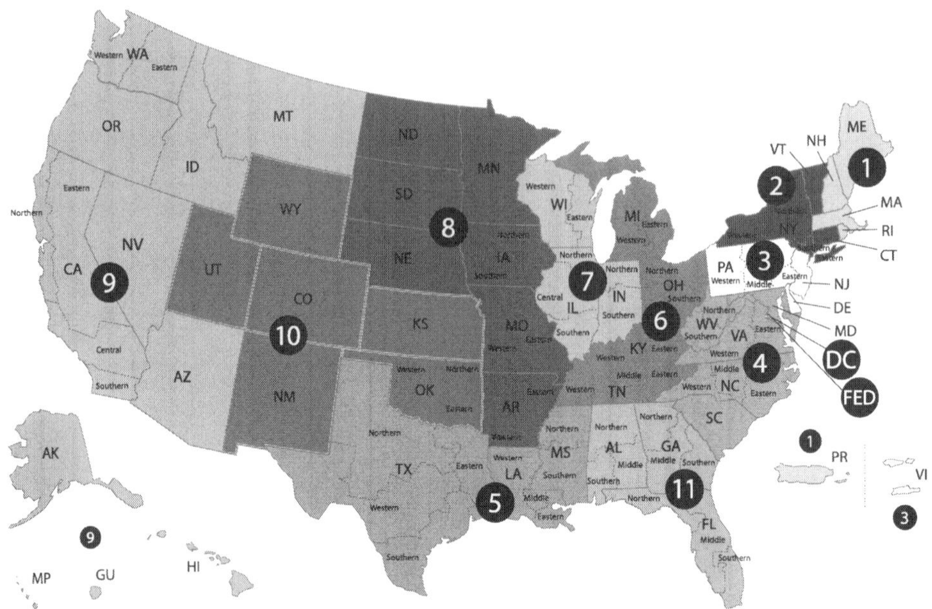

There are other federal judges, for example, magistrate judges and bankruptcy judges, but these judges are judicial officers of the district court, not "Article III" judges. This means that they are selected by the district court judges, not nominated by the President and confirmed by the Senate as required for Article III judges. *See* U.S. Const. art. II, § 2. Parties cannot be forced to try a case before a federal magistrate judge or a bankruptcy judge, as these judges are not Article III judges, but many parties will choose to do so.

Notes on Agencies

1. There is another aspect of the federal government that has grown in impact: administrative agencies. One role of administrative agencies is rulemaking. (The enforcement role of agencies is discussed in section B of Chapter 6.) Congress can give an agency the ability to regulate, so long as Congress gives the agency an "intelligible principle" on which to base its regulations. *JW Hampton, Jr. & Co. v. United States*, 276 U.S. 394, 409

(1928). Thus, although Congress cannot completely delegate its legislative powers to administrative agencies, *A.L.A. Schechter Poultry Corp. v. United States*, 295 U.S. 495, 529–30 (1935), the intelligible-principle standard has been interpreted so broadly that the Supreme Court has not used it to strike down legislation since 1935. *See Gundy v. United States*, 139 S. Ct. 2116, 2123 (2019) (a recent example, finding an "intelligible principle" in the Sex Offender Registration and Notification Act, thus permitting agency rulemaking).

2. The process of creating regulations (or "rulemaking") is governed by the Administrative Procedure Act (APA), 5 U.S.C. § 551 et seq. The APA generally requires publication of the proposed rules in a notice of proposed rulemaking, a period thereafter for public comments, followed by adoption and publication of the final rule in the *Federal Register.*
3. Administrative-created rules (also known as regulations) are reported in the Code of Federal Regulations (C.F.R.). The *Federal Register* differs from the C.F.R. in that the former is a chronological list of regulations whereas the latter collects the regulations by subject-matter.
4. In 2019, the C.F.R. was over 180,000 pages in length! That reflects a sizeable number of regulations. Many critics bemoan this growth in regulation and the rise of the resulting "administrative state." The concern is that the administrative bodies have quasi-legislative authority, yet they exist outside of the legislative branch. The reasons justifying the rise in regulations, and growth of the administrative or regulatory state, have varied over time, but there is no doubt the regulatory state is here to stay:

   > Since its inception, the regulatory state has witnessed different theories or "models" of administrative law that purport to answer questions of agency legitimacy. The earliest model was the "transmission belt" model, which understood agencies as merely implementing statutory instructions. If simply obeying statutory instructions, agency officials assumed the virtues of their authors; agency officials were viewed as accountable, faction-proof, and efficacious as was Congress. In the 1930s, another model arose. The "expertise" model understood agencies as committed to an ethic of professionalism and rationality. Because they were disciplined, if not objective, agency officials were better positioned to produce sound regulation and good government than elected officials. By the 1970s, a third model emerged. The "interest group representation" model understood agencies as open to all affected interests. In this respect,

> agency officials were even more accessible and responsive to the public than were elected officials. A fourth model appeared in the 1980s. The "presidential control" model understood agencies as subject to the oversight and management of the chief executive. For legitimacy purposes, agency officials stood in the shoes of their boss; they were as accountable, faction-resistant, and efficacious as the president.

Lisa S. Bressman & Michael P. Vandenbergh, *Inside the Administrative State: A Critical Look at the Practice of Presidential Control*, 105 Mich. L. Rev. 47, 53 (2006).

Notes on State Governments

1. The Constitution requires that each state have a "republican form of government." U.S. Const. art. IV, § 4. The Constitution does not require that this "republican form of government" replicate the structure of the federal government, but nevertheless, all 50 states have a constitution and the same three branches as the federal government (legislative, executive, and judicial). *See* https://www.whitehouse.gov/about-the-white-house/our-government/state-local-government/.
2. The state legislatures, in all states but Nebraska, consist of two chambers, not unlike the two-chamber federal legislature. *Id.* The governor is the chief executive in the states. And the states have courts of general jurisdiction and specialty courts with limited jurisdiction such as family courts, probate courts, traffic courts, and small claims courts, to name a few.

— ★ —

FOUR

CHOOSING A COURT

A. OVERVIEW

Every judicial decision that you will read was rendered as part of a lawsuit, so it is helpful to understand that legal process. As students trained in law in another country, this need is particularly compelling for you because you may have assumptions about litigation based on your prior learning. One significant difference between the U.S. system and the systems in many other countries is the role of the parties. The parties — not the judges or any other government personnel — bear primary responsibility for the progress of civil litigation in the United States. Indeed, the very decision *whether* to start civil litigation belongs solely to the plaintiff.

After making the decision to file a lawsuit, the plaintiff next must choose in which court to file the claim. In some situations, the plaintiff will have the choice of filing the claim in the courts of one or more states.

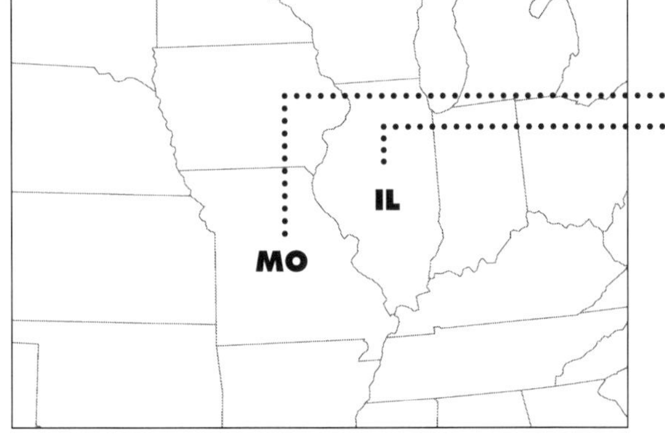

For example, if a car accident occurs in **Missouri** between an **Illinois** resident and a Missouri resident, the Missouri resident could likely file suit against the driver in Illinois (where the other driver lives) or Missouri (where the accident occurred).

In other situations, the plaintiff may properly file the claim in only one state, but there may be various courts in different geographic areas within that state in which the plaintiff could file the claim.

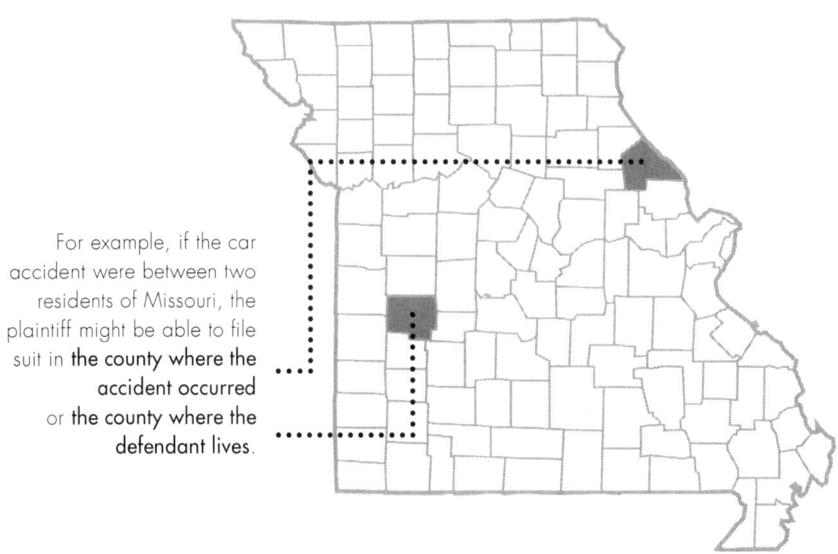

In addition to those possible choices, the plaintiff may also have the option of filing the claim in federal court. Choosing between state and federal court is not simply a function of whether the case presents issues of state or federal law. State courts can adjudicate federal-law claims (as well as state-law claims), and federal courts can adjudicate state-law claims (as well as federal-law claims). The options available to plaintiffs will vary from case to case based on the facts and the nature of the claim. The next sections in this Chapter will introduce you to some of the limits on the plaintiff's available choices of courts in which to file a claim.

B. SELECTING A COURT: SUBJECT-MATTER JURISDICTION

1. Overview

Subject-matter jurisdiction is a limit on the *types* of cases a court has authority to adjudicate. If the plaintiff's case is of a type over which the court does not have subject-matter jurisdiction, the court has no authority over the case.

Federal courts are described as courts of limited jurisdiction. Their subject-matter jurisdiction extends only as far as permitted by federal statute. In contrast, most state courts are courts of general jurisdiction. There are far fewer limits on their ability to hear certain types of claims, and whatever limits do exist for state courts will vary considerably from state to state. This section will focus, therefore, on the subject-matter jurisdiction of federal courts.

Two of the most common forms of federal court subject-matter jurisdiction are federal-question jurisdiction and diversity jurisdiction. Federal-question jurisdiction exists when the plaintiff's claims present a question of federal law, either concerning a federal statute or the Constitution. *See* 28 U.S.C. § 1331. A more precise understanding of when a case presents a federal question must be left for a class on civil procedure. At this time, it is enough if you understand that a claim premised on a federal statute (such as, a claim alleging discrimination in violation of a federal statute prohibiting certain conduct) or alleging a violation of the U.S. Constitution would present a federal question. A federal district court could therefore consider such claims.

Diversity jurisdiction—the type of jurisdiction alleged in *Capron v. Van Noorden*—is another form of subject-matter jurisdiction. *See* 28 U.S.C. § 1332. When the claims are between citizens of different states and when the amount in controversy exceeds the statutory minimum, courts have diversity jurisdiction: "The district courts shall have original jurisdiction of all civil actions where the matter in controversy exceeds the sum or value of $75,000, exclusive of interest and costs, and is between—(1) citizens of different States...." 28 U.S.C. § 1332(a).

The requirement of subject-matter jurisdiction is so fundamental that, as *Capron v. Van Noorden* illustrates, even the party who files the suit and then *loses* can challenge the court's jurisdiction—and in *Capron*, win on the jurisdictional issue!

Capron v. Van Noorden

Supreme Court of the United States

6 U.S. 126 (1804)

A *plaintiff* may assign for error the want of jurisdiction in that court to which he has chosen to resort.

...

The Courts of the U.S. have not jurisdiction unless the record shews that the parties [meet the requirement for subject-matter jurisdiction, in this case, diversity of citizenship].

...

Upon the general issue, in an action of trespass on the case, a verdict was found for the defendant, *Van Noorden,* upon which judgment was rendered.

The writ of Error was sued out by *Capron,* the plaintiff below, who assigned for error, among other things, first "That the circuit court aforesaid is a court of limited jurisdiction, and that [the diversity necessary for subject-matter jurisdiction did not exist]." ...

And secondly, "That by the record aforesaid it manifestly appeareth that the said Circuit Court had not any jurisdiction of the cause aforesaid, nor ought to have held plea thereof, or given judgment therein, but ought to have dismissed the same, whereas the said Court hath proceeded to final judgment therein."

... [T]he only question [is] whether the plaintiff had a right to assign for error, the want of jurisdiction in that Court to which he had chosen to resort.

It is true, as a general rule, that a man cannot reverse a judgment... unless he can shew that the error was to his disadvantage; but it is also a rule, that he may reverse a judgment for an error of *the Court,* even though it be for his advantage....

Here it was the duty of the Court to see that they had jurisdiction, for the consent of parties could not give it.

It is therefore an *error of the Court,* and the plaintiff has a right to take advantage of it.

The... judgment [is] reversed.

Notes

1. This case is a good example of why the year of the decision is useful information. The year of the *Capron* decision helps to explain the unusual language that the Court used: the strange spelling of "shows" as "shews" and the use of the word "appeareth," a word that is no longer listed in most dictionaries.

   The year should also help you realize the fundamental nature of the conclusion regarding subject-matter jurisdiction. How long had federal courts even existed before the Supreme Court rendered this decision?

2. Who filed suit? Who lost in the trial court? Who challenged the propriety of bringing the action in federal court? The answer to each question is the same. So why would the Court allow the plaintiff to choose federal court and then complain that the federal court was an improper court to adjudicate the plaintiff's claim? Does that seem fair?
3. What does this decision mean about who bears the ultimate obligation to ensure the federal court has jurisdiction? Given the nature of subject-matter jurisdiction, why does it make sense to place the burden there?
4. Most challenges to the trial court's actions must first be raised in the trial court or they cannot be raised on appeal. This prerequisite ensures that the trial court has an opportunity to remedy any potential error before more proceedings follow, thus promoting judicial efficiency. If raising an issue for the first time on appeal were generally permitted, trial courts would have invested the time in various rulings, and possibly even an entire trial, only for the appellate court to reverse the trial court's result and send it back for retrial based on an issue that the trial court never had an opportunity to consider. If that approach makes sense for most issues, why is subject-matter jurisdiction handled differently?
5. A reading tip: The decisions that you read may have many ellipses (…). These indicate that the author of the textbook has not included some of the text that is in the published decision.

Notes on the Responsibilities of Attorneys

1. Note 4 above explained that parties generally must raise in the trial court any challenges they may have to trial-court action if they are to have the right to raise that issue on appeal. Some issues must even be presented to the trial court at the precisely correct time or they will be deemed forfeited or "waived." Look for this timeliness requirement when reading about personal jurisdiction, evidence, and judgments as a matter of law later in this textbook.
2. What if a party believes his or her attorney has not made the proper arguments in the trial court or failed to preserve key issues? The party has a couple of options. The party has the option to sue the attorney for malpractice. But succeeding on such a claim would require proving, in part, that the attorney's action or inaction caused harm to the plaintiff.

In other words, the party must prove that the case would have come out differently if only the attorney had taken certain action. That standard is difficult to meet because most errors or omissions are "harmless," meaning they do not affect the outcome of the litigation. A second option is to report the attorney to the bar. Every practicing attorney is licensed (i.e., is a member of the bar) in at least one state in the country. Each state's bar has a mechanism for reporting complaints about attorneys and a disciplinary committee to evaluate those complaints and determine if any discipline (such as suspension or additional training) is warranted.

3. Most attorneys, though, are adequately prepared to perform their tasks well. Most bars require that applicants have a J.D. degree from a law school accredited by the American Bar Association. A few states permit applicants who have both a law degree from another country and an LL.M. degree from a U.S. law school to apply to their bars. Entry into the bar also requires successful completion of the state's bar exam (with a few exceptions, such as when an attorney has practiced for many years as a member of another state's bar or when, as in Wisconsin, the applicant graduated from a law school in that state). Another component of the bar admission process is an evaluation of the applicant's character and fitness to be a lawyer. This portion of the application may ask questions about the applicant's past involvement in criminal or civil proceedings, traffic tickets, mental health, or substance abuse issues, and academic disciplinary actions, to name a few. Thus, attorneys admitted to the bar have received required education, passed a proficiency test, and been vetted for good character.
4. The education for lawyers does not end with law school, though. Annual continuing legal education is also required. A portion of these hours must be on the topic of legal ethics. And many states now include requirements on continuing education on issues related to bias and inclusion.
5. Attorneys practice in a wide range of settings — e.g., in-house, government, courts, private practice — and focus on a wide range of substantive areas — e.g., family law, corporate law, criminal law, employment law. The type of conduct that constitutes a significant error for these attorneys may be different from that of a litigator, but these attorneys, like all attorneys, are subject to the same supervision by the bar and vulnerable to the same sanctions for harmful errors.

2. Diversity Jurisdiction: Diversity Requirement

One requirement of diversity jurisdiction is that each plaintiff must have a different citizenship from each defendant. But what does it mean to be a "citizen" of a state? U.S. citizens can move freely from state to state. No permission is needed to pick up and leave one state to take up residence in a different state. How, then, do we determine an individual's state citizenship for purposes of diversity jurisdiction? The next case sheds light on this question. Notice also that the case introduces you to a different type of "diversity," the "diversity" that would allow you as a foreign citizen temporarily in the United States to file suit in federal court against any U.S. citizen.

Mas v. Perry

United States Court of Appeals for the Fifth Circuit

489 F.2d 1396 (1974)

AINSWORTH, Circuit Judge:

This case presents questions pertaining to federal diversity jurisdiction under 28 U.S.C. § 1332(a)(1), which ... provides for original jurisdiction in federal district courts of all civil actions ... between ... citizens of different States or citizens of a State and citizens of foreign states and in which the amount in controversy is more than $10,000.

Appellees Jean Paul Mas, a citizen of France, and Judy Mas were married at her home in Jackson, Mississippi. Prior to their marriage, Mr. and Mrs. Mas were graduate assistants, pursuing coursework as well as performing teaching duties, for approximately nine months and one year, respectively, at Louisiana State University in Baton Rouge, Louisiana. Shortly after their marriage, they returned to Baton Rouge to resume their duties as graduate assistants at LSU. They remained in Baton Rouge for approximately two more years, after which they moved to Park Ridge, Illinois. At the time of the trial in this case, it was their intention to return to Baton Rouge while Mr. Mas finished his studies for the degree of Doctor of Philosophy. Mr. and Mrs. Mas were undecided as to where they would reside after that.

Upon their return to Baton Rouge after their marriage, appellees rented an apartment from appellant Oliver H. Perry, a citizen of Louisiana. This appeal arises from a final judgment entered on a jury verdict [in favor of Mr. Mas and

Mrs. Mas] for damages incurred by them as a result of the discovery that their bedroom and bathroom contained "two-way" mirrors and that they had been watched through them by the appellant during three of the first four months of their marriage.

At the close of the appellees' case at trial, appellant made an oral motion to dismiss for lack of jurisdiction. The motion was denied by the district court. Before this Court, appellant challenges the final judgment below solely on jurisdictional grounds, contending that appellees failed to prove diversity of citizenship among the parties.... Finding no merit to these contentions, we affirm. Under section 1332(a)(2), the federal judicial power extends to the claim of Mr. Mas, a citizen of France, against the appellant, a citizen of Louisiana. Since we conclude that Mrs. Mas is a citizen of Mississippi for diversity purposes, the district court also properly had jurisdiction under section 1332(a)(1) of her claim.

It has long been the general rule that complete diversity of parties is required in order that diversity jurisdiction obtain; that is, no party on one side may be a citizen of the same State as any party on the other side. This determination of one's State Citizenship for diversity purposes is controlled by federal law, not by the law of any State. As is the case in other areas of federal jurisdiction, the diverse citizenship among adverse parties must be present at the time the complaint is filed. Jurisdiction is unaffected by subsequent changes in the citizenship of the parties....

To be a citizen of a State within the meaning of section 1332, a natural person must be both a citizen of the United States, and a domiciliary of that State. For diversity purposes, [State] citizenship means domicile; mere residence in the State is not sufficient.

A person's domicile is the place of "his true, fixed, and permanent home and principal establishment, and to which he has the intention of returning whenever he is absent therefrom...."... A change of domicile may be effected by a combination of two elements: (a) taking up residence in a different domicile with (b) the intention to remain there.

It is clear that at the time of her marriage, Mrs. Mas was a domiciliary of the State of Mississippi.... Mrs. Mas's Mississippi domicile was disturbed neither by her year in Louisiana prior to her marriage nor as a result of the time she and her husband spent at LSU after their marriage, since for both periods she was a graduate assistant at LSU. Though she testified that after her marriage she had no intention of returning to her parents' home in Mississippi, Mrs. Mas did not effect a change of domicile since she and Mr. Mas were in Louisiana only as students and lacked the requisite intention to remain there. Until she acquires a new domicile, she remains a domiciliary, and thus a citizen, of Mississippi.[2] ... Thus the power of the federal district court to entertain the claims of appellees in this case stands on two separate legs of diversity jurisdiction: a claim by an alien against a State citizen; and an action between citizens of different States.

Affirmed.

Notes

1. Judicial decisions generally contain many citations to statutes and prior judicial decisions that support the court's assertions. These citations allow the reader to see how existing law and prior decisions lead to the result that the court reaches in the case then before it. The actual published version of the decision in *Mas* contains such citations at the end of most of its sentences. Those cites have been removed in the version of *Mas* reported above and most are removed in the other cases in this book to streamline the decisions and permit you to focus on the concepts the decisions present. Many textbooks will use some variation of this approach, removing some, but not necessarily all citations. Please note that if you read a decision in this book, or another textbook, with citations to other legal authorities, you are not expected to look them up or read them.
2. In this case, the Court was interpreting and applying the federal statute, 28 U.S.C. § 1332(a)(1), which currently reads: "(a) The district courts shall have original jurisdiction of all civil actions where the matter in controversy exceeds the sum or value of $75,000, exclusive of interest and costs, and is between — (1) citizens of different States." The decision in *Mas* focuses on the diversity of citizenship requirement of this statute.

---

2. The original complaint in this case was filed... quite some time before [Mr. and Mrs. Mas] moved to Park Ridge, Illinois. Because the district court's jurisdiction is not affected by actions of the parties subsequent to the commencement of the suit, the testimony concerning Mr. and Mrs. Mas's moves after that time is not determinative of the issue of diverse citizenship, though it is of interest insofar as it supports their lack of intent to remain permanently in Louisiana.

3. For purposes of assessing diversity jurisdiction, what was the citizenship of Mr. Mas? Of Mrs. Mas? Of Mr. Perry?
4. Why was the move to Louisiana insufficient to change Mrs. Mas's state citizenship to Louisiana? Did Mrs. Mas have any intention to return to Mississippi?
5. Why was the move to Illinois insufficient to change Mrs. Mas's state citizenship from Mississippi to Illinois? Would the court have reached a different conclusion if Mrs. Mas had intended to make Illinois her permanent home?
6. What if Mr. Mas had been offered a job in New York and he and his wife had intended to move there when he graduated. Would that change the court's assessment of Mrs. Mas's citizenship? Why or why not?
7. The court focused on the citizenship of Mrs. Mas. It had no doubt that Mr. Mas could sue Mr. Perry in federal district court. Why was the court confident it had jurisdiction over Mr. Mas's claim? Section 1332(a)(2) and (a)(3) address when non-U.S. citizens are diverse from that of an opposing party. These sections grant jurisdiction to district courts for certain suits between:

    > (2) citizens of a State and citizens or subjects of a foreign state, except that the district courts shall not have original jurisdiction under this subsection of an action between citizens of a State and citizens or subjects of a foreign state who are lawfully admitted for permanent residence in the United States and are domiciled in the same State;
    >
    > (3) citizens of different States and in which citizens or subjects of a foreign state are additional parties....

    28 U.S.C. § 1332(a).
8. If the court had not had jurisdiction, what action would the court have been required to take?
9. Different rules apply to determining the citizenship of corporations. A corporation is a citizen of "every State and foreign state by which it has been incorporated and of the State or foreign state where it has its principal place of business." 28 U.S.C. § 1332(c). Thus, while a human being can have only one citizenship, corporations can have multiple citizenships. Would the diversity requirement of diversity jurisdiction be satisfied if a corporation incorporated in Delaware with its principal place

of business in New York is sued by a New York citizen injured by the corporation's product? How does *Mas* define the requirement of complete diversity?

3. Diversity Jurisdiction: Amount-in-Controversy Requirement

The Constitution permits, but does not require, Congress to grant federal courts jurisdiction over all controversies "between Citizens of different States." U.S. Const. art. III, § 2. And this permissive grant of power does not limit Congress to recognizing diversity jurisdiction only when the plaintiff's claims exceed a certain value. Nevertheless, Congress has chosen to limit the federal court's diversity jurisdiction to civil actions between Citizens of different States "where the matter in controversy *exceeds the sum or value of $75,000*, exclusive of interest and costs." 28 U.S.C. § 1332(a) (emphasis added). The $75,000 requirement is often called the "amount in controversy." In 1948, when § 1332 was first enacted, that amount was $500. Congress has incrementally raised the amount in controversy on many occasions since the original version of § 1332. At the time of *Mas*, the required amount in controversy was $10,000. This amount-in-controversy requirement applies to all forms of diversity cases, not just claims between diverse citizens of the United States. So, even when diversity is satisfied because the suit is between a foreign citizen and a U.S. citizen, for example, the amount-in controversy requirement still applies.

The Supreme Court has long interpreted the amount-in-controversy requirement as referring to the damages the plaintiff seeks to recover or the value of the right that the plaintiff seeks to enforce or protect. Typically, challenges to the adequacy of the amount-in-controversy arise early in litigation when the means of assessing the amount in controversy is often limited to the allegations in the complaint. If the complaint requests a specified sum in damages, for example, the courts will generally defer to that figure as reflecting the amount in controversy. This plaintiff-favorable approach to evaluating the amount in controversy has been called a legal-certainty test: "[U]nless the law gives a different rule, the sum claimed by the plaintiff controls if the claim is apparently made in good faith. It must appear to a legal certainty that the claim is really for less than the jurisdictional amount to justify dismissal." *St. Paul Mercury Indem. Co. v. Red Cab Co.*, 303 U.S. 283, 288–89 (1938). Therefore, absent a situation where no reasonable jury could award the amount requested, the complaint's requested amount controls.

Notes

1. Federal-question jurisdiction, mentioned in section A of this Chapter, is another common form of jurisdiction. *See* 28 U.S.C. § 1331. Prior to 1980, the statute creating federal-question jurisdiction included an amount-in-controversy requirement, limiting jurisdiction over claims arising under federal law to those where "the matter in controversy exceeds the sum or value of $10,000, exclusive of interest and costs, unless such action is brought against the United States, any agency thereof, or any officer or employee thereof in his official capacity." In 1980, Congress removed the amount-in-controversy requirement for federal-question jurisdiction so that now all claims based on federal law, regardless of the amount at stake, may be brought in federal court.
2. This discussion of the amount in controversy skims the surface of the issue, intentionally leaving many questions unanswered because a complete chapter could be written on this topic alone. For example, you may be wondering if the claims of each plaintiff must satisfy the amount in controversy or is it sufficient if the claims of just one plaintiff reaches this amount? It depends on the relationship between the claims. Can the value of plaintiff's various claims against a single defendant be aggregated to meet the amount-in-controversy requirement? Yes, but the value of claims by a single plaintiff against multiple defendants cannot usually be aggregated to meet the amount-in-controversy requirement. Fuller answers to these questions are left for a class on civil procedure.

Notes on Damages

1. The measure and types of recoverable damages in the United States are quite different from those in other countries. For example, there are no schedules specifying the values of various physical injuries. Instead, the factfinder (generally, the jury) is responsible for assigning a value to the plaintiff's harm based on the evidence provided at trial.
2. Assume an individual is hit by something protruding from a train, for example (the facts of the case in *Erie Railroad Co. v. Tompkins* in Chapter 5). You might immediately realize that the medical expenses of the individual would be a recoverable damage. And the jury would assign a value to the

injury itself. But plaintiffs can also recover, where the facts support it, an amount to compensate for (1) pain and suffering, (2) permanent or temporary loss of use of a portion of the body, (3) a shortened life span, (4) loss of physical relationships with a spouse, (5) limitations on the ability to be an active parent with his or her children, (6) lost past and anticipated lost future wages, (7) anticipated future medical expenses, and others.

3. All of the damages described in the prior paragraph are compensatory. They are intended to compensate the plaintiff for the plaintiff's injuries. In Chapter 6, you will read about punitive damages, a form of damages that are not compensatory but instead meant to punish defendants for their past conduct and discourage defendants from performing in a similar way in the future.
4. Compensatory damages are intended to return the plaintiff to the position the plaintiff would have been in had the wrong not occurred. For a physical injury, that result is technically not possible because a person cannot be restored to a prior physical condition. So, the plaintiff instead seeks a monetary equivalent. But for breach of a contract or loss of a job due to illegal discrimination, an amount can often be computed to reflect the amount of money a plaintiff would have had but for the wrong.

C. SELECTING A COURT: PERSONAL JURISDICTION

Subject-matter jurisdiction limits which claims can be brought in federal court. If subject-matter jurisdiction is lacking, the case cannot be brought in *any* federal court. In contrast, personal jurisdiction limits federal and state court power over people, not claims. The focus of personal jurisdiction is on when is it fair to ask defendants to defend themselves against litigation in a court located in a state with which the defendants may have limited connection. The absence of personal jurisdiction does not foreclose litigation in *all* courts, just those courts in states with which the defendants do not have sufficient contacts.

Another key distinction between subject-matter jurisdiction and personal jurisdiction is that the Constitution expressly grants Congress the authority to define the federal courts' subject-matter jurisdiction. See, e.g., U.S. Const. art. III, § 2. Congress has used that authority and enacted statutes establishing federal court subject-matter jurisdiction in various situations. See 28. U.S.C. §§ 1331–1369. When evaluating subject-matter jurisdiction, the federal courts are interpreting and applying those statutes. In contrast, the bounds of personal jurisdiction are rooted in the Due Process Clause of the Fourteenth Amendment of the Constitution: "No state shall...deprive any person of life, liberty, or property, without due process of law." U.S. Const. amend. XIV, § 1. The Constitution leaves the parameters of the due-process requirement unstated and unexplained. The vagueness of this language has left vast room for the courts to interpret the scope of personal jurisdiction.

International Shoe Co. v. Washington

Supreme Court of the United States

326 U.S. 310 (1945)

Mr. Chief Justice STONE delivered the opinion of the Court.

The question[] for decision [is]...whether, within the limitations of the due process clause of the Fourteenth Amendment, appellant, a Delaware corporation, has, by its activities in the State of Washington, rendered itself amenable to proceedings in the courts of that state to recover unpaid contributions to the state unemployment compensation fund exacted by state statutes.

The statutes in question set up a comprehensive scheme of unemployment compensation, the costs of which are defrayed by contributions required to be made by employers to a state unemployment compensation fund. The contributions are a specified percentage of the wages payable annually by each employer for his employees' services in the state. The assessment and collection of the contributions and the fund are administered by appellees....

...

[The state enforced the requirements of this statute against Appellant International Shoe.] The facts...are not in dispute. Appellant is a Delaware corporation, having its principal place of business in St. Louis, Missouri, and is engaged in the manufacture and sale of shoes and other footwear. It maintains places of business in several states other than Washington, at which its manufacturing is carried on and from which its merchandise is distributed interstate through several sales units or branches located outside the State of Washington.

Appellant has no office in Washington, and makes no contracts either for sale or purchase of merchandise there. It maintains no stock of merchandise in that state, and makes there no deliveries of goods in intrastate commerce. During the years from 1937 to 1940, now in question, appellant employed eleven to thirteen salesmen under direct supervision and control of sales managers located in St. Louis. These salesmen resided in Washington; their principal activities were confined to that state, and they were compensated by commissions based upon the amount of their sales. The commissions for each year totaled more than $31,000. Appellant supplies its salesmen with a line of samples, each consisting of one shoe of a pair, which they display to prospective purchasers. On occasion, they rent permanent sample rooms, for exhibiting samples, in business buildings, or rent rooms in hotels or business buildings temporarily for that purpose. The cost of such rentals is reimbursed by appellant.

The authority of the salesmen is limited to exhibiting their samples and soliciting orders from prospective buyers, at prices and on terms fixed by appellant. The salesmen transmit the orders to appellant's office in St. Louis for acceptance or rejection, and, when accepted, the merchandise for filling the orders is shipped... from points outside Washington to the purchasers within the state. All the merchandise shipped into Washington is invoiced at the place of shipment, from which collections are made. No salesman has authority to enter into contracts or to make collections.

The Supreme Court of Washington was of opinion that the regular and systematic solicitation of orders in the state by appellant's salesmen, resulting in a continuous flow of appellant's product into the state, was sufficient to constitute doing business in the state so as to make appellant amenable to suit in its courts. But it was also of opinion that there were sufficient additional activities shown to bring the case within the rule, frequently stated, that solicitation within a state by the agents of a foreign corporation plus some additional activities there are sufficient to render the corporation amenable to suit brought in the courts of the state to enforce an obligation arising out of its activities there. The court found such additional activities in the salesmen's display of samples sometimes in permanent display rooms, and the salesmen's residence within the state, continued over a period of years, all resulting in a substantial volume of merchandise regularly shipped by appellant to purchasers within the state....

...

Appellant [] insists that its activities within the state were not sufficient to manifest its "presence" there, and that, in its absence, the state courts were without jurisdiction, that, consequently, it was a denial of due process for the state to subject appellant to suit....

Historically, the jurisdiction of courts to render judgment *in personam* is grounded on their *de facto* power over the defendant's person. Hence, his presence within the territorial jurisdiction of a court was prerequisite to its rendition of a judgment personally binding him. But now... due process requires only that, in order to subject a defendant to a judgment *in personam,* if he be not present within the territory of the forum, he have certain minimum contacts with it such that the maintenance of the suit does not offend "traditional notions of fair play and substantial justice."

Since the corporate personality is a fiction, although a fiction intended to be acted upon as though it were a fact, it is clear that, unlike an individual, its "presence" without, as well as within, the state of its origin can be manifested only by activities carried on in its behalf by those who are authorized to act for it.... For the terms "present" or "presence" are used merely to symbolize those activities of the corporation's agent within the state which courts will deem to be sufficient to satisfy the demands of due process. Those demands may be met by such contacts of the corporation with the state of the forum as make it reasonable, in the context of our federal system of government, to require the corporation to defend the particular suit which is brought there. An "estimate of the inconveniences" which would result to the corporation from a trial away from its "home" or principal place of business is relevant in this connection.

"Presence" in the state in this sense has never been doubted when the activities of the corporation there have not only been continuous and systematic, but also give rise to the liabilities sued on.... Conversely, it has been generally recognized that the casual presence of the corporate agent, or even his conduct of single or isolated items of activities in a state in the corporation's behalf, are not enough to subject it to suit on causes of action unconnected with the activities there. To require the corporation in such circumstances to defend the suit away from its home or other jurisdiction where it carries on more substantial activities has been thought to lay too great and unreasonable a burden on the corporation to comport with due process. While it has been held, in cases on which appellant relies, that continuous activity of some sorts within a state is not enough to support the demand that the corporation be amenable to suits unrelated to that activity, there have been instances in which the continuous corporate operations within a state were thought so substantial and of such a nature as to justify suit against it on causes of action arising from dealings entirely distinct from those activities.

. . .

It is evident that the criteria by which we mark the boundary line between those activities which justify the subjection of a corporation to suit and those which do not cannot be simply mechanical or quantitative. The test is not merely, as has sometimes been suggested, whether the activity, which the corporation has seen fit to procure through its agents in another state, is a little more or a little less. Whether due process is satisfied must depend, rather, upon the quality and nature of the activity in relation to the fair and orderly administration of the laws which it was the purpose of the due process clause to insure. That clause does not contemplate that a state may make binding a judgment *in personam* against an individual or corporate defendant with which the state has no contacts, ties, or relations.

But, to the extent that a corporation exercises the privilege of conducting activities within a state, it enjoys the benefits and protection of the laws of that state. The exercise of that privilege may give rise to obligations, and, so far as those obligations arise out of or are connected with the activities within the state, a procedure which requires the corporation to respond to a suit brought to enforce them can, in most instances, hardly be said to be undue.

Applying these standards, the activities carried on in behalf of appellant in the State of Washington were neither irregular nor casual. They were systematic and continuous throughout the years in question. They resulted in a large volume of interstate business, in the course of which appellant received the benefits and protection of the laws of the state, including the right to resort to the courts for the enforcement of its rights. The obligation which is here sued upon arose out of those very activities. It is evident that these operations establish sufficient contacts or ties with the state of the forum to make it reasonable and just, according to our traditional conception of fair play and substantial justice, to permit the state to enforce the obligations which appellant has incurred there. Hence, we cannot say that the maintenance of the present suit in the State of Washington involves an unreasonable or undue procedure.

...

Appellant having rendered itself amenable to suit upon obligations arising out of the activities of its salesmen in Washington, the state may maintain the present suit *in personam* to collect the tax laid upon the exercise of the privilege of employing appellant's salesmen within the state. For Washington has made one of those activities which, taken together, establish appellant's "presence" there for purposes of suit the taxable event by which the state brings appellant within the reach of its taxing power. The state thus has constitutional power to lay the tax and to subject appellant to a suit to recover it. The activities which establish its "presence" subject it alike to taxation by the state and to suit to recover the tax.

Affirmed.

Mr. Justice JACKSON took no part in the consideration or decision of this case.

Mr. Justice BLACK delivered the following opinion. [Omitted.]

Notes

1. The determination of whether or not personal jurisdiction exists will always turn on the relevant facts. Your understanding of those facts is therefore imperative. This fact-focused analysis may be quite different from the methods of legal analysis that you learned in your earlier legal studies in another country, but that difference is one of several reasons why personal jurisdiction is a good starting point for your study of some of the unique aspects of U.S. law.
2. There are many facts discussed in *International Shoe*. Underlining every fact or copying every sentence that describes a fact into a separate case brief will not help you answer questions during class. That approach would collect too many facts. The challenge is to identify only the legally significant facts. Consider this sentence: "During the years from 1937 to 1940, now in question, appellant employed eleven to thirteen salesmen under direct supervision and control of sales managers located in St. Louis." Are the years important? Not really, as they are simply the relevant years. Is the exact number of salesmen important? Not necessarily, but the sense that

it was more than a few salesmen might be important. You might possibly note that appellant had "about a dozen" salesmen in Washington.

3. Margin notes would be extremely beneficial in a case such as *International Shoe.* Consider this paragraph of text below (on the left) taken from the opinion and the margin notes (on the right) that you could have written next to it.

Opinion Text	Margin Notes
[The state enforced the requirements of this statute against Appellant International Shoe.] The facts... are not in dispute. Appellant is a Delaware corporation, having its principal place of business in St. Louis, Missouri, and is engaged in the manufacture and sale of shoes and other footwear. It maintains places of business in several states other than Washington, at which its manufacturing is carried on and from which its merchandise is distributed interstate through several sales units or branches located outside the State of Washington.	Int'l Shoe — **NOT** in Wash. (all outside of Wash.) – Incorporation – Principal place of bus. – Manufacturing – Distribution of shoes

Make similar margin notes next to the paragraph that begins, "Appellant has no office in Washington,..." and the paragraph after that one.

4. Now that you know the facts well, consider what the court says about the relevant standard for assessing whether those facts support exercising personal jurisdiction over a defendant. One paragraph of the legal discussion in the case is included on the following page. A key phrase is underlined. In the margins is a summary of the point of the paragraph.

Opinion Text	Margin Notes
But, to the extent that a corporation exercises the privilege of conducting activities within a state, it enjoys the benefits and protection of the laws of that state. The exercise of that privilege may give rise to obligations, and, so far as those obligations arise out of or are connected with the activities within the state, a procedure which requires the corporation to respond to a suit brought to enforce them can, in most instances, hardly be said to be undue.	Corp. doing business in a state gets benefits from that state. ← So this is fair!

Repeat this exercise for the other paragraphs of legal discussion in the decision.

5. Also, note or highlight any words or phrases that you do not understand. For example, *in personam* might be on your list. Listen carefully in class to hear if anything is said to eliminate your confusion about this phrase.
6. The Fifth Amendment, which applies to federal courts, contains very similar language as the Fourteenth Amendment regarding due process, but the personal jurisdiction requirements in federal court are more of an open question than in state court. *See Omni Capital Int'l, Ltd. v. Rudolf Wolff & Co.*, 484 U.S. 97, 102, n. 5 (1987). This class will focus on personal jurisdiction in state courts.
7. The decision that you read was written by the Supreme Court of the United States, a federal court. But the Court referenced the Fourteenth Amendment, not the Fifth Amendment. Why? Which court must have personal jurisdiction? In other words, where did the case originate?

Notes on Citing and Quoting Cases in Practice and School

1. All cites have been removed from this version of *International Shoe*, just as the cites were removed in the edited version of *Mas* included in this textbook. The edited version of the case above does not even indicate where such citations have been removed. The next case, *World-Wide Volkswagen Corp. v. Woodson*, will be the first case to include some of the many citations that are included in the published opinion, but will continue not to indicate where citations have been omitted.
2. The liberties taken in editing cases for a textbook are very different from those that govern paraphrasing or quoting language from cases for legal practice or law school assignments. An elaborate set of rules govern the proper citation of cases, including quotes from cases, and are reported in *The Bluebook: A Uniform System of Citations.* Most courts, but not all, expect practitioners to follow the rules of the *Bluebook* when submitting documents to that court. As an example of an exception, California courts use their own variant on the *Bluebook*, known as the *California Style Manual: A Handbook of Legal Style for California Courts and Lawyers.* One thing that these various approaches have in common are rules about attribution whenever quoting another source.
3. Rules against plagiarism apply as well when submitting assignments in school (the context most important to you, but not the only context in which these rules apply). These rules prohibit the use of material created by another person without proper attribution or use of quotation marks, where appropriate. Do not assume that plagiarism as it is understood in any other country is the same as it is understood in the United States. Carefully consult the plagiarism rules as they are defined and applied at your U.S. law school. Failure to adhere to the rules against plagiarism can lead to serious, adverse consequences for the student.

Personal jurisdiction has been the topic of many Supreme Court decisions. This book includes only three of the many more Supreme Court decisions that have considered the scope of personal jurisdiction. Notice how, in each subsequent case, the Supreme Court refines and revises the principles articulated in its earlier decisions. This development of the law through judicial decisions is a hallmark of the U.S. common-law system. As you read the next three cases, continue writing margin notes as you did for *International Shoe.*

World-Wide Volkswagen Corp. v. Woodson

Supreme Court of the United States

444 U.S. 286 (1980)

Mr. Justice WHITE delivered the opinion of the Court.

The issue before us is whether, consistently with the Due Process Clause of the Fourteenth Amendment, an Oklahoma court may exercise *in personam* jurisdiction over a nonresident automobile retailer and its wholesale distributor in a products liability action, when the defendants' only connection with Oklahoma is the fact that an automobile sold in New York to New York residents became involved in an accident in Oklahoma.

I

Respondents Harry and Kay Robinson purchased a new Audi automobile from petitioner Seaway Volkswagen, Inc. (Seaway), in Massena, N.Y. in 1976. The following year, the Robinson family, who resided in New York, left that State for a new home in Arizona. As they passed through the State of Oklahoma, another car struck their Audi in the rear, causing a fire which severely burned Kay Robinson and her two children.

The Robinsons subsequently brought a products liability action in the District Court for Creek County, Okla., claiming that their injuries resulted from defective design and placement of the Audi's gas tank and fuel system. They joined as defendants the automobile's manufacturer, Audi NSU Auto Union Aktiengesellschaft (Audi); its importer, Volkswagen of America, Inc. (Volkswagen); its regional distributor, petitioner World-Wide Volkswagen Corp. (World-Wide); and its retail dealer, petitioner Seaway. Seaway and World-Wide...claim[ed] that Oklahoma's exercise of jurisdiction over them would offend the limitations on the State's jurisdiction imposed by the Due Process Clause of the Fourteenth Amendment.

The facts presented to the District Court showed that World-Wide is incorporated and has its business office in New York. It distributes vehicles, parts, and accessories, under contract with Volkswagen, to retail dealers in New York, New Jersey, and Connecticut. Seaway, one of these retail dealers, is incorporated and has its place of business in New York. Insofar as the record reveals, Seaway and World-Wide are fully independent corporations whose relations with each other and with Volkswagen and Audi are contractual only. Respondents adduced no evidence that either World-Wide or Seaway does any business in Oklahoma, ships or sells any products to or in that State, has an agent to receive process there, or purchases advertisements in any media calculated to reach Oklahoma. In fact, as respondents' counsel conceded at oral argument, there was no showing that any automobile sold by World-Wide or Seaway has ever entered Oklahoma, with the single exception of the vehicle involved in the present case.

Despite the apparent paucity of contacts between petitioners and Oklahoma, the District Court rejected their constitutional claim and reaffirmed that ruling in denying petitioners' motion for reconsideration. Petitioners then sought a writ of prohibition in the Supreme Court of Oklahoma to restrain the District Judge...from exercising *in personam* jurisdiction over them. They renewed their contention that, because they had no "minimal contacts," with the State of Oklahoma, the actions of the District Judge were in violation of their rights under the Due Process Clause.

The Supreme Court of Oklahoma denied the writ....

We granted certiorari to consider an important constitutional question with respect to state court jurisdiction and to resolve a conflict between the Supreme Court of Oklahoma and the highest courts of at least four other States. We reverse.

II

The Due Process Clause of the Fourteenth Amendment limits the power of a state court to render a valid personal judgment against a nonresident defendant.... Due process requires that the defendant be given adequate notice of the suit, and be subject to the personal jurisdiction of the court, *International Shoe Co. v. Washington,* 326 U.S. 310 (1945). In the present case,...the only question is whether these particular petitioners were subject to the jurisdiction of the Oklahoma courts.

As has long been settled, and as we reaffirm today, a state court may exercise personal jurisdiction over a nonresident defendant only so long as there exist "minimum contacts" between the defendant and the forum State. The concept of minimum contacts, in turn, can be seen to perform two related, but distinguishable, functions. It protects the defendant against the burdens of litigating in a distant or inconvenient forum. And it acts to ensure that the States, through their courts, do not reach out beyond the limits imposed on them by their status as coequal sovereigns in a federal system.

The protection against inconvenient litigation is typically described in terms of "reasonableness" or "fairness." We have said that the defendant's contacts with the forum State must be such that maintenance of the suit "does not offend traditional notions of fair play and substantial justice." *International Shoe Co. v. Washington*, *supra*, at 316. The relationship between the defendant and the forum must be such that it is "reasonable... to require the corporation to defend the particular suit which is brought there." 326 U.S., at 317. Implicit in this emphasis on reasonableness is the understanding that the burden on the defendant, while always a primary concern, will in an appropriate case be considered in light of other relevant factors, including the forum State's interest in adjudicating the dispute; the plaintiff's interest in obtaining convenient and effective relief, at least when that interest is not adequately protected by the plaintiff's power to choose the forum; the interstate judicial system's interest in obtaining the most efficient resolution of controversies; and the shared interest of the several States in furthering fundamental substantive social policies.

The limits imposed on state jurisdiction by the Due Process Clause, in its role as a guarantor against inconvenient litigation, have been substantially relaxed over the years. As we noted in *McGee v. International Life Ins. Co.*, 355 U.S. [220,] 222–223 [(1957)], this trend is largely attributable to a fundamental transformation in the American economy:

> "Today many commercial transactions touch two or more States, and may involve parties separated by the full continent. With this increasing nationalization of commerce has come a great increase in the amount of business conducted by mail across state lines. At the same time, modern transportation and communication have made it much less burdensome for a party sued to defend himself in a State where he engages in economic activity."
>
> ...

Nevertheless, we have never accepted the proposition that state lines are irrelevant for jurisdictional purposes, nor could we and remain faithful to the principles of interstate federalism embodied in the Constitution. The economic interdependence of the States was foreseen and desired by the Framers. In the Commerce Clause, they provided that the Nation was to be a common market, a "free trade unit" in which the States are debarred from acting as separable economic entities. But the Framers also intended that the States retain many essential attributes of sovereignty, including, in particular, the sovereign power to try causes in their courts. The sovereignty of each State, in turn, implied a limitation on the sovereignty of all of its sister States — a limitation express or implicit in both the original scheme of the Constitution and the Fourteenth Amendment.

Hence, . . . , we emphasized that the reasonableness of asserting jurisdiction over the defendant must be assessed "in the context of our federal system of government," *International Shoe Co. v. Washington,* 326 U.S., at 317, and stressed that the Due Process Clause ensures not only fairness, but also the "orderly administration of the laws," *id.,* at 319. As we noted in *Hanson v. Denckla,* 357 U.S. 235, 250–251 (1958):

> "As technological progress has increased the flow of commerce between the States, the need for jurisdiction over nonresidents has undergone a similar increase. At the same time, progress in communications and transportation has made the defense of a suit in a foreign tribunal less burdensome. In response to these changes, the requirements for personal jurisdiction over nonresidents have evolved from the rigid rule of *Pennoyer v. Neff,* 95 U.S. 714 [(1877)], to the flexible standard of *International Shoe Co. v. Washington,* 326 U.S. 310. But it is a mistake to assume that this trend heralds the eventual demise of all restrictions on the personal jurisdiction of state courts. [Citation omitted.] Those restrictions are more than a guarantee of immunity from inconvenient or distant litigation. They are a consequence of territorial limitations on the power of the respective States."

. . . Even if the defendant would suffer minimal or no inconvenience from being forced to litigate before the tribunals of another State; even if the forum State has a strong interest in applying its law to the controversy; even if the forum State is the most convenient location for litigation, the Due Process Clause, acting as an instrument of interstate federalism, may sometimes act to divest the State of its power to render a valid judgment. *Hanson v. Denckla, supra,* at 251.

III

Applying these principles to the case at hand, we find in the record before us a total absence of those affiliating circumstances that are a necessary predicate to any exercise of state court jurisdiction. Petitioners carry on no activity whatsoever in Oklahoma. They close no sales and perform no services there. They avail themselves of none of the privileges and benefits of Oklahoma law. They solicit no business there either through salespersons or through advertising reasonably calculated to reach the State. Nor does the record show that they regularly sell cars at wholesale or retail to Oklahoma customers or residents, or that they indirectly, through others, serve or seek to serve the Oklahoma market. In short, respondents seek to base jurisdiction on one, isolated occurrence and whatever inferences can be drawn therefrom: the fortuitous circumstance that a single Audi automobile, sold in New York to New York residents, happened to suffer an accident while passing through Oklahoma.

It is argued, however, that, because an automobile is mobile by its very design and purpose, it was "foreseeable" that the Robinsons' Audi would cause injury in Oklahoma. Yet "foreseeability" alone has never been a sufficient benchmark for personal jurisdiction under the Due Process Clause. In *Hanson v. Denckla, supra,* it was no doubt foreseeable that the settlor of a Delaware trust would subsequently move to Florida and seek to exercise a power of appointment there; yet we held that Florida courts could not constitutionally exercise jurisdiction over a Delaware trustee that had no other contacts with the forum State. In *Kulko v. California Superior Court,* 436 U.S. 84 (1978), it was surely "foreseeable" that a divorced wife would move to California from New York, the domicile of the marriage, and that a minor daughter would live with the mother. Yet we held that California could not exercise jurisdiction in a child support action over the former husband, who had remained in New York.

If foreseeability were the criterion,... [e]very seller of chattels would, in effect, appoint the chattel his agent for service of process. His amenability to suit would travel with the chattel. [W]e are unwilling to endorse [that] principle in the present case. This is not to say, of course, that foreseeability is wholly irrelevant. But the foreseeability that is critical to due process analysis is not the mere likelihood that a product will find its way into the forum State. Rather, it is that the defendant's conduct and connection with the forum State are such that he should reasonably anticipate being haled into court there. The Due Process Clause, by ensuring the "orderly administration of the laws," *International Shoe Co. v. Washington,* 326 U.S., at 319, gives a degree of predictability to the legal system that allows potential defendants to structure their primary conduct with some minimum assurance as to where that conduct will and will not render them liable to suit.

When a corporation "purposefully avails itself of the privilege of conducting activities within the forum State," it has clear notice that it is subject to suit there, and can act to alleviate the risk of burdensome litigation by procuring insurance, passing the expected costs on to customers, or, if the risks are too great, severing its connection with the State. Hence if the sale of a product of a manufacturer or distributor such as Audi or Volkswagen is not simply an isolated occurrence, but arises from the efforts of the manufacturer or distributor to serve, directly or indirectly, the market for its product in other States, it is not unreasonable to subject it to suit in one of those States if its allegedly defective merchandise has there been the source of injury to its owner or to others. The forum State does not exceed its powers under the Due Process Clause if it asserts personal jurisdiction over a corporation that delivers its products into the stream of commerce with the expectation that they will be purchased by consumers in the forum State. *Cf. Gray v. American Radiator & Standard Sanitary Corp.*, 22 Ill. 2d 432, 176 N.E.2d 761 (1961).

But there is no such or similar basis for Oklahoma jurisdiction over World-Wide or Seaway in this case. Seaway's sales are made in Massena, N.Y. World-Wide's market, although substantially larger, is limited to dealers in New York, New Jersey, and Connecticut. There is no evidence of record that any automobiles distributed by World-Wide are sold to retail customers outside this tristate area. It is foreseeable that the purchasers of automobiles sold by World-Wide and Seaway may take them to Oklahoma. But the mere "unilateral activity of those who claim some relationship with a nonresident defendant cannot satisfy the requirement of contact with the forum State." *Hanson v. Denckla, supra,* at 253.

In a variant on the previous argument, it is contended that jurisdiction can be supported by the fact that petitioners earn substantial revenue from goods used in Oklahoma.... This argument seems to make the point that the purchase of automobiles in New York, from which the petitioners earn substantial revenue, would not occur *but for* the fact that the automobiles are capable of use in distant States like Oklahoma. Respondents observe that the very purpose of an automobile is to travel, and that travel of automobiles sold by petitioners is facilitated by an extensive chain of Volkswagen service centers throughout the country, including some in Oklahoma. However, financial benefits accruing to the defendant from a collateral relation to the forum State will not support jurisdiction if they do not stem from a constitutionally cognizable contact with that State. In our view, whatever marginal revenues petitioners may receive by virtue of the fact that their products are capable of use in Oklahoma is far too attenuated a contact to justify that State's exercise of *in personam* jurisdiction over them.

Because we find that petitioners have no "contacts, ties, or relations" with the State of Oklahoma, *International Shoe Co. v. Washington, supra,* at 319, the judgment of the Supreme Court of Oklahoma is

Reversed.

Mr. Justice BRENNAN, dissenting.

...Because I believe that the Court reads *International Shoe* and its progeny too narrowly, and because I believe that the standards enunciated by those cases may already be obsolete as constitutional boundaries, I dissent.

I

The Court's opinions focus tightly on the existence of contacts between the forum and the defendant. In so doing, they accord too little weight to the strength of the forum State's interest in the case, and fail to explore whether there would be any actual inconvenience to the defendant.... The clear focus in *International Shoe* was on fairness and reasonableness....

...The existence of contacts, so long as there were some, was merely one way of giving content to the determination of fairness and reasonableness.

Surely *International Shoe* contemplated that the significance of the contacts necessary to support jurisdiction would diminish if some other consideration helped establish that jurisdiction would be fair and reasonable. The interests of the State and other parties in proceeding with the case in a particular forum are such considerations....

Another consideration is the actual burden a defendant must bear in defending the suit in the forum. *McGee, supra.* Because lesser burdens reduce the unfairness to the defendant, jurisdiction may be justified despite less significant contacts....

...

II

...I would find that the forum State has an interest in permitting the litigation to go forward[:] the litigation is connected to the forum, the defendant is linked to the forum, and the burden of defending is not unreasonable. Accordingly, I would hold that it is neither unfair nor unreasonable to require these defendants to defend in the forum State.

...

[T]he interest of the forum State and its connection to the litigation is strong. The automobile accident underlying the litigation occurred in Oklahoma. The plaintiffs were hospitalized in Oklahoma when they brought suit. Essential witnesses and evidence were in Oklahoma. The State has a legitimate interest in enforcing its laws designed to keep its highway system safe, and the trial can proceed at least as efficiently in Oklahoma as anywhere else.

...

Thus, the Court errs in its conclusion that petitioners have no contacts, ties, or relations" with Oklahoma. There obviously are contacts, and, given Oklahoma's connection to the litigation, the contacts are sufficiently significant to make it fair and reasonable for the petitioners to submit to Oklahoma's jurisdiction.

...

...I am not convinced that the defendants would suffer any "heavy and disproportionate burden" in defending the suits. Accordingly, I would hold that the Constitution should not shield the defendants from appearing and defending in the plaintiffs' chosen fora.

Mr. Justice MARSHALL, with whom Mr. Justice BLACKMUN joins, dissenting.

For over 30 years, the standard by which to measure the constitutionally permissible reach of state court jurisdiction has been well established.... The concepts of fairness and substantial justice as applied to an evaluation of "the quality and nature of the [defendant's] activity," are not readily susceptible of further definition, however, and it is not surprising that the constitutional standard is easier to state than to apply.

This is a difficult case, and reasonable minds may differ as to whether respondents have alleged a sufficient "relationship among the defendant[s], the forum, and the litigation" to satisfy the requirements of *International Shoe.* I am concerned, however, that the majority has reached its result by taking an unnecessarily narrow view of petitioners' forum-related conduct. The majority asserts that

> "respondents seek to base jurisdiction on one, isolated occurrence and whatever inferences can be drawn therefrom: the fortuitous circumstance that a single Audi automobile, sold in New York to New York residents, happened to suffer an accident while passing through Oklahoma."

If that were the case, I would readily agree that the minimum contacts necessary to sustain jurisdiction are not present. But the basis for the assertion of jurisdiction is not the happenstance that an individual over whom petitioners had no control made a unilateral decision to take a chattel with him to a distant State. Rather, jurisdiction is premised on the deliberate and purposeful actions of the defendants themselves in choosing to become part of a nationwide, indeed a global, network for marketing and servicing automobiles.

Petitioners are sellers of a product whose utility derives from its mobility. The unique importance of the automobile in today's society needs no further elaboration. Petitioners know that their customers buy cars not only to make short trips, but also to travel long distances. In fact, the nationwide service network with which they are affiliated was designed to facilitate and encourage such travel. Seaway would be unlikely to sell many cars if authorized service were available only in Massena, N.Y. Moreover, local dealers normally derive a substantial portion of their revenues from their service operations, and thereby obtain a further economic benefit from the opportunity to service cars which were sold in other States. It is apparent that petitioners have not attempted to minimize the chance that their activities will have effects in other States; on the contrary, they have chosen to do business in a way that increases that chance, because it is to their economic advantage to do so.

To be sure, petitioners could not know in advance that this particular automobile would be driven to Oklahoma. They must have anticipated, however, that a substantial portion of the cars they sold would travel out of New York. Seaway, a local dealer in the second most populous State, and World-Wide, one of only seven regional Audi distributors in the entire country, would scarcely have been surprised to learn that a car sold by them had been driven in Oklahoma on Interstate 44, a heavily traveled transcontinental highway. In the case of the distributor, in particular, the probability that some of the cars it sells will be driven in every one of the contiguous States must amount to a virtual certainty. This knowledge should alert a reasonable businessman to the likelihood that a defect in the product might manifest itself in the forum State — not because of some unpredictable, aberrant, unilateral action by a single buyer, but in the normal course of the operation of the vehicles for their intended purpose.

. . .

Accordingly, I dissent.

Mr. Justice BLACKMUN, dissenting.

. . .

I would affirm the judgment of the Supreme Court of Oklahoma. Because the Court reverses that judgment, it will now be about parsing every variant in the myriad of motor vehicle fact situations that present themselves. Some will justify jurisdiction and others will not. All will depend on the "contact" that the Court sees fit to perceive in the individual case.

Notes

1. Which defendants challenged personal jurisdiction? Which defendants apparently did not challenge personal jurisdiction? Why do you think those defendants did not challenge personal jurisdiction? Why did the Court conclude that there was no personal jurisdiction over Seaway and World-Wide? What was the effect of there being no personal jurisdiction over Seaway and World-Wide?
2. Does *World-Wide Volkswagen* change or refine the principles or test applied in *International Shoe*? In other words, do you think you could have predicted the result of *World-Wide Volkswagen* based on the guidance provided in *International Shoe*? Why or why not? If *World-Wide Volkswagen* changed or refined the test, in what way?
3. The decision in *World-Wide Volkswagen* generated four opinions. The majority opinion, which is controlling authority in this and future cases, and three dissenting opinions. The dissenting opinions have no precedential value. Why would a Justice take the time to write an opinion that has no precedential effect?
4. Blackmun "joined" Marshall's dissenting opinion. What do you think that means? Why do you think Blackmun also wrote a separate opinion?
5. Regardless of whether you consider any or all of the dissents more persuasive than the majority opinion, the majority is still the controlling opinion. Nevertheless, it is important to develop your own opinions and critical

reasoning skills. Which of the four separate opinions do you find most persuasive and why?

6. Personal jurisdiction protects a defendant's right to refuse to defend against a lawsuit in certain forums when there are inadequate connections between the defendant and the forum. Notice that personal jurisdiction protects a *defendant's* rights, not the rights or authority of the court. When it concerns the authority of the court, as with subject-matter jurisdiction, the issue can be raised at any time, even after the plaintiff has lost the case, as was shown in *Capron.* Because personal jurisdiction is a right personal to the defendant, the defendant must challenge the court's personal jurisdiction at the first opportunity. Fed. R. Civ. P. 12(b)(2). If the defendant delays, the defendant will be deemed to have consented to and waived the right to challenge the court's personal jurisdiction. Fed. R. Civ. P. 12(h)(1). Not included in the opinion above is the fact that "Petitioners entered special appearances" in the district court. This language means that the first pleadings filed by Seaway and World-Wide in the case were for the sole purpose of challenging personal jurisdiction.

Burger King Corp. v. Rudzewicz

Supreme Court of United States

471 U.S. 462 (1985)

Justice BRENNAN delivered the opinion of the Court.

The State of Florida's long-arm statute extends jurisdiction to "[a]ny person, whether or not a citizen or resident of this state," who, *inter alia*, "[b]reach[es] a contract in this state by failing to perform acts required by the contract to be performed in this state," so long as the cause of action arises from the alleged contractual breach. Fla. Stat. §48.193(1)(g) (Supp. 1984). The United States District Court for the Southern District of Florida, sitting in diversity, relied on this provision in exercising personal jurisdiction over a Michigan resident who allegedly had breached a franchise agreement with a Florida corporation by failing to make required payments in Florida. The question presented is whether this exercise of long-arm jurisdiction offended "traditional conception[s] of fair play and substantial justice" embodied in the Due Process Clause of the Fourteenth Amendment. *International Shoe Co. v. Washington*, 326 U.S. 310, 320 (1945).

I

A

Burger King Corporation is a Florida corporation whose principal offices are in Miami. It is one of the world's largest restaurant organizations, with over 3,000 outlets in the 50 States, the Commonwealth of Puerto Rico, and 8 foreign nations. Burger King conducts approximately 80% of its business through a franchise operation that the company styles the "Burger King System"—"a comprehensive restaurant format and operating system for the sale of uniform and quality food products." Burger King licenses its franchisees to use its trademarks and service marks for a period of 20 years and leases standardized restaurant facilities to them for the same term. In addition, franchisees acquire a variety of proprietary information concerning the "standards, specifications, procedures and methods for operating a Burger King Restaurant." They also receive market research and advertising assistance; ongoing training in restaurant management; and accounting, cost-control, and inventory-control guidance. By permitting franchisees to tap into Burger King's established national reputation and to benefit from proven procedures for dispensing standardized fare, this system enables them to go into the restaurant business with significantly lowered barriers to entry.

In exchange for these benefits, franchisees pay Burger King an initial $40,000 franchise fee and commit themselves to payment of monthly royalties, advertising and sales promotion fees, and rent computed in part from monthly gross sales. Franchisees also agree to submit to the national organization's exacting regulation of virtually every conceivable aspect of their operations. Burger King imposes these standards and undertakes its rigid regulation out of conviction that "[u]niformity of service, appearance, and quality of product is essential to the preservation of the Burger King image and the benefits accruing therefrom to both Franchisee and Franchisor."

Burger King oversees its franchise system through a two-tiered administrative structure. The governing contracts provide that the franchise relationship is established in Miami and governed by Florida law, and call for payment of all required fees and forwarding of all relevant notices to the Miami headquarters. The Miami headquarters sets policy and works directly with its franchisees in attempting to resolve major problems. Day-to-day monitoring of franchisees, however, is conducted through a network of 10 district offices which in turn report to the Miami headquarters.

The instant litigation grows out of Burger King's termination of one of its franchisees, and is aptly described by the franchisee as "a divorce proceeding among commercial partners." The appellee John Rudzewicz, a Michigan citizen and resident, is the senior partner in a Detroit accounting firm. In 1978, he was approached by Brian MacShara, the son of a business acquaintance, who suggested that they jointly apply to Burger King for a franchise in the Detroit area. MacShara proposed to serve as the manager of the restaurant if Rudzewicz would put up the investment capital; in exchange, the two would evenly share the profits. Believing that MacShara's idea offered attractive investment and tax-deferral opportunities, Rudzewicz agreed to the venture.

Rudzewicz and MacShara jointly applied for a franchise to Burger King's Birmingham, Michigan, district office in the autumn of 1978. Their application was forwarded to Burger King's Miami headquarters, which entered into a preliminary agreement with them in February 1979. During the ensuing four months it was agreed that Rudzewicz and MacShara would assume operation of an existing facility in Drayton Plains, Michigan. MacShara attended the prescribed management courses in Miami during this period, and the franchisees purchased $165,000 worth of restaurant equipment from Burger King's Davmor Industries division in Miami. Even before the final agreements were signed, however, the parties began to disagree over site-development fees, building design, computation of monthly rent, and whether the franchisees would be able to assign their liabilities to a corporation they had formed. During these disputes Rudzewicz and MacShara negotiated both with the Birmingham district office and with the Miami headquarters. With some misgivings, Rudzewicz and MacShara finally obtained limited concessions from the Miami headquarters, signed the final agreements, and commenced operations in June 1979. By signing the final agreements, Rudzewicz obligated himself personally to payments exceeding $1 million over the 20-year franchise relationship.

The Drayton Plains facility apparently enjoyed steady business during the summer of 1979, but patronage declined after a recession began later that year. Rudzewicz and MacShara soon fell far behind in their monthly payments to Miami. Headquarters sent notices of default, and an extended period of negotiations began among the franchisees, the Birmingham district office, and the Miami headquarters. After several Burger King officials in Miami had engaged in prolonged but ultimately unsuccessful negotiations with the franchisees by mail and by telephone, headquarters terminated the franchise and ordered

Rudzewicz and MacShara to vacate the premises. They refused and continued to occupy and operate the facility as a Burger King restaurant.

B

Burger King commenced the instant action in the United States District Court for the Southern District of Florida in May 1981.... Burger King alleged that Rudzewicz and MacShara had breached their franchise obligations "within [the jurisdiction of] this district court" by failing to make the required payments "at plaintiff's place of business in Miami, Dade County, Florida," and also charged that they were tortiously infringing its trademarks and service marks through their continued, unauthorized operation as a Burger King restaurant, Burger King sought damages, injunctive relief, and costs and attorney's fees. Rudzewicz and MacShara entered special appearances and argued, *inter alia*, that because they were Michigan residents and because Burger King's claim did not "arise" within the Southern District of Florida, the District Court lacked personal jurisdiction over them. The District Court denied their motions after a hearing, holding that, pursuant to Florida's long-arm statute, "a non-resident Burger King franchisee is subject to the personal jurisdiction of this Court in actions arising out of its franchise agreements." Rudzewicz and MacShara then filed an answer and a counterclaim seeking damages for alleged violations by Burger King of Michigan's Franchise Investment Law.

After a 3-day bench trial, the court [ruled in favor of Burger King on the merits of its claims.]....

Rudzewicz appealed to the Court of Appeals for the Eleventh Circuit. A divided panel of that Circuit reversed the judgment, concluding that the District Court could not properly exercise personal jurisdiction over Rudzewicz... because "the circumstances of the Drayton Plains franchise and the negotiations which led to it left Rudzewicz bereft of reasonable notice and financially unprepared for the prospect of franchise litigation in Florida." Accordingly, the panel majority concluded that "[j]urisdiction under these circumstances would offend the fundamental fairness which is the touchstone of due process."

... [W]e grant [certiorari] and now reverse.

II

A

The Due Process Clause protects an individual's liberty interest in not being subject to the binding judgments of a forum with which he has established no meaningful "contacts, ties, or relations." *International Shoe Co. v. Washington*, 326 U.S., at 319. By requiring that individuals have "fair warning that a particular activity may subject [them] to the jurisdiction of a foreign sovereign," the Due Process Clause "gives a degree of predictability to the legal system that allows potential defendants to structure their primary conduct with some minimum assurance as to where that conduct will and will not render them liable to suit," *World-Wide Volkswagen Corp. v. Woodson*, 444 U.S. 286, 297 (1980).

Where a forum seeks to assert specific jurisdiction over an out-of-state defendant who has not consented to suit there, this "fair warning" requirement is satisfied if the defendant has "purposefully directed" his activities at residents of the forum, and the litigation results from alleged injuries that "arise out of or relate to" those activities....

We have noted several reasons why a forum legitimately may exercise personal jurisdiction over a nonresident who "purposefully directs" his activities toward forum residents. A State generally has a "manifest interest" in providing its residents with a convenient forum for redressing injuries inflicted by out-of-state actors. Moreover, where individuals "purposefully derive benefit" from their interstate activities, it may well be unfair to allow them to escape having to account in other States for consequences that arise proximately from such activities; the Due Process Clause may not readily be wielded as a territorial shield to avoid interstate obligations that have been voluntarily assumed. And because "modern transportation and communications have made it much less burdensome for a party sued to defend himself in a State where he engages in economic activity," it usually will not be unfair to subject him to the burdens of litigating in another forum for disputes relating to such activity.

Notwithstanding these considerations, the constitutional touchstone remains whether the defendant purposefully established "minimum contacts" in the forum State. *International Shoe Co. v. Washington*, *supra*, at 316. Although it has been argued that foreseeability of causing *injury* in another State should be sufficient to establish such contacts there when policy considerations so require, the Court has consistently held that this kind of foreseeability is not a "sufficient benchmark" for exercising personal jurisdiction. *World-Wide Volkswagen Corp. v. Woodson*, 444 U.S., at 295. Instead, "the foreseeability that is critical to due process analysis... is that the defendant's conduct and connection with the forum State are such that he should reasonably anticipate being haled into court there." *Id.*, at 297....

This "purposeful availment" requirement ensures that... [j]urisdiction is proper [] where the contacts proximately result from actions by the defendant *himself* that create a "substantial connection" with the forum State. Thus where the defendant "deliberately" has engaged in significant activities within a State, or has created "continuing obligations" between himself and residents of the forum, he manifestly has availed himself of the privilege of conducting business there, and because his activities are shielded by "the benefits and protections" of the forum's laws it is presumptively not unreasonable to require him to submit to the burdens of litigation in that forum as well.

...

Once it has been decided that a defendant purposefully established minimum contacts within the forum State, these contacts may be considered in light of other factors to determine whether the assertion of personal jurisdiction would comport with "fair play and substantial justice."... Thus courts in "appropriate case[s]" may evaluate "the burden on the defendant," "the forum State's interest in adjudicating the dispute," "the plaintiff's interest in obtaining convenient and effective relief," "the interstate judicial system's interest in obtaining the most efficient resolution of controversies," and the "shared interest of the several States in furthering fundamental substantive social policies." *World-Wide Volkswagen Corp. v. Woodson*, 444 U.S., at 292. These considerations sometimes serve to establish the reasonableness of jurisdiction upon a lesser showing of minimum contacts than would otherwise be required. On the other hand, where a defendant who purposefully has directed his activities at forum residents seeks to defeat jurisdiction, he must present a compelling case that the presence of some other considerations would render jurisdiction unreasonable....

...

B

(1)

Applying these principles to the case at hand, we believe there is substantial record evidence supporting the District Court's conclusion that the assertion of personal jurisdiction over Rudzewicz in Florida for the alleged breach of his franchise agreement did not offend due process.... If the question is whether an individual's contract with an out-of-state party *alone* can automatically establish sufficient minimum contacts in the other party's home forum, we believe the answer clearly is that it cannot.... Instead, we have emphasized the need for a "highly realistic" approach that recognizes that a "contract" is "ordinarily but an intermediate step serving to tie up prior business negotiations with future consequences which themselves are the real object of the business transaction." *Id.*, at 316–317. It is these factors — prior negotiations and contemplated future consequences, along with the terms of the contract and the parties' actual course of dealing — that must be evaluated in determining whether the defendant purposefully established minimum contacts within the forum.

In this case, no physical ties to Florida can be attributed to Rudzewicz other than MacShara's brief training course in Miami. Rudzewicz did not maintain offices in Florida and, for all that appears from the record, has never even visited there. Yet this franchise dispute grew directly out of "a contract which had a *substantial* connection with that State." *McGee v. International Life Insurance Co.*, 355 U.S., at 223 (emphasis added).... Rudzewicz deliberately "reach[ed] out beyond" Michigan and negotiated with a Florida corporation for the purchase of a long-term franchise and the manifold benefits that would derive from affiliation with a nationwide organization. Upon approval, he entered into a carefully structured 20-year relationship that envisioned continuing and wide-reaching contacts with Burger King in Florida. In light of Rudzewicz' voluntary acceptance of the long-term and exacting regulation of his business from Burger King's Miami headquarters, the "quality and nature" of his relationship to the company in Florida can in no sense be viewed as "random," "fortuitous," or "attenuated." Rudzewicz' refusal to make the contractually required payments in Miami, and his continued use of Burger King's trademarks and confidential business information after his termination, caused foreseeable injuries to the corporation in Florida. For these reasons it was, at the very least, presumptively reasonable for Rudzewicz to be called to account there for such injuries.

...

(2)

Nor has Rudzewicz pointed to other factors that can be said persuasively to outweigh the considerations discussed above and to establish the *uncon-*

stitutionality of Florida's assertion of jurisdiction. We cannot conclude that Florida had no "legitimate interest in holding [Rudzewicz] answerable on a claim related to" the contacts he had established in that State. Moreover, although Rudzewicz has argued at some length that Michigan's Franchise Investment Law governs many aspects of this franchise relationship, he has not demonstrated how Michigan's acknowledged interest might possibly render jurisdiction in Florida *unconstitutional.* Finally, the Court of Appeals' assertion that the Florida litigation "severely impaired [Rudzewicz'] ability to call Michigan witnesses who might be essential to his defense and counterclaim" is wholly without support in the record. And even to the extent that it is inconvenient for a party who has minimum contacts with a forum to litigate there, such considerations most frequently can be accommodated through a change of venue. Although the Court has suggested that inconvenience may at some point become so substantial as to achieve *constitutional* magnitude, this is not such a case.

...

III

... Because Rudzewicz established a substantial and continuing relationship with Burger King's Miami headquarters, received fair notice from the contract documents and the course of dealing that he might be subject to suit in Florida, and has failed to demonstrate how jurisdiction in that forum would otherwise be fundamentally unfair, we conclude that the District Court's exercise of jurisdiction pursuant to Fla. Stat. § 48.193(1)(g) (Supp. 1984) did not offend due process. The judgment of the Court of Appeals is accordingly reversed, and the case is remanded for further proceedings consistent with this opinion.

It is so ordered.

Justice POWELL took no part in the consideration or decision of this case.

Justice STEVENS, with whom Justice WHITE joins, dissenting.

In my opinion, there is a significant element of unfairness in requiring a franchisee to defend a case of this kind in the forum chosen by the franchisor. It is undisputed that appellee maintained no place of business in Florida, that he had no employees in that State, and that he was not licensed to do business there. Appellee did not prepare his French fries, shakes, and hamburgers in Michigan, and then deliver them into the stream of commerce "with the expectation that they [would] be purchased by consumers in" Florida. To the contrary, appellee did business only in Michigan, his business, property, and payroll taxes were payable in that State, and he sold all of his products there.

Throughout the business relationship, appellee's principal contacts with appellant were with its Michigan office. Notwithstanding its disclaimer, the Court seems ultimately to rely on nothing more than standard boilerplate language contained in various documents, to establish that appellee "purposefully availed himself of the benefits and protections of Florida's laws." Such superficial analysis creates a potential for unfairness not only in negotiations between franchisors and their franchisees but, more significantly, in the resolution of the disputes that inevitably arise from time to time in such relationships.

Notes

1. How are the facts of this case similar to and different from the facts in *International Shoe and World-Wide Volkswagen?* Do the differences warrant a different conclusion regarding personal jurisdiction than was reached in *World-Wide Volkswagen*? Or do you think the facts are more similar to *International Shoe*? Alternatively, do the facts of *Burger King* bear no meaningful similarity to either *International Shoe* or *World-Wide Volkswagen?*
2. Does *Burger King* add to the principles recognized in *International Shoe* and *World-Wide Volkswagen*? Does it vary those principles? Does it refine those principles? If so, in what way or ways?

If you feel ill-equipped at this point to predict when personal jurisdiction will or will not exist, do not be unduly concerned. You are in good company. As you can see in the next case, the Supreme Court has on occasion likewise struggled to reach consensus on whether personal jurisdiction does or does not exist.

J. McIntyre Machinery, Ltd. v. Nicastro

Supreme Court of the United States

564 U.S. 873 (2011)

Justice KENNEDY announced the judgment of the Court and delivered an opinion, in which THE CHIEF JUSTICE, Justice SCALIA, and Justice THOMAS join.

Whether a person or entity is subject to the jurisdiction of a state court despite not having been present in the State either at the time of suit or at the time of the alleged injury, and despite not having consented to the exercise of jurisdiction, is a question that arises with great frequency in the routine course of litigation. The rules and standards for determining when a State does or does not have jurisdiction over an absent party have been unclear because of decades-old questions left open in *Asahi Metal Industry Co. v. Superior Court of Cal., Solano Cty.*, 480 U.S. 102 (1987).

Here, the Supreme Court of New Jersey, relying in part on *Asahi*, held that New Jersey's courts can exercise jurisdiction over a foreign manufacturer of a product so long as the manufacturer "knows or reasonably should know that its products are distributed through a nationwide distribution system that might lead to those products being sold in any of the fifty states." *Nicastro v. McIntyre Machinery America, Ltd.*, 201 N.J. 48, 76, 77, 987 A.2d 575, 591, 592 (2010). Applying that test, the court concluded that a British manufacturer of scrap metal machines was subject to jurisdiction in New Jersey, even though at no time had it advertised in, sent goods to, or in any relevant sense targeted the State.

That decision cannot be sustained. Although the New Jersey Supreme Court issued an extensive opinion with careful attention to this Court's cases and to its own precedent, the "stream of commerce" metaphor carried the decision far afield. Due process protects the defendant's right not to be coerced except by lawful judicial power. As a general rule, the exercise of judicial power is not lawful unless the defendant "purposefully avails itself of the privilege of conducting activities within the forum State, thus invoking the benefits and protections of its laws." *Hanson v. Denckla*, 357 U.S. 235, 253 (1958). There may be exceptions, say, for instance, in cases involving an intentional tort. But the general rule is applicable in this products-liability case, and the so-called "stream-of-commerce" doctrine cannot displace it.

I

This case arises from a products-liability suit filed in New Jersey state court. Robert Nicastro seriously injured his hand while using a metal-shearing machine manufactured by J. McIntyre Machinery, Ltd. (J. McIntyre). The accident occurred in New Jersey, but the machine was manufactured in England, where J. McIntyre is incorporated and operates. The question here is whether the New Jersey courts have jurisdiction over J. McIntyre, notwithstanding the fact that the company at no time either marketed goods in the State or shipped them there. Nicastro was a plaintiff in the New Jersey trial court and is the respondent here; J. McIntyre was a defendant and is now the petitioner.

At oral argument in this Court, Nicastro's counsel stressed three primary facts in defense of New Jersey's assertion of jurisdiction over J. McIntyre.

First, an independent company agreed to sell J. McIntyre's machines in the United States. J. McIntyre itself did not sell its machines to buyers in this country beyond the U.S. distributor, and there is no allegation that the distributor was under J. McIntyre's control.

Second, J. McIntyre officials attended annual conventions for the scrap recycling industry to advertise J. McIntyre's machines alongside the distributor. The conventions took place in various States, but never in New Jersey.

Third, no more than four machines (the record suggests only one), including the machine that caused the injuries that are the basis for this suit, ended up in New Jersey.

In addition to these facts emphasized by petitioner, the New Jersey Supreme Court noted that J. McIntyre held both United States and European patents on its recycling technology. It also noted that the U.S. distributor "structured [its] advertising and sales efforts in accordance with" J. McIntyre's "direction and guidance whenever possible," and that "at least some of the machines were sold on consignment to" the distributor.

In light of these facts, the New Jersey Supreme Court concluded that New Jersey courts could exercise jurisdiction over petitioner without contravention of the Due Process Clause. Jurisdiction was proper, in that court's view, because the injury occurred in New Jersey; because petitioner knew or reasonably should have known "that its products are distributed through a nationwide distribution system that might lead to those products being sold in any of the fifty states;" and because petitioner failed to "take some reasonable step to prevent the distribution of its products in this State."

. . .

II

. . .

A court may subject a defendant to judgment only when the defendant has sufficient contacts with the sovereign "such that the maintenance of the suit does not offend 'traditional notions of fair play and substantial justice.'" *International Shoe Co. v. Washington, 326 U.S. 310,* 316 (1945) (quoting *Milliken v. Meyer*, 311 U.S. 457, 463 (1940)). Freeform notions of fundamental fairness divorced from traditional practice cannot transform a judgment rendered in the absence of authority into law. As a general rule, the sovereign's exercise of power requires some act by which the defendant "purposefully avails itself of the privilege of conducting activities within the forum State, thus invoking the benefits and protections of its laws," *Hanson*, 357 U.S., at 253, though in some cases, as with an intentional tort, the defendant might well fall within the State's authority by reason of his attempt to obstruct its laws. In products-liability cases like this one, it is the defendant's purposeful availment that makes jurisdiction consistent with "traditional notions of fair play and substantial justice."

. . .

There is [a] limited form of submission to a State's authority for disputes that "arise out of or are connected with the activities within the state." *International Shoe Co., supra*, at 319. Where a defendant "purposefully avails itself of the privilege of conducting activities within the forum State, thus invoking the benefits and protections of its laws," *Hanson, supra*, at 253, it submits to the judicial power of an otherwise foreign sovereign to the extent that power is exercised in connection with the defendant's activities touching on the State....

The imprecision arising from *Asahi*, for the most part, results from its statement of the relation between jurisdiction and the "stream of commerce." The stream of commerce, like other metaphors, has its deficiencies as well as its utility. It refers to the movement of goods from manufacturers through distributors to consumers, yet beyond that descriptive purpose its meaning is far from exact. This Court has stated that a defendant's placing goods into the stream of commerce "with the expectation that they will be purchased by consumers within the forum State" may indicate purposeful availment. *World-Wide Volkswagen Corp. v. Woodson*, 444 U.S. 286, 298 (1980) (finding that expectation lacking). But that statement does not amend the general rule of personal jurisdiction. It merely observes that a defendant may in an appropriate case be subject to jurisdiction without entering the forum — itself an unexceptional proposition — as where manufacturers or distributors "seek to serve" a given State's market. *Id.*, at 295. The principal inquiry in cases of this sort is whether the defendant's activities manifest an intention to submit to the power of a sovereign. In other words, the defendant must "purposefully avai[l] itself of the privilege of conducting activities within the forum State, thus invoking the benefits and protections of its laws." *Hanson*, *supra*, at 253. Sometimes a defendant does so by sending its goods rather than its agents. The defendant's transmission of goods permits the exercise of jurisdiction only where the defendant can be said to have targeted the forum; as a general rule, it is not enough that the defendant might have predicted that its goods will reach the forum State.

In *Asahi*, an opinion by Justice Brennan for four Justices outlined a different approach. It discarded the central concept of sovereign authority in favor of considerations of fairness and foreseeability. As that concurrence contended, "jurisdiction premised on the placement of a product into the stream of commerce [without more] is consistent with the Due Process Clause," for "[a]s long as a participant in this process is aware that the final product is being marketed in the forum State, the possibility of a lawsuit there cannot come as a surprise." 480 U.S., at 117 (opinion concurring in part and concurring in judgment). It was the premise of the concurring opinion that the defendant's ability to anticipate suit renders the assertion of jurisdiction fair. In this way, the opinion made foreseeability the touchstone of jurisdiction.

The standard set forth in Justice Brennan's concurrence was rejected in an opinion written by Justice O'Connor; but the relevant part of that opinion, too, commanded the assent of only four Justices, not a majority of the Court. That opinion stated: "The 'substantial connection' between the defendant and the forum State necessary for a finding of minimum contacts must come about by an action of the defendant purposefully directed toward the forum State. The placement of a product into the stream of commerce, without more, is not an act of the defendant purposefully directed toward the forum State." *Id.*, at 112 (emphasis deleted; citations omitted).

Since *Asahi* was decided, the courts have sought to reconcile the competing opinions. But Justice Brennan's concurrence, advocating a rule based on general notions of fairness and foreseeability, is inconsistent with the premises of lawful judicial power. This Court's precedents make clear that it is the defendant's actions, not his expectations, that empower a State's courts to subject him to judgment.

... [J]urisdiction is in the first instance a question of authority rather than fairness....

... [P]ersonal jurisdiction requires a forum-by-forum, or sovereign-by-sovereign, analysis. The question is whether a defendant has followed a course of conduct directed at the society or economy existing within the jurisdiction of a given sovereign, so that the sovereign has the power to subject the defendant to judgment concerning that conduct. Personal jurisdiction, of course, restricts "judicial power not as a matter of sovereignty, but as a matter of individual liberty," for due process protects the individual's right to be subject only to lawful power. But whether a judicial judgment is lawful depends on whether the sovereign has authority to render it.

...

It must be remembered, however, that although this case and *Asahi* both involve foreign manufacturers, the undesirable consequences of Justice Brennan's approach are no less significant for domestic producers. The owner of a small Florida farm might sell crops to a large nearby distributor, for example, who might then distribute them to grocers across the country. If foreseeability were the controlling criterion, the farmer could be sued in Alaska or any number of other States' courts without ever leaving town. And the issue of foreseeability may itself be contested so that significant expenses are incurred just on the preliminary issue of jurisdiction. Jurisdictional rules should avoid these costs whenever possible.

The conclusion that the authority to subject a defendant to judgment depends on purposeful availment, consistent with Justice O'Connor's opinion in *Asahi*, does not by itself resolve many difficult questions of jurisdiction that will arise in particular cases. The defendant's conduct and the economic realities of the market the defendant seeks to serve will differ across cases, and judicial exposition will, in common-law fashion, clarify the contours of that principle.

III

In this case, petitioner directed marketing and sales efforts at the United States.... Here the question concerns the authority of a New Jersey state court to exercise jurisdiction, so it is petitioner's purposeful contacts with New Jersey, not with the United States, that alone are relevant.

Respondent has not established that J. McIntyre engaged in conduct purposefully directed at New Jersey. Recall that respondent's claim of jurisdiction centers on three facts: The distributor agreed to sell J. McIntyre's machines in the United States; J. McIntyre officials attended trade shows in several States but not in New Jersey; and up to four machines ended up in New Jersey. The British manufacturer had no office in New Jersey; it neither paid taxes nor owned property there; and it neither advertised in, nor sent any employees to, the State. Indeed, after discovery the trial court found that the "defendant does not have a single contact with New Jersey short of the machine in question ending up in this state." These facts may reveal an intent to serve the U.S. market, but they do not show that J. McIntyre purposefully availed itself of the New Jersey market.

...

Due process protects petitioner's right to be subject only to lawful authority. At no time did petitioner engage in any activities in New Jersey that reveal an intent to invoke or benefit from the protection of its laws. New Jersey is without power to adjudge the rights and liabilities of J. McIntyre, and its exercise of jurisdiction would violate due process. The contrary judgment of the New Jersey Supreme Court is

Reversed.

Justice BREYER, with whom Justice ALITO joins, concurring in the judgment.

The Supreme Court of New Jersey adopted a broad understanding of the scope of personal jurisdiction based on its view that "[t]he increasingly fast-paced globalization of the world economy has removed national borders as barriers to trade." *Nicastro v. McIntyre Machinery America, Ltd.*, 201 N.J. 48, 52, 987 A.2d 575, 577 (2010). I do not doubt that there have been many recent changes in commerce and communication, many of which are not anticipated by our precedents. But this case does not present any of those issues. So I think it unwise to announce a rule of broad applicability without full consideration of the modern-day consequences.

In my view, the outcome of this case is determined by our precedents. Based on the facts found by the New Jersey courts, respondent Robert Nicastro failed to meet his burden to demonstrate that it was constitutionally proper to exercise jurisdiction over petitioner J. McIntyre Machinery, Ltd.

(British Manufacturer), a British firm that manufactures scrap-metal machines in Great Britain and sells them through an independent distributor in the United States (American Distributor). On that basis, I agree with the plurality that the contrary judgment of the Supreme Court of New Jersey should be reversed.

. . .

None of our precedents finds that a single isolated sale, even if accompanied by the kind of sales effort indicated here, is sufficient. Rather, this Court's previous holdings suggest the contrary. The Court has held that a single sale to a customer who takes an accident-causing product to a different State (where the accident takes place) is not a sufficient basis for asserting jurisdiction. *See World-Wide Volkswagen Corp. v. Woodson*, 444 U.S. 286 (1980). And the Court, in separate opinions, has strongly suggested that a single sale of a product in a State does not constitute an adequate basis for asserting jurisdiction over an out-of-state defendant, even if that defendant places his goods in the stream of commerce, fully aware (and hoping) that such a sale will take place. *See Asahi Metal Industry Co. v. Superior Court of Cal., Solano Cty.*, 480 U.S. 102, 111, 112 (1987) (opinion of O'Connor, J.) (requiring "something more" than simply placing "a product into the stream of commerce," even if defendant is "awar[e]" that the stream "may or will sweep the product into the forum State"); *id.*, at 117 (Brennan, J., concurring in part and concurring in judgment) (jurisdiction should lie where a sale in a State is part of "the regular and anticipated flow" of commerce into the State, but not where that sale is only an "edd[y]," *i.e.*, an isolated occurrence); *id.*, at 122 (Stevens, J., concurring in part and concurring in judgment) (indicating that "the volume, the value, and the hazardous character" of a good may affect the jurisdictional inquiry and emphasizing Asahi's "regular course of dealing").

. . .

. . . I would not work such a change to the law in the way either the plurality or the New Jersey Supreme Court suggests without a better understanding of the relevant contemporary commercial circumstances. . . .

This case presents no such occasion, and so I again reiterate that I would adhere strictly to our precedents and the limited facts found by the New Jersey Supreme Court. And on those grounds, I do not think we can find jurisdiction in this case. Accordingly, though I agree with the plurality as to the outcome of this case, I concur only in the judgment of that opinion and not its reasoning.

Justice GINSBURG, with whom Justice SOTOMAYOR and Justice KAGAN join, dissenting.

A foreign industrialist seeks to develop a market in the United States for machines it manufactures. It hopes to derive substantial revenue from sales it makes to United States purchasers. Where in the United States buyers reside does not matter to this manufacturer. Its goal is simply to sell as much as it can, wherever it can. It excludes no region or State from the market it wishes to reach. But, all things considered, it prefers to avoid products liability litigation in the United States. To that end, it engages a U.S. distributor to ship its machines stateside. Has it succeeded in escaping personal jurisdiction in a State where one of its products is sold and causes injury or even death to a local user?

Under this Court's pathmarking precedent in *International Shoe Co. v. Washington*, 326 U.S. 310 (1945), and subsequent decisions, one would expect the answer to be unequivocally, "No." But instead, six Justices of this Court, in divergent opinions, tell us that the manufacturer has avoided the jurisdiction of our state courts, except perhaps in States where its products are sold in sizeable quantities. Inconceivable as it may have seemed yesterday, the splintered majority today "turn[s] the clock back to the days before modern long-arm statutes when a manufacturer, to avoid being haled into court where a user is injured, need only Pilate-like wash its hands of a product by having independent distributors market it." Weintraub, A Map Out of the Personal Jurisdiction Labyrinth, 28 U.C.D.L. Rev. 531, 555 (1995).

...

This case is illustrative of marketing arrangements for sales in the United States common in today's commercial world. A foreign-country manufacturer engages a U.S. company to promote and distribute the manufacturer's products, not in any particular State, but anywhere and everywhere in the United States the distributor can attract purchasers. The product proves defective and injures a user in the State where the user lives or works....

...

The modern approach to jurisdiction over corporations and other legal entities, ushered in by *International Shoe*, gave prime place to reason and fairness. Is it not fair and reasonable, given the mode of trading of which this case is an example, to require the international seller to defend at the place its products cause injury? Do not litigational convenience and choice-of-law considerations point in that direction? On what measure of reason and fairness can it be considered undue to require McIntyre UK to defend in New Jersey as an incident of its efforts to develop a market for its industrial machines anywhere and everywhere in the United States? Is not the burden on McIntyre UK to defend in New Jersey fair, *i.e.*, a reasonable cost of transacting business internationally, in comparison to the burden on Nicastro to go to Nottingham, England, to gain recompense for an injury he sustained using McIntyre's product at his workplace in Saddle Brook, New Jersey?

McIntyre UK dealt with the United States as a single market. Like most foreign manufacturers, it was concerned not with the prospect of suit in State X as opposed to State Y, but rather with its subjection to suit anywhere in the United States....

In sum, McIntyre UK, by engaging McIntyre America to promote and sell its machines in the United States, "purposefully availed itself "of the United States market nationwide, not a market in a single State or a discrete collection of States. McIntyre UK thereby availed itself of the market of all States in which its products were sold by its exclusive distributor. "Th[e] 'purposeful availment' requirement," this Court has explained, simply "ensures that a defendant will not be haled into a jurisdiction solely as a result of 'random,' 'fortuitous,' or 'attenuated' contacts." *Burger King*, 471 U.S., at 475. Adjudicatory authority is appropriately exercised where "actions by the defendant *himself*" give rise to the affiliation with the forum. *Ibid.* How could McIntyre UK not have intended, by its actions targeting a national market, to sell products in the fourth largest destination for imports among all States of the United States and the largest scrap metal market?

...

For the reasons stated, I would hold McIntyre UK answerable in New Jersey for the harm Nicastro suffered at his workplace in that State using McIntyre UK's shearing machine. While I dissent from the Court's judgment, I take heart that the plurality opinion does not speak for the Court, for that opinion would take a giant step away from the "notions of fair play and substantial justice" underlying *International Shoe*. 326 U.S., at 316 (internal quotation marks omitted).

Notes

1. The Supreme Court consists of nine Justices. Which opinion in *J. McIntyre* received a majority of the votes of the Supreme Court? Which *result*, i.e., personal jurisdiction or no personal jurisdiction, received a majority of the votes of the Supreme Court?
2. Part of the problem that the Court faced in *J. McIntyre* was the uncertainty created by the Court's earlier decision in *Asahi Metal Industry Co. v. Superior Court*, 480 U.S. 102 (1987). The New Jersey Supreme Court attempted to follow *Asahi*, but the plurality in *J. McIntyre* concluded that the New Jersey Supreme Court's efforts, although well-intentioned, were unsuccessful. And yet, despite the uncertainty created by the lack of a majority as to key aspects of the analysis in *Asahi*, the Court failed again to reach a majority as to its reasoning in *J. McIntyre.*
3. The main opinion in *Asahi* had multiple sections: I, II-A, II-B, and III. The decision begins with a list of which Justices voted for which sections, and which Justices wrote separately and who supported those separate opinions:

   > O'CONNOR, J., announced the judgment of the Court and delivered the opinion for a unanimous Court with respect to Part I, the opinion of the Court with respect to Part II-B, in which REHNQUIST, C.J., and BRENNAN, WHITE, MARSHALL, BLACKMUN, POWELL, and STEVENS, JJ., joined, and an opinion with respect to Parts II-A and III, in which REHNQUIST, C.J., and POWELL and SCALIA, JJ., joined. BRENNAN, J., filed an opinion concurring in part and concurring in the judgment, in which WHITE, MARSHALL, and BLACKMUN, JJ., joined. STEVENS, J., filed an opinion concurring in part and concurring in the judgment, in which WHITE and BLACKMUN, JJ., joined.

   Note that four Justices supported section II-A. Four other Justices, in an opinion written by Justice Brennan, supported an alternative theory to section II-A. Thus, neither discussion received a majority of the votes. *J. McIntyre* illustrates the problems created by these types of opinions. In *J. McIntyre*, the New Jersey Supreme Court had followed the plurality approach offered by Justice Brennan. The *J. McIntyre* decision concludes that the New Jersey Supreme Court should have used the plurality approach offered by Justice O'Connor.

4. These cases — *International Shoe* through *J. McIntyre* — discuss the scope of *specific* personal jurisdiction. *General* personal jurisdiction is a different concept. The Supreme Court recently explained: "A state court may exercise general jurisdiction only when a defendant is 'essentially at home' in the State. General jurisdiction, as its name implies, extends to 'any and all claims' brought against a defendant. Those claims need not relate to the forum State or the defendant's activity there; they may concern events and conduct anywhere in the world.... In what we have called the 'paradigm' case, an individual is subject to general jurisdiction in her place of domicile. And the 'equivalent' forums for a corporation are its place of incorporation and principal place of business." *Ford Motor Co. v. Montana Eighth Judicial Dist.*, 592 U.S. ___,141 S. Ct. 1017, 1024 (2021). Nevertheless, in *Ford,* the Court concluded that Ford was subject to specific, not general, personal jurisdiction because it had "purposefully avail[ed] itself of the privilege of conducting activities" in the state even though the defendant's specific conduct in the forum did not give rise to the plaintiff 's claims.

Notes on Personal Jurisdiction Over Plaintiffs: Class Actions

1. Personal jurisdiction over the plaintiff will rarely be questioned. Why do you think that issue rarely arises? Personal jurisdiction is about protecting the party, unlike subject-matter jurisdiction which is about ensuring the court has the power to consider a case. If personal jurisdiction is about protecting the party, why does it make sense not to analyze the court's personal jurisdiction as to a plaintiff who chose to file the lawsuit in that particular court?
2. Background on class actions: When many individuals have been injured in the same way by the same action or policy, it is sometimes more efficient for the action to proceed as a "class," rather than requiring each individual to sue separately. In a class action, a few "named plaintiffs" bring an action on behalf of themselves and a large class of unnamed plaintiffs. Because the named plaintiffs are representing many other similarly injured people, most of whom the named plaintiffs likely do not know personally, there are extensive prerequisites to bringing a class action. The first set

of requirements for a class action are a class "so numerous that joinder of all members is impracticable," the existence of common questions of fact or law, the claims or defenses of the named plaintiffs are "typical of the claims or defenses of the class," and the named plaintiffs will "fairly and adequately protect the interests of the class." *See* Fed. R. Civ. P. 23(a). The shorthand for these four requirements is numerosity, commonality, typicality, and adequacy.

The court must also find that "prosecuting separate actions by or against individual class members would create a risk of" inconsistent judgments arising from litigation based on the same events; that class-wide relief, such as an injunction, is appropriate; or that the questions of law or "fact common to class members predominate over any questions affecting only individual members, and that a class action is superior to other available methods for fairly and efficiently adjudicating the controversy." Fed. R. Civ. P. 23(b). When both sets of these requirements are met, a handful of plaintiffs may bring suit on behalf of themselves and all of the absent plaintiffs they represent.

3. Hopefully you noticed that class actions present questions about personal jurisdiction over plaintiffs that do not arise in non-class-action litigation. Most of the plaintiffs in a class action are "unnamed" in the lawsuit or "absent," so they have not expressly consented to the court's personal jurisdiction. The Supreme Court has concluded that in class actions in which notice of an opportunity to opt out of the litigation is mailed to absent plaintiffs, the plaintiffs who do not affirmatively choose to opt out have impliedly consented to the court's personal jurisdiction. *Phillips Petroleum Co. v. Shutts*, 472 U.S. 797, 812–13 (1985).

D. REMOVAL: OVERRIDING THE PLAINTIFF'S CHOICE OF STATE COURT

1. Overview

State courts can apply most federal law. The state courts can also entertain lawsuits over which the federal courts would have had diversity jurisdiction. Although the plaintiff could file either of these types of actions in federal court, the plaintiff can instead choose to file them in state court, and the state court can adjudicate them.

But what about the defendant's preference? The defendant might prefer that the action proceed in federal, not state court. In that situation, the defendant can remove the case to federal court, and, if the plaintiff thinks removal should not have been permitted, the plaintiff can challenge the propriety of that removal through a motion to remand.

2. Removal

"Except as otherwise expressly provided by Act of Congress, any civil action brought in a State court of which the district courts of the United States have original jurisdiction, may be removed by the defendant...." 28 U.S.C. § 1441(a). The case is removed "to the district court of the United States for the district and division embracing the place where such action is pending." 28 U.S.C. § 1441(a). In other words, a case pending in a state court in Los Angeles will be removed to the federal district court for the Central District of California, the district that includes Los Angeles.

The right to removal is not completely coextensive with the right to file a case in a federal court in the first instance. For example, Congress has eliminated removal as an option for claims based on some federal statutes, even though those claims would have otherwise supported subject-matter jurisdiction based on a federal question if the plaintiff had initially filed the claim in federal court. 28 U.S.C. §§ 1331, 1445. For diversity claims, Congress has foreclosed removal of cases in which any of the properly joined defendants is "a citizen of the State in which such action is brought." 28 U.S.C. § 1441(b)(2). There are also time limits on removal and a requirement that "all defendants who have been properly joined and served must join in or consent to the removal of the action." *See, e.g.*, 28 U.S.C. § 1446(b)(1), (b)(2) & (c). Thus, even though in each of these instances, the action could have been filed in federal court, the possibility of removing it to federal court may not exist.

The next decision explores one of these limitations. In *Breuer v. Jim's Concrete of Brevard, Inc.*, the Supreme Court considered whether language in the Fair Labor Standards Act constituted an express prohibition by Congress on the removal of actions alleging violations of that statute.

Breuer v. Jim's Concrete of Brevard, Inc.

Supreme Court of the United States

538 U.S. 691 (2003)

Justice SOUTER delivered the opinion of the Court.

The question is whether the provision of the Fair Labor Standards Act of 1938 (FLSA or Act), that suit under the Act "may be maintained... in any Federal or State court of competent jurisdiction," 52 Stat. 1069, as amended, 29 U.S.C. § 216(b), bars removal of a suit from state to federal court. We hold there is no bar.

I

Petitioner, Phillip T. Breuer, sued respondent, his former employer, Jim's Concrete of Brevard, Inc., in a state court of Florida for unpaid wages.... Section 216(b) provides not only that an employer who violates its minimum wage and overtime provisions is liable to an employee, but that "[a]n action to recover the liability prescribed... may be maintained against any employer (including a public agency) in any Federal or State court of competent jurisdiction."

Jim's Concrete removed the case to the United States District Court for the Middle District of Florida under 28 U.S.C. § 1441(a), which reads that "[e]xcept as otherwise expressly provided by Act of Congress, any civil action brought in a State court of which the district courts of the United States have original jurisdiction, may be removed by the defendant or the defendants, to the district court of the United States for the district and division embracing the place where such action is pending." Breuer sought an order remanding the case to state court, arguing that removal was improper owing to the FLSA's provision that an action "may be maintained" in any state court, a provision that Breuer put forward as an express exception to the general authorization of removal under § 1441(a). Though the District Court denied Breuer's motion, it certified the issue for interlocutory appeal under § 1292(b). The Eleventh Circuit affirmed, saying that Congress had expressly barred removal in "direct, unequivocal language" in other statutes, 292 F.3d 1308, 1310 (2002), but was not comparably prohibitory in § 216(b). The Eleventh Circuit thus joined the First [Circuit], *see Cosme Nieves v. Deshler*, 786 F.2d 445 (1986), but placed itself at odds with the Eighth [Circuit], *see Johnson v. Butler Bros.*, 162 F.2d 87 (1947) (denying removability under FLSA). We granted certiorari to resolve the conflict, and now affirm.

II

A

There is no question that Breuer could have begun his action in the District Court. The FLSA provides that an action "may be maintained . . . in any Federal or State court of competent jurisdiction," 29 U.S.C. § 216(b), and the district courts would in any event have original jurisdiction over FLSA claims under 28 U.S.C. § 1331, as "arising under the Constitution, laws, or treaties of the United States," and § 1337(a), as "arising under any Act of Congress regulating commerce." Removal of FLSA actions is thus prohibited under § 1441(a) only if Congress expressly provided as much.

Nothing on the face of 29 U.S.C. § 216(b) looks like an express prohibition of removal, there being no mention of removal, let alone of prohibition. While § 216(b) provides that an action "may be maintained . . . in any . . . State court of competent jurisdiction," the word "maintain" enjoys a breadth of meaning that leaves its bearing on removal ambiguous at best. "To maintain an action" may mean "to continue" to litigate, as opposed to "commence" an action. Black's Law Dictionary 1143 (3d ed.1933). But "maintain" in reference to a legal action is often read as "bring" or "file"; "[t]o maintain an action or suit may mean to commence or institute it; the term imports the existence of a cause of action." *Ibid.* The most, then, that Breuer can claim simply from the use of the term "maintain" is that any text, even when ambiguous, that might be read as inconsistent with removal is an "express" prohibiting provision under the statute. But if an ambiguous term like "maintain" qualified as an express provision for purposes of 28 U.S.C. § 1441(a), then the requirement of an "expres[s] provi[-sion]" would call for nothing more than a "provision," pure and simple, leaving the word "expressly" with no consequence whatever. "[E]xpres[s] provi[sion]" must mean something more than any verbal hook for an argument.

The need to take the express exception requirement seriously is underscored by examples of indisputable prohibitions of removal in a number of other statutes. Section 1445, for example, provides that

> "(a) A civil action in any State court against a railroad or its receivers or trustees . . . may not be removed to any district court of the United States.
>
> "(b) A civil action in any State court against a carrier or its receivers or trustees to recover damages for delay, loss, or injury of shipments . . . may not be removed to any district court of the United States unless the matter in controversy exceeds $10,000, exclusive of interest and costs.

> "(c) A civil action in any State court arising under the workmen's compensation laws of such State may not be removed to any district court of the United States.
>
> "(d) A civil action in any State court arising under... the Violence Against Women Act of 1994 may not be removed to any district court of the United States."

See also 15 U.S.C. § 77v(a) ("[N]o case arising under [the Securities Act of 1933] and brought in any State court of competent jurisdiction shall be removed to any court of the United States"); § 1719 ("No case arising under [the Interstate Land Sales Full Disclosure Act] and brought in any State court of competent jurisdiction shall be removed to any court of the United States, except where the United States or any officer or employee of the United States in his official capacity is a party"); § 3612 ("No case arising under [the Condominium and Cooperative Abuse Relief Act of 1980] and brought in any State court of competent jurisdiction shall be removed to any court of the United States, except where any officer or employee of the United States in his official capacity is a party"). When Congress has "wished to give plaintiffs an absolute choice of forum, it has shown itself capable of doing so in unmistakable terms." *Cosme Nieves*, 786 F.2d, at 451. It has not done so here.

B

None of Breuer's refinements on his basic argument from the term "maintain" puts him in a stronger position. He goes on to say, for example, that interpretation does not stop at the dictionary, and he argues that the statutory phrase "may be maintained" shows up as sufficiently prohibitory once it is coupled with a federal policy of construing removal jurisdiction narrowly. Breuer relies heavily on our statement... that "the policy of the successive acts of Congress regulating the jurisdiction of federal courts is one calling for the strict construction of [removal legislation] .... 'Due regard for the rightful independence of state governments, which should actuate federal courts, requires that they scrupulously confine their own jurisdiction to the precise limits... the statute has defined.'" But whatever apparent force this argument might have claimed when [initially stated it] has been qualified by later statutory development. At th[at earlier] time..., § 1441 provided simply that any action within original federal subject-matter jurisdiction could be removed. Fourteen years later, however, it was amended into its present form, requiring any exception to the general removability rule to be express. *See* Act of June

25, 1948, § 1441(a), 62 Stat. 937 (authorizing removal over civil suits within the district courts' original jurisdiction "[e]xcept as otherwise expressly provided by Act of Congress"). Since 1948, therefore, there has been no question that whenever the subject matter of an action qualifies it for removal, the burden is on a plaintiff to find an express exception, and congressional insistence on express exception is hardly satisfied by the malleability of the term "maintain" in the text Breuer relies upon.

...

But even if the text of § 216(b) were not itself reason enough to doubt that the provision conveys any right to remain in the original forum, the implication of Breuer's position would certainly raise misgivings about his point. For if the phrase "[a]n action... may be maintained" meant that a plaintiff could insist on keeping an FLSA case wherever he filed it in the first place, it would seem that an FLSA case brought in a federal district court could never be transferred to a different one over the plaintiff's objection, a result that would plainly clash with the provision for change of venue, 28 U.S.C. § 1404(a) ("For the convenience of parties and witnesses, in the interest of justice, a district court may transfer any civil action to any other district or division where it might have been brought").

It is, finally, a like concern about consequences that leaves us with fatal reservations about Breuer's pragmatic appeal that many claims under the FLSA are for such small amounts that removal to a sometimes distant federal court may make it less convenient and more expensive for employees to vindicate their rights effectively. This may often be true, but even if its truth somehow justified winking at the ambiguity of the term "maintain," the implications would keep us from going Breuer's way. A number of other statutes incorporate or use the same language as § 216(b), *see* 29 U.S.C. § 626(b) (providing that the Age Discrimination in Employment Act of 1967 "shall be enforced in accordance with the powers, remedies, and procedures provided in" § 216(b) and other sections of the FLSA); § 2005(c)(2) ("An action to recover the liability prescribed [under the Employee Polygraph Protection Act of 1988] in paragraph (1) may be maintained against the employer in any Federal or State court of competent jurisdiction"); § 2617(a)(2) ("An action to recover the damages or equitable relief [under the Family and Medical Leave Act of 1993] prescribed in paragraph (1) may be maintained against any employer (including a public agency) in any Federal or State court of competent jurisdiction by any one or more employees"). Breuer, then, cannot have a removal exception for the FLSA without entailing exceptions for other statutory actions, to the point that it becomes just too hard to believe that a right to "maintain" an action was ever meant to displace the right to remove.

III

Breuer's case was properly removed under 28 U.S.C. § 1441, and the judgment of the Eleventh Circuit is affirmed.

It is so ordered.

Notes

1. This decision focuses on interpreting a provision of the Fair Labor Standards Act (FLSA). What word in the FLSA was the focus of the Court's analysis? What meaning did the plaintiff argue should be given to that word? What meaning did the Court give to that word? Be sure to understand the arguments that the Court made to support its interpretation.
2. The Court considered the implication of the plaintiff's argument on another statute. What other statute was the Court concerned would be seriously undermined if it were to accept plaintiff's argument?
3. The Court concluded that removal was appropriate in *Breuer.* After removal from state court, a case is fully and solely in the federal court and no longer in the state court. To accomplish this transfer, the defendant who removed the case is required to attach a copy of all of the pleadings that had been filed in state court. 28 U.S.C. § 1446(a).
4. Some claims are barred from removal to federal court. *See, e.g.,* 28 U.S.C. § 1445. For example, a defendant cannot remove a civil action arising under the Federal Employers' Liability Act. That statute permits railroad workers to recover damages from their employers for injuries the workers sustained as a result, in whole or in part, from the negligence of any of the officers, agents, or employees of the railroad, or by reason of any defect due to the railroad's negligence. Why might Congress choose to foreclose removal of such actions? What effect does removal have on the choice of a plaintiff's forum?
5. If the plaintiff is in charge of the case and has the authority to choose the forum in which the plaintiff would prefer to bring the claims, why would removal ever be permissible? What rights or interests are furthered by permitting removal?

6. What purposes do time limits on removal serve? Why should removal be an option that is generally only available early in the litigation? Who would be harmed by late removal? What about considerations of efficiency? Who or what would be adversely affected if removal were permitted at any time during the state court action?

Notes on Statutory Interpretation

1. When a court interprets a statute, its task is to determine the legislature's intent. The language of the statute is considered the best indicator of that intent. So, if the statute is not ambiguous, the language of the statute will control.
2. When examining the language of the statute, courts employ a variety of "rules" of statutory construction. The term "rules" is a misnomer, because these so-called "rules" are more like guidelines than binding rules. Courts choose among the guidelines to support their interpretation of the statute.
3. One rule of statutory construction, known as the "plain meaning rule," requires courts to interpret a statute using the ordinary meaning of the words in the statute, absent some contrary statutory directive. Courts often consult the dictionary for the ordinary meaning of a word, as the court did in *Breuer*.
4. Although the Court did not mention the rule by name, the Court in *Breuer* applied the "rule against surplusage." Under this rule, courts should interpret statutes to give meaning to every word. For example, the Court was concerned that treating the FLSA statute as prohibiting removal would effectively read the word "expressly" out of the removal statute. That potential omission counseled against plaintiff's interpretation of the FLSA.
5. The *Breuer* decision also compares the language of the FLSA to the language of other statutes that plainly prohibit removal. The point of this comparison is to show that Congress knew how to be clear when it wanted to prevent removal. The Court therefore assumed that had Congress wanted to prevent removal for FLSA cases, it knew how to do it more clearly. Having not chosen to use such clear language, Congress must not have intended to prevent removal of those claims.

6. Another common technique for interpreting statutes is to explore what effect the interpretation would have beyond the precise question at issue in the case. This technique is also used in *Breuer*. The Court expressed skepticism at the results that would follow from plaintiff's interpretation of the FLSA. Can you identify the results that the Court thought would be unreasonable?
7. One challenging aspect of the rules of statutory construction for all students, but particularly for non-native English speakers, is that the rules themselves are often named using yet another language, albeit one no longer spoken—Latin! For example, *ejusdem generis* is the name of the rule that requires courts to interpret general words that follow specific words by using the specific words as a guide to the meaning of the general words. Another frequent rule of construction is *expressio unius est exclusio alterius*, or the expression of one thing excludes all others.
8. Thus far, these notes have focused on rules for interpreting the statutory language itself. Sometimes, no matter what rules the Court uses, the statutory language will remain ambiguous. In those situations, the court can examine the legislative history of the statute and the statute's purpose to determine the correct interpretation. Legislative history includes congressional committee reports, committee hearings, and floor debates, and any and all documents created by Congress during drafting and consideration of a statute. Reliance on these materials has often been criticized because enacting a statute is a collective exercise, so no statement by one individual can reflect the intent of *all* of the members of Congress who voted for the statute. A single person's statement as to the meaning of the statute, therefore, has only arguable relevance. That relevance increases, though, if the person whose statement on which the court relies was involved in the statute's proposal or drafting. But even then, it is still just one person's opinion. Nevertheless, courts will resort to these legislative materials when necessary.

What if states do not want cases to be removed from their courts? Do they have any way to stop removal?

Donald v. Philadelphia & Reading Coal & Iron Co.

Supreme Court of the United States

241 U.S. 329 (1916)

Mr. Justice McREYNOLDS delivered the opinion of the court:

These appeals bring up for consideration the validity of a Wisconsin statute providing for revocation of licenses granted to corporations not organized under the laws of that state....

Terms and conditions upon which foreign corporations might do local business, and penalties for failure to comply therewith, were first prescribed by the legislature of Wisconsin in 1898. Amendatory and supplemental statutes were enacted, and finally the act of June 20, 1905, added four new sections to the statutes of 1898, one of which follows:

Sec. 1770f. 'Whenever any foreign corporation doing business in this state shall remove or make application to remove into any district or circuit court of the United States any action or proceeding commenced against it by any citizen of this state, upon any claim or cause of action arising within this state, it shall be the duty of the secretary of state, upon such fact being made to appear to him, to revoke the license of such corporation to do business within this state.'

Since 1860 the Western Union Telegraph Company, a New York corporation, has been continuously carrying on within Wisconsin both intra and interstate commerce, and for use therein has acquired and owns a large amount of property. In 1907 it filed with the secretary of state a copy of its charter, paid the prescribed fee, and took out a license to do intrastate business.

The Philadelphia & Reading Coal & Iron Company, a Pennsylvania corporation, since prior to 1898, within Wisconsin has been continuously shipping and selling coal both in intrastate and interstate commerce, and for use therein has purchased at great expense docks and other properties. Having paid required fees and filed its charter with the secretary of state, it received a license, November 10, 1898.

The Western Union Telegraph Company removed to the United States district court a civil suit begun against it in the circuit court, Dane county, Wisconsin, during 1911; and in 1912 an action against the Philadelphia & Reading Coal & Iron Company was likewise removed. Averring that so far as the same directs or attempts to direct annulment of its right to do business, § 1770f, above quoted, is in conflict with the Federal Constitution, each of the appellees filed an original bill praying an injunction restraining the secretary of state from revoking its license because of such removal. The lower court sustained the claim of unconstitutionality, granted preliminary injunctions, and these direct appeals were taken.

Consideration of the Wisconsin statutes convinces us that they seek to prevent appellees and other foreign commercial corporations doing local business from exercising their constitutional right to remove suits into Federal courts. To accomplish this is beyond the state's power. The action of the court below in holding § 1770f inoperative, and enjoining its enforcement as to appellees, was correct and its decree must be affirmed.

We are asked in effect to reconsider the question discussed and definitely determined in *Harrison v. St. Louis & S. F. R. Co.*, 232 U.S. 318. We there said: 'The judicial power of the United States as created by the Constitution and provided for by Congress pursuant to its constitutional authority is a power wholly independent of state action, and which therefore the several states may not, by any exertion of authority in any form, directly or indirectly, destroy, abridge, limit, or render inefficacious.'

Affirmed.

Notes

1. Wisconsin did not outright prohibit removal. It instead tried to discourage removal by imposing a penalty for removing a case from state to federal court. What was that penalty?
2. The penalty was limited to foreign corporations. Why would Wisconsin not extend this penalty to Wisconsin corporations?
3. What was the Court's conclusion about the Wisconsin statute and why? How does that conclusion reflect the relationship between federal and state laws?

3. Remand

Students often think that the federal court is standing as a gatekeeper as removed cases arrive to that court from state court. The assumption often is that the federal courts review cases as they arrive from state court to determine whether the removal was proper, allowing those cases for which removal was proper to stay and sending back to state court those cases for which removal was not proper. But that is not how the process works. As with all other aspects of litigation, the parties, not the court, bear the initial responsibility of evaluating whether removal was proper. If the plaintiff believes removal was improper, the plaintiff brings that issue to the court's attention by filing a motion to remand. The court will rule on the motion, either permitting the case to stay in federal court or sending it back to state court.

Notes

1. There are time-limits for filing a motion to remand if the motion challenges defendants' compliance with procedural requirements. On the other hand, plaintiffs have no time limit for filing a motion to remand that challenges the court's subject-matter jurisdiction. Why would the time for challenging compliance with procedural requirements be limited, but the time for filing motions for lack of subject-matter jurisdiction not be similarly limited?
2. The plaintiff in *Breuer* made his argument regarding the non-removability of FLSA claims in a motion to remand. Did that argument challenge procedure or the court's subject-matter jurisdiction?

— ★ —

FIVE

WHAT LAW APPLIES?

If a plaintiff chooses to file suit in a federal court (assuming the court has subject-matter and personal jurisdiction), the next question that may arise is what law will that court apply. If the plaintiff brings a federal claim (i.e., a claim based on a federal statute or the U.S. Constitution), the applicable law is entirely federal law. But the question is a little trickier if the plaintiff's lawsuit presents a state-based claim.

There are two primary sources of law in each state: statutes and common law. While the statutes are codified by the state's legislature and reported in a single source, state common law is developed through judicial decisions. As a result, a state does not have a single statement or source of common law that parties can reference. Instead, understanding a state's common law requires research and reading of possibly numerous decisions of that state's courts.

The plaintiff in *Erie Railroad Co. v. Tompkins* brought a claim for negligence (a tort) under Pennsylvania law. There were no state statutes governing the claim, so the claim was governed by common law. The question the federal court faced in *Erie* was who determines the applicable common law of the state: must the federal court apply the common law as interpreted by Pennsylvania judicial decisions or could the federal court make its own independent decision regarding the applicable common law? (The latter law is described as "general law" in the opinion.) As you read *Erie*, be sure to understand how courts answered that question under the *Swift v. Tyson* doctrine. After *Erie*, however, how should courts answer that question? How does *Erie* eliminate some of the problems created by the *Swift v. Tyson* doctrine?

The notes after the case guide you through the marks you might make on the text itself (i.e., underlining, highlighting, arrows) and the information that you might want to write in the margins. So, consult the Notes as you read the case and follow the suggestions. The purpose of this exercise is to help you identify the right amount of additional writing and highlighting in the text to help you easily find key information if called on in class. The hazard of highlighting and noting too much is just as great as the hazard of doing too little. Striking the right balance is the challenge.

Erie Railroad Co. v. Tompkins

Supreme Court of the United States

304 U.S. 64 (1938)

Mr. Justice BRANDEIS delivered the opinion of the Court.

The question for decision is whether the oft-challenged doctrine of *Swift v. Tyson* shall now be disapproved.

Tompkins, a citizen of Pennsylvania, was injured on a dark night by a passing freight train of the Erie Railroad Company while walking along its right of way at Hughestown in that state. He claimed that the accident occurred through negligence in the operation, or maintenance, of the train;...and that he was struck by something which looked like a door projecting from one of the moving cars. To enforce that claim he brought an action in the federal court for Southern New York, which had jurisdiction because the company is a corporation of that state. [The company, Erie,] denied liability; and the case was tried by a jury.

The Erie...contended among other things, that its duty to Tompkins, and hence its liability, should be determined in accordance with the Pennsylvania law; that under the law of Pennsylvania, as declared by its highest court, persons who use pathways along the railroad right of way...are to be deemed trespassers; and that the railroad is not liable for injuries to undiscovered trespassers resulting from its negligence, unless it be wanton or willful. Tompkins denied that any such rule had been established by the decisions of the Pennsylvania courts; and contended that, since there was no statute of the state on the subject, the railroad's duty and liability is to be determined in federal courts as a matter of general law.

The trial judge refused to rule that the applicable law precluded recovery. The jury brought in a verdict of $30,000; and the judgment entered thereon was affirmed by the Circuit Court of Appeals, which held that it was unnecessary to consider whether the law of Pennsylvania was as contended, because the question was one not of local, but of general, law, and that 'upon questions of general law the federal courts are free, in absence of a local statute, to exercise their independent judgment as to what the law is; and it is well settled that the question of the responsibility of a railroad for injuries caused by its servants is one of general law.... Where the public has made open and notorious use of a railroad right of way for a long period of time and without objection, the company owes to persons on such permissive pathway a duty of care in the operation of its trains.... It is likewise generally recognized law that a jury may find that negligence exists toward a pedestrian using a permissive path on the railroad right of way if he is hit by some object projecting from the side of the train.'

The Erie had contended that application of the Pennsylvania rule was required, among other things, by section 34 of the Federal Judiciary Act of September 24, 1789, 28 U.S.C. § 725, which provides: 'The laws of the several States, except where the Constitution, treaties, or statutes of the United States otherwise require or provide, shall be regarded as rules of decision in trials at common law, in the courts of the United States, in cases where they apply.'

Because of the importance of the question whether the federal court was free to disregard the alleged rule of the Pennsylvania common law, we granted certiorari.

First, *Swift v. Tyson* held that federal courts exercising jurisdiction on the ground of diversity of citizenship need not, in matters of general jurisprudence, apply the unwritten law of the state as declared by its highest court; that they are free to exercise an independent judgment as to what the common law of the state is-or should be; and that... 'the true interpretation of the 34th section limited its application to... the positive statutes of the state, and the construction thereof adopted by the local tribunals, and to rights and titles to thing having a permanent locality, such as the rights and titles to real estate, and other matters immovable and intra-territorial in their nature and character.... '

Criticism of the doctrine became widespread after the decision of *Black & White Taxicab & Transfer Co. v. Brown & Yellow Taxicab & Transfer Co.* There, Brown & Yellow, a Kentucky corporation..., and the Louisville & Nashville Railroad, also a Kentucky corporation, wished that the former should have the exclusive privilege of soliciting passenger and baggage transportation at the Bowling Green, Ky., Railroad station; and that the Black & White, a competing Kentucky corporation, should be prevented from interfering with that privilege. Knowing that such a contract would be void under the common law of Kentucky, it was arranged that the Brown & Yellow reincorporate under the law of Tennessee, and that the contract with the railroad should be executed there. The suit was then brought by the Tennessee corporation in the federal court for Western Kentucky to enjoin competition by the Black & White; an injunction issued by the District Court was sustained by the Court of Appeals; and this Court, citing many decisions in which the doctrine of *Swift & Tyson* had been applied, affirmed the decree.

Second. Experience in applying the doctrine of *Swift v. Tyson*, had revealed its defects, political and social; and the benefits expected to flow from the rule did not accrue. Persistence of state courts in their own opinions on questions of common law prevented uniformity, and the impossibility of discovering a satisfactory line of demarcation between the province of general law and that of local law developed a new well of uncertainties.

On the other hand, the mischievous results of the doctrine had become apparent. Diversity of citizenship jurisdiction was conferred in order to prevent apprehended discrimination in state courts against those not citizens of the state. *Swift v. Tyson* introduced grave discrimination by noncitizens against citizens. It made rights enjoyed under the unwritten 'general law' vary according to whether enforcement was sought in the state or in the federal court; and the privilege of selecting the court in which the right should be determined was conferred upon the noncitizen. Thus, the doctrine rendered impossible equal protection of the law. In attempting to promote uniformity of law throughout the United States, the doctrine had prevented uniformity in the administration of the law of the state.

...

[E]xcept in matters governed by the Federal Constitution or by acts of Congress, the law to be applied in any case is the law of the state. And whether the law of the state shall be declared by its Legislature in a statute or by its highest court in a decision is not a matter of federal concern. There is no federal general common law. Congress has no power to declare substantive rules of common law applicable in a state whether they be local in their nature or 'general'.... And no clause in the Constitution purports to confer such a power upon the federal courts. As stated by Mr. Justice Field when protesting in *Baltimore & Ohio R.R. Co. v. Baugh*, 149 U.S. 368, against ignoring the Ohio common law of fellow-servant liability: '...Supervision over either the legislative or the judicial action of the states is in no case permissible except as to matters by the constitution specifically authorized or delegated to the United States. Any interference with either, except as thus permitted, is an invasion of the authority of the state, and, to that extent, a denial of its independence.'

...

Thus the doctrine of *Swift v. Tyson* is... 'an unconstitutional assumption of powers by the Courts of the United States which no lapse of time or respectable array of opinion should make us hesitate to correct.'...

...The Circuit Court of Appeals ruled that the question of liability is one of general law; and on that ground declined to decide the issue of state law. As we hold this was error, the judgment is reversed and the case remanded to it for further proceedings in conformity with our opinion.

Reversed.

Mr. Justice CARDOZO took no part in the consideration or decision of this case.

Mr. Justice BUTLER (dissenting). [Opinion omitted.]

Mr. Justice McREYNOLDS, concurs in this opinion.

Mr. Justice REED (concurring in part).

...

The line between procedural and substantive law is hazy, but no one doubts federal power over procedure....

Notes

1. What events formed the factual basis for the plaintiff's claim? In other words, what happened to the plaintiff? What did he contend that the defendant (Erie) had done wrong? Very briefly describe that conduct in the margins of the case next to the discussion of those facts in the opinion. (Note that π is often used as a symbol for the plaintiff and Δ is often used as a symbol for the defendant. You can use these symbols in the margins.)
2. Find the word "negligence" and highlight it. It is the name of the plaintiff's legal theory. Is that legal theory based on federal law? Is it based on a federal statute? The federal constitution? If not, on what law was it based?
3. In the paragraph beginning, "The Erie..." the court describes the defendant's and the plaintiff's arguments as to the applicable law. Circle the word "Erie" and underline the most key aspects of Erie's characterization of the applica-

ble law. For example, the key aspect might be "the railroad is not liable for injuries to undiscovered trespassers resulting from its negligence, unless it be wanton or willful." You might even draw an arrow from the word "Erie" to the underlined text to make explicit the connection between the two.

Circle the word "Tompkins." This particular paragraph says only that Tompkins contends "general law" applies. Where do you find the description of the specific "general law" that governs the negligence claim that the plaintiff has brought? Underline that description and draw an arrow connecting "Tompkins" to that underlined text.

Understanding the difference between the applicable law as contended by Erie and as contended by Tompkins will help you understand how the result in the case—plaintiff wins or loses—turns in large part on which law applies. If the standard advocated by Erie applies, the plaintiff (Tompkins) will almost surely lose. If the standard advocated by Tompkins applies, Tompkins will and did win.

4. The paragraph that begins "The trial judge refused..." describes the result in the trial court and on appeal. How was the case resolved in the trial court? Who filed an appeal? Did the appellate court reverse or affirm the trial court's judgment? What procedure was required to bring the case before the Supreme Court? Make notes in the margin about all of that information.
5. The paragraph that begins "First,..." references "section 34" but does not describe the content of section 34. Where can you find the content of section 34? What was the key phrase in section 34 that the Court had arguably interpreted in *Swift v. Tyson*? What had *Swift v. Tyson* interpreted that phrase to mean? What were some of the problems that resulted from this interpretation? Underline text or add margin notes that explain the point of *Swift v. Tyson*. It is important that you understand this information, because the Court next explained why *Swift v. Tyson* created problems.
6. The next paragraph begins with the word "Criticism." This word signals the point of the paragraph and is therefore an important word for you to notice as you are reading. You might even highlight it. In the margin, explain, in the briefest way possible, the unfairness that existed in the *Black & White* case. (Hint: What was the basis of the federal court's jurisdiction in that case? How did the basis for jurisdiction come into existence? What difference would it make to the outcome of *Black & White* if the federal court had not had jurisdiction? Where would the case have been tried and who likely would have won?)

7. In the paragraph that begins "Second," key words to highlight are "defects" and "uncertainties." Those are the points of this paragraph. Can you paraphrase the "defect" and how it created "uncertainties"? This paragraph also references "uniformity." What did the court mean by "uniformity"? What should be uniform with what else? And who was the Court worried about being harmed by this lack of uniformity? Defendant? Plaintiff? Help in answering these questions comes in the next paragraph of the opinion.

8. A key phrase in the next paragraph is "mischievous results." This paragraph reviews the purpose of diversity jurisdiction (the basis of the lower court's jurisdiction in *Erie*) and explains how plaintiffs had been using diversity jurisdiction in a way that was contrary to the reasons why Congress created diversity jurisdiction.

9. The paragraph that begins with the word "[E]xcept . ." contains the Court's conclusion. Do you understand it? Can you paraphrase it in the margin? The next paragraph concludes that applying federal law on questions of state substantive law was an "unconstitutional assumption of powers," but the explanation for this conclusion is in the "[E]xcept" paragraph. Can you find that explanation?

10. What will happen on remand? Has one party won or lost? Will there be further proceedings? If so, what law — state or federal — will apply during those proceedings?

11. The opinion begins by saying, "The question for decision is whether the oft-challenged doctrine of *Swift v. Tyson* shall now be disapproved." Having fully read and analyzed the case, do you think that is the best description of what the case concludes? Can you articulate the Court's holding in a more accurate and helpful way?

12. Justice Reed's concurrence recognizes a distinction between substantive and procedural law. Although the distinction between the two is not always clear, some matters are clearly substantive or clearly procedural. For example, the elements necessary to prove a claim are matters of substantive law. So, the elements of negligence — duty, breach, causation, and damages — are a matter of substantive law. The interpretation of these elements would be a matter of substantive law as well. For example, the law relevant to when an individual does or does not have a duty is substantive.

At the opposite end of the spectrum, there are issues that are purely procedural. For example, the permissible page length of a brief, i.e., how long a party's brief may be, is a purely procedural issue. Whether or not the court allows argument on a motion is a procedural issue as well.

But between these two sets of rather obvious examples there lies a wealth of situations that are neither clearly substantive nor clearly procedural. And the uncertainty of that boundary has, in part, generated considerable litigation.

13. If you find that the federal case that you are reading primarily concerns an issue of state law, you should ask yourself why the author of the textbook would use a federal case, rather than a state case, to illustrate a point of state law. The answer could be, for example, that the state's courts had not adequately addressed the issue and the federal court was therefore required to make an educated guess as to how the state supreme court would define or interpret the law if presented with the opportunity. But remember that state courts are not required to follow the federal court decision and instead could properly choose to ignore it completely. Similar questions can be asked if the decision arises from a state court, but concerns a federal issue. You might ask yourself if there is something unique about the case that makes a decision of the state court on a federal issue particularly worthy of study.
14. Does this mean that states always have the final say on state law? Not always. A decision of a state's highest court is generally the final authority on that state's law. In other words, if the Supreme Court of the United States and the California Supreme Court disagree on an issue of California law, the California Supreme Court's interpretation governs. But federal courts are not bound by a state's interpretation or application of its law if that interpretation runs afoul of any federal law or the federal Constitution. For example, an award of punitive damages, proper under state law, might be excessive in light of the Constitution's Due Process Clause. Thus, even if that award were affirmed by the state's highest court, the Supreme Court of the United States could reverse the award because that Court is the final authority on any question of federal law, including the question of whether a state law offends federal law or the Constitution.

Notes on Choosing Which State's Law Should Apply

1. There seemed to be no dispute in *Erie* that if a state's law were to apply, it would be the law of Pennsylvania. Did you notice, though, that the lawsuit was brought in a New York federal court against a New York company? So why Pennsylvania law? The simple answer is that the accident occurred in Pennsylvania. The more complex answer is that in the United States, the choice of which state's law to apply can be such a complicated subject that the topic warrants its own course, generally called Conflict of Laws or Choice of Laws. You will see those two descriptors used interchangeably to describe this topic in cases and legal literature.

   If the lawsuit in *Erie* had instead been brought in a state court in New York, would Pennsylvania law still apply? Yes. State courts are sometimes required to apply the law of another state. That challenge is much easier now that technological research tools are widely available.

2. The American Law Institute has created several treatises, called "Restatements." The American Law Institute consists of law professors, practicing attorneys, and judges. Restatements have no binding effect on *any* jurisdiction, but they are generally considered very persuasive authority because considerable thought, discussion, and legal research went into drafting the standards the Restatement proposes. One Restatement is on the topic of Conflict of Laws. The most current Restatement on this topic is the second series, finalized in 1971. A third series is in development, although not yet complete as this book goes to press.

3. With respect to personal injury actions, such as the action in *Erie*, the Restatement proposes a general rule that "the local law of the state where the injury occurred determines the rights and liabilities of the parties...." *Restatement (Second) of Conflict of* Laws § 146 (1971). The Restatement recognizes exceptions to this rule if "some other state has a more significant relationship... to the occurrence and the parties." *Id.* But generally, the law of the place of the personal injury will control.

4. What law applies, though, if one car strikes a second car while the two cars are in Florida, but just about to cross the state line into Georgia? The driver of the second car does not immediately crash and instead struggles to keep the car on the road. After crossing the state line into Georgia, the second car crashes and bursts into flames. Should the law of Florida apply

because the first event occurred in that state or should the law of Georgia apply because the last event occurred in that state? You can see how a simple rule can quickly become inadequate when multiple states are involved in events. (Note: This issue is only of significance if the laws of the two states are different.)

5. And what about a claim for defamation, for example, where there is no tangible physical injury? The general principle for defamation is that the "law of the state where the publication occurs determines the rights and liabilities of the parties," but of course there are numerous exceptions to that general principle as well. *See Restatement (Second) of Conflict of Laws* § 149 (1971).
6. In the absence of any applicable rule, the Restatement generally directs consideration of: "(a) the needs of the interstate and international systems, (b) the relevant policies of the forum, (c) the relevant policies of other interested states and the relative interests of those states in the determination of the particular issue, (d) the protection of justified expectations, (e) the basic policies underlying the particular field of law, (f) certainty, predictability and uniformity of result, and (g) ease in the determination and application of the law to be applied." *Restatement (Second) of Conflict of Laws* § 6 (1971).
7. Contracts provide an opportunity to avoid the uncertainty that accompanies a choice-of-law analysis. Parties can specify in the contract the law that will control the contract's interpretation. Most parties will choose the law of a state with some connection to their activities, such as the state where the contract was signed, where one or both parties operate a business, or where the subject of the contract is located. If the parties choose the law of a state with no relation to the parties or the contract, there is the potential that the court would ignore the choice-of-law provision, despite the parties having agreed to it.

Erie is a landmark case that established what might appear to be a new "rule," but rules in the common law system are not always as firm as they may seem at first glance. In the common law system, the facts are always very important to the court's decision. The facts provide the context in which the court's decision is made. Change the facts (in other words, change the context) and the result may be different, as the court refines the formulation of its initial "rule." The following are just three of the many cases that have examined the "rule" of *Erie* and applied it to a different set of facts. How does each decision further refine the initial idea articulated in *Erie*?

Cohen v. Beneficial Industrial Loan Corp.

Supreme Court of the United States

337 U.S. 541 (1949)

Mr. Justice JACKSON delivered the opinion of the Court.

The ultimate question here is whether a federal court, having jurisdiction of a stockholder's derivative action only because the parties are of diverse citizenship, must apply a statute of the forum state which makes the plaintiff, if unsuccessful, liable for all expenses, including attorney's fees, of the defense and requires security for their payment as a condition of prosecuting the action....

[The general effect of the statute at issue in the case was] to make a plaintiff... liable for all expenses and attorney's fees of the defense if he fails to make good his complaint and to entitle the corporation to indemnity before the case can be prosecuted.... The corporate defendant therefore moved to require security... and averred that a bond of $125,000 would be appropriate.

The District Court was of the opinion that the state enactment is not applicable to such an action when pending in a federal court. The Court of Appeals was of a contrary opinion and reversed, and we granted certiorari....

This Court in *Erie R. Co. v. Tompkins*, 304 U.S. 64, held that judicial decisions are laws of the states.... But *Erie R. Co. v. Tompkins* and its progeny have wrought a more far-reaching change in the relation of state and federal courts and the application of state law in the latter whereby in diversity cases the federal court administers the state system of law in all except details related to its own conduct of business. The only substantial argument that this New Jersey statute is not applicable here is that its provisions are mere rules of procedure rather than rules of substantive law.

Even if we were to agree that the New Jersey statute is procedural, it would not determine that it is not applicable. Rules which lawyers call procedural do not always exhaust their effect by regulating procedure. But this statute is not merely a regulation of procedure. With it or without it the main action takes the same course. However, it creates a new liability where none existed before, for it makes a stockholder who institutes a derivative action liable for the expense to which he puts the corporation and other defendants, if he does not make good his claims. Such liability is not usual and it goes beyond payment of what we know as "costs." If all the Act did was to create this liability, it would clearly be substantive. But this new liability would be without meaning and value in many cases if it resulted in nothing but a judgment for expenses at or after the end of the case. Therefore, a procedure is prescribed by which the liability is insured by entitling the corporate defendant to a bond of indemnity before the outlay is incurred. We do not think a statute which so conditions the stockholder's action can be disregarded by the federal court as a mere procedural device....

We hold that the New Jersey statute applies in federal courts and that the District Court erred in declining to fix the amount of indemnity reasonably to be exacted as a condition of further prosecution of the suit.

The judgment of the Court of Appeals is affirmed.

Mr. Justice DOUGLAS, with whom Mr. Justice FRANKFURTER concurs, dissenting in part.

...This New Jersey statute does not add one iota to nor subtract one iota from [the] cause of action. It merely prescribes the method by which stockholders may enforce it. Each state has numerous regulations governing the institution of suits in its courts. They may favor the litigation or they may affect it adversely. But they do not fall under the principle of *Erie R. Co. v. Tompkins*, 304 U.S. 64, unless they define, qualify or delimit the cause of action or otherwise relate to it.

This New Jersey statute, like statutes governing security for costs, regulates only the procedure for instituting a particular cause of action and hence need not be applied in this diversity suit in the federal court....

Mr. Justice RUTLEDGE, dissenting.

...

What is being applied is a gloss on the *Erie* rule, not the rule itself. That case held that federal courts in diversity cases must apply state law, decisional as well as statutory, in determining matters of substantive law, in particular and apart from procedural limitations upon its assertion....

But the *Erie* case made no ruling that in so deciding diversity cases a federal court is "merely another court of the state in which it sits," and hence that in every situation in which the doors of state courts are closed to a suitor, so must be also those of the federal courts. Not only is this not true when the state bar is raised by a purely procedural obstacle. There is sound historical reason for believing that one of the purposes of the diversity clause was to afford a federal court remedy when, for at least some reasons of state policy, none would be available in the state courts. It is the gloss which has been put upon the *Erie* ruling by later decisions, which in my opinion is being applied to extend the *Erie* ruling far beyond its original purpose or intent and, in my judgment, with consequences and implications seriously impairing Congress' power, within its proper sphere of action, to control this type of litigation in the federal courts.

The accepted dichotomy is the familiar "procedural-substantive" one. This of course is a subject of endless discussion, which hardly needs to be repeated here. Suffice it to say that actually in many situations procedure and substance are so interwoven that rational separation becomes well-nigh impossible. But, even so, this fact cannot dispense with the necessity of making a distinction. For, as the matter stands, it is Congress which has the power to govern the procedure of the federal courts in diversity cases, and the states which have that power over matters clearly substantive in nature. Judges therefore cannot escape making the division.... The real question is not whether the separation shall be made, but how it shall be made, whether mechanically by reference to whether the state courts' doors are open or closed, or by a consideration of the policies which close them and their relation to accommodating the policy of the *Erie* rule with Congress' power to govern the incidents of litigation in diversity suits.

It is in these close cases, this borderland area, that I think we are going too far. It is one thing to decide that Pennsylvania does or does not create a cause of action in tort for injuries inflicted by specified conduct and to have that determination govern the outcome of a diversity suit in Pennsylvania or New York. It is another, in my view, to require a bond for costs or for payment of the opposing party's expenses and attorney's fees in the event the claimant is unsuccessful. Whether or not the latter is conceived as creating a new substantive right, it is too close to controlling the incidents of the litigation rather than its outcome to be identified with the former. It is a matter which in my opinion lies within Congress' control for diversity cases, not one for state control or to be governed by the fact that the state shuts the doors of its courts unless the state requirements concerning such incidents of litigation are complied with.

...

Notes

1. Justice Reed, in his concurrence in *Erie,* foreshadowed an issue for future cases—do state rules of procedure govern in federal cases that present state-law claims? He concluded that they surely did not. The issue anticipated by Justice Reed presents itself in *Cohen.* How did the Supreme Court resolve the issue? The relevant state law required that unsuccessful plaintiffs must pay the defendant's expenses, including attorney's fees, and that before they could proceed with the litigation, plaintiffs must post a bond or other security for the anticipated amount of those expenses. In other words, plaintiffs had to prove to the trial court at the beginning of litigation that they had the money or other resources necessary to pay the defendant's expenses if that became necessary after the trial. If the plaintiffs could not make such a showing (by posting a bond or other security), plaintiffs could not proceed with their claims. Did the Supreme Court decide that this was a procedural rule? Substantive rule? A combination of both?
2. The state's requirement had two components: 1) payment of defense expenses after trial and 2) posting security at the beginning of litigation sufficient to cover anticipated defense expenses. Did the court consider these two requirements separately? Should it have? Does one seem more procedural than the other? Does one seem more substantive than the other?
3. What was the source of the state law—statute or common law? Was that distinction important to the Court's decision?
4. Justice Douglas disagreed with the majority as to the scope of "substantive" law. If we can understand his dissent, we can understand a little better what "substantive" law is *not* limited to because Justice Douglas's opinion did not win out. For purposes of the federal-state choice-of-law analysis, what would Justice Douglas consider "substantive" law? His notion was narrower than that of the majority. In what way?
5. Justice Rutledge indicated that he would reach a different conclusion from the majority. How does Justice Rutledge's reasoning differ from that of the majority? How does Justice Rutledge's reasoning differ from that of Justice Douglas?

According to Justice Rutledge, do the federal government or state governments (both courts and legislature) have the power to make decisions regarding the requirements for initiating a lawsuit in federal court?

Byrd v. Blue Ridge Rural Electric Cooperative, Inc.

Supreme Court of the United States

356 U.S. 525 (1958)

Mr. Justice BRENNAN delivered the opinion of the Court.

This case was brought in the District Court for the Western District of South Carolina. Jurisdiction was based on diversity of citizenship. The petitioner, a resident of North Carolina, sued respondent, a South Carolina corporation, for damages for injuries allegedly caused by the respondent's negligence. He had a judgment on a jury verdict. The Court of Appeals for the Fourth Circuit reversed and directed the entry of judgment for the respondent....

One of the respondent's affirmative defenses [concerned an issue of immunity from suit. One of the questions raised in the Supreme Court was whether a decision regarding the respondent's immunity was a question to be resolved by a jury, as was the practice in federal courts, or was to be resolved by the court, as was the practice in state court. The Court also analyzed an issue unrelated to immunity and concluded that an error had occurred. For that reason, the Court reversed and remanded the case. In section II, which is included in this excerpt, the Court gives guidance to the trial court as to who should decide the issue of immunity on remand.]...

II.

A question is also presented as to whether on remand the [issue of immunity] is to be decided by the judge or by the jury. The respondent argues on the basis of the decision of the Supreme Court of South Carolina that the issue of immunity should be decided by the judge and not by the jury.... The respondent argues that this state-court decision governs the present diversity case and "divests the jury of its normal function" to decide the disputed fact question of the respondent's immunity.... This is to contend that the federal court is bound under *Erie R. Co. v. Tompkins*, 304 U.S. 64, to follow the state court's holding [that immunity is a question to be resolved by the court] to secure uniform enforcement of the immunity created by the State.

First. It was decided in *Erie R. Co. v. Tompkins* that the federal courts in diversity cases must respect the definition of state-created rights and obligations by the state courts. We must, therefore, first examine the rule [stated in a South Carolina Supreme Court decision] to determine whether it is bound up with these rights and obligations in such a way that its application in the federal court is required.... The South Carolina Supreme Court states no reasons...why, although the jury decides all other factual issues raised by the cause of action and defenses, the jury is displaced as to the factual issue raised by the affirmative defense [of immunity].... A State may, of course, distribute the functions of its judicial machinery as it sees fit. The decisions relied upon, however, furnish no reason for selecting the judge rather than the jury to decide this single affirmative defense in the negligence action.... Thus the requirement appears to be merely a form and mode of enforcing the immunity and not a rule intended to be bound up with the definition of the rights and obligations of the parties.

Second. But cases following *Erie* have evinced a broader policy to the effect that the federal courts should conform as near as may be — in the absence of other considerations — to state rules even of form and mode where the state rules may bear substantially on the question whether the litigation would come out one way in the federal court and another way in the state court if the federal court failed to apply a particular local rule. Concededly the nature of the tribunal which tries issues may be important in the enforcement of the parcel of rights making up a cause of action or defense, and bear significantly upon achievement of uniform enforcement of the right. It may well be that in the instant personal-injury case the outcome would be substantially affected by whether the issue of immunity is decided by a judge or a jury. Therefore, were "outcome" the only consideration, a strong case might appear for saying that the federal court should follow the state practice.

But there are affirmative countervailing considerations at work here. The federal system is an independent system for administering justice to litigants who properly invoke its jurisdiction. An essential characteristic of that system is the manner in which, in civil common-law actions, it distributes trial functions between judge and jury and, under the influence — if not the command — of the Seventh Amendment, assigns the decisions of disputed questions of fact to the jury. The policy of uniform enforcement of state-created rights and obligations cannot in every case exact compliance with a state rule — not bound up with rights and obligations — which disrupts the federal system of allocating functions between judge and jury. Thus the inquiry here is whether the federal policy favoring jury decisions of disputed fact questions should yield to the state rule in the interest of furthering the objective that the litigation should not come out one way in the federal court and another way in the state court.

We think that in the circumstances of this case the federal court should not follow the state rule. It cannot be gainsaid that there is a strong federal policy against allowing state rules to disrupt the judge-jury relationship in the federal courts....

Third. We have discussed the problem upon the assumption that the outcome of the litigation may be substantially affected by whether the issue of immunity is decided by a judge or a jury. But clearly there is not present here the certainty that a different result would follow, or even the strong possibility that this would be the case. There are factors present here which might reduce that possibility. The trial judge in the federal system has powers denied the judges of many States to comment on the weight of evidence and credibility of witnesses, and discretion to grant a new trial if the verdict appears to him to be against the weight of the evidence. We do not think the likelihood of a different result is so strong as to require the federal practice of jury determination of disputed factual issues to yield to the state rule in the interest of uniformity of outcome.

...

Mr. Justice WHITTAKER concurring in part and dissenting in part. [Omitted.]

Mr. Justice FRANKFURTER, whom Mr. Justice HARLAN joins, dissenting. [Omitted.]

Mr. Justice HARLAN, dissenting. [Omitted.]

Notes

1. What was the basic point of each of the sections marked "First," "Second," and "Third"? Be sure to write that basic point in the margins next to the pertinent discussion.
2. The Court twice discussed the impact of the choice of law on the outcome. Can you reconcile the two discussions? And what does the Court mean by affecting the outcome? Does it just mean changing the result from a win to

a loss or vice versa? Does it also mean affecting the extent of the plaintiff's success, such as affecting the amount of the damages? In thinking about these questions, remember back to the concerns expressed in *Erie* and *Cohen*. What kind of outcome-difference is the Court concerned with?

3. *Byrd* doesn't explicitly discuss the procedural/substantive distinction that is discussed more expressly in *Cohen*, but there are hints of that distinction in *Byrd*. Which of the three main points of the decision implicitly evaluates whether the use of a jury was a procedural or substantive matter?
4. The Court concluded that an essential characteristic of the federal court system is the way in which "it distributes trial functions between judge and jury and, under the influence — if not the command — of the Seventh Amendment assigns the decisions of disputed questions of fact to the jury." The Seventh Amendment guarantees the right to a jury trial in federal court. What did the Court mean by "influence — if not the command — of the Seventh Amendment"? If the issue had not implicated a constitutional amendment, would the court have reached the same result?

The next decision — *Hanna v. Plumer* — ties together and elaborates on many of the ideas discussed in *Erie*, *Cohen*, and *Byrd*.

Hanna v. Plumer

Supreme Court of the United States

380 U.S. 460 (1965)

Mr. Chief Justice WARREN delivered the opinion of the Court.

The question to be decided is whether, in a civil action where the jurisdiction of the United States district court is based upon diversity of citizenship between the parties, service of process shall be made in the manner prescribed by state law or that set forth in Rule 4(d)(1) of the Federal Rules of Civil Procedure.

On February 6, 1963, petitioner, a citizen of Ohio, filed her complaint in the District Court for the District of Massachusetts, claiming damages in excess of $10,000 for personal injuries resulting from an automobile accident in South Carolina, allegedly caused by the negligence of one Louise Plumer Osgood, a

Massachusetts citizen deceased at the time of the filing of the complaint. Respondent, Mrs. Osgood's executor and also a Massachusetts citizen, was named as defendant. On February 8, service was made by leaving copies of the summons and the complaint with respondent's wife at his residence, concededly in compliance with Rule 4(d)(1), which provides:

> "The summons and complaint shall be served together. The plaintiff shall furnish the person making service with such copies as are necessary. Service shall be made as follows:
>
> "(1) Upon an individual other than an infant or an incompetent person, by delivering a copy of the summons and of the complaint to him personally or by leaving copies thereof at his dwelling house or usual place of abode with some person of suitable age and discretion then residing therein...."

Respondent filed his answer on February 26, alleging, *inter alia*, that the action could not be maintained because it had been brought "contrary to and in violation of the provisions of Massachusetts General Laws Chapter 197, Section 9." That section provides:

> "Except as provided in this chapter, an executor or administrator shall not be held to answer to an action by a creditor of the deceased which is not commenced within one year from the time of his giving bond for the performance of his trust, or to such an action which is commenced within said year unless before the expiration thereof the writ in such action has been served by delivery in hand upon such executor or administrator or service thereof accepted by him or a notice stating the name of the estate, the name and address of the creditor, the amount of the claim and the court in which the action has been brought has been filed in the proper registry of probate...."

Mass. Gen. Laws Ann., c. 197, § 9 (1958). On October 17, 1963, the District Court granted respondent's motion for summary judgment, [concluding] that the adequacy of the service was to be measured by § 9, with which, the court held, petitioner had not complied. On appeal, petitioner admitted noncompliance with § 9, but argued that Rule 4(d)(1) defines the method by which service of process is to be effected in diversity actions. The Court of Appeals for the First Circuit, finding that "[r]elatively recent amendments [to § 9] evince a clear legislative purpose to require personal notification within the year," concluded that the conflict of state and federal rules was over "a substantive, rather than a procedural, matter," and unanimously affirmed. Because of the threat to the goal of uniformity of federal procedure posed by the decision below, we granted certiorari.

We conclude that the adoption of Rule 4(d)(1), designed to control service of process in diversity actions, neither exceeded the congressional mandate embodied in the Rules Enabling Act nor transgressed constitutional bounds, and that the Rule is therefore the standard against which the District Court should have measured the adequacy of the service. Accordingly, we reverse the decision of the Court of Appeals.

The Rules Enabling Act, 28 U.S.C. § 2072 (1958 ed.), provides, in pertinent part:

> "The Supreme Court shall have the power to prescribe, by general rules, the forms of process, writs, pleadings, and motions, and the practice and procedure of the district courts of the United States in civil actions."
>
> "Such rules shall not abridge, enlarge or modify any substantive right, and shall preserve the right of trial by jury...."

Under the cases construing the scope of the Enabling Act, Rule 4(d)(1) clearly passes muster. Prescribing the manner in which a defendant is to be notified that a suit has been instituted against him, it relates to the "practice and procedure of the district courts."

> "The test must be whether a rule really regulates procedure — the judicial process for enforcing rights and duties recognized by substantive law and for justly administering remedy and redress for disregard or infraction of them."

In *Mississippi Pub. Corp. v. Murphree,* this Court upheld Rule 4(f), which permits service of a summons anywhere within the State (and not merely the district) in which a district court sits:

> "...The fact that the application of Rule 4(f) will operate to subject petitioner's rights to adjudication by the district court for northern Mississippi will undoubtedly affect those rights. But it does not operate to abridge, enlarge or modify the rules of decision by which that court will adjudicate its rights." *Id.* at 326 U.S. 445-446.

Thus, were there no conflicting state procedure, Rule 4(d)(1) would clearly control. However, respondent, focusing on the contrary Massachusetts rule, calls to the Court's attention another line of cases, a line which — like the Federal Rules — had its birth in 1938. *Erie R. Co. v. Tompkins,* 304 U.S. 64, *overruling Swift v. Tyson,* 16 Pet. 1, held that federal courts sitting in diversity cases, when deciding questions of "substantive" law, are bound by state court decisions as well as state statutes. The broad command of *Erie* was therefore identical to that of the Enabling Act: federal courts are to apply state substantive law and federal procedural law. However, as subsequent cases sharpened the distinction between substance and procedure, the line of cases following *Erie* diverged markedly from the line construing the Enabling Act....

...

Respondent... suggests that the *Erie* doctrine acts as a check on the Federal Rules of Civil Procedure, that, despite the clear command of Rule 4(d)(1), *Erie* and its progeny demand the application of the Massachusetts rule. Reduced to essentials, the argument is: (1) *Erie*... demands that federal courts apply state law whenever application of federal law in its stead will alter the outcome of the case. (2) In this case, a determination that the Massachusetts service requirements obtain will result in immediate victory for respondent. If, on the other hand, it should be held that Rule 4(d)(1) is applicable, the litigation will continue, with possible victory for petitioner. (3) Therefore, *Erie* demands application of the Massachusetts rule. The syllogism possesses an appealing simplicity, but is, for several reasons, invalid.

In the first place, it is doubtful that, even if there were no Federal Rule making it clear that in-hand service is not required in diversity actions, the *Erie* rule would have obligated the District Court to follow the Massachusetts procedure. "Outcome-determination" analysis was never intended to serve as a talisman. *Byrd v. Blue Ridge Rural Elec. Cooperative,* 356 U.S. 525, 537.... [C]hoices between state and federal law are to be made not by application of any automatic "litmus paper" criterion, but rather by reference to the policies underlying the *Erie* rule

The *Erie* rule is rooted in part in a realization that it would be unfair for the character of result of a litigation materially to differ because the suit had been brought in a federal court.

...

The decision was also, in part, a reaction to the practice of "forum-shopping" which had grown up in response to the rule of *Swift v. Tyson*.... Not only are nonsubstantial, or trivial, variations not likely to raise the sort of equal protection problems which troubled the Court in *Erie*; they are also unlikely to influence the choice of a forum. The "outcome determination" test therefore cannot be read without reference to the twin aims of the *Erie* rule: discouragement of forum shopping and avoidance of inequitable administration of the laws.

The difference between the conclusion that the Massachusetts rule is applicable, and the conclusion that it is not is, of course, at this point, "outcome determinative" in the sense that, if we hold the state rule to apply, respondent prevails, whereas, if we hold that Rule 4(d)(1) governs, the litigation will continue. But, in this sense, every procedural variation is "outcome determinative." For example, having brought suit in a federal court, a plaintiff cannot then insist on the right to file subsequent pleadings in accord with the time limits applicable in state courts, even though enforcement of the federal timetable will, if he continues to insist that he must meet only the state time limit, result in determination of the controversy against him. So it is here. Though choice of the federal or state rule will at this point have a marked effect upon the outcome of the litigation, the difference between the two rules would be of scant, if any, relevance to the choice of a forum. Petitioner, in choosing her forum, was not presented with a situation where application of the state rule would wholly bar recovery; rather, adherence to the state rule would have resulted only in altering the way in which process was served. Moreover, it is difficult to argue that permitting service of defendant's wife to take the place of in-hand service of defendant himself alters the mode of enforcement of state-created rights in a fashion sufficiently "substantial" to raise the sort of equal protection problems to which the *Erie* opinion alluded.

There is, however, a more fundamental flaw in respondent's syllogism: the incorrect assumption that the rule of *Erie R. Co. v. Tompkins* constitutes the appropriate test of the validity, and therefore the applicability, of a Federal Rule of Civil Procedure. The *Erie* rule has never been invoked to void a Federal Rule. It is true that there have been cases where this Court has held applicable a state rule in the face of an argument that the situation was governed by one of the Federal Rules. But the holding of each such case was not that *Erie* commanded displacement of a Federal Rule by an inconsistent state rule, but rather that the scope of the Federal Rule was not as broad as the losing party urged, and therefore, there being no Federal Rule which covered the point in dispute, *Erie* commanded the enforcement of state law.

...

.... It is true that both the Enabling Act and the *Erie* rule say, roughly, that federal courts are to apply state "substantive" law and federal "procedural" law, but from that it need not follow that the tests are identical. For they were designed to control very different sorts of decisions. When a situation is covered by one of the Federal Rules, the question facing the court is a far cry from the typical, relatively unguided *Erie* Choice: the court has been instructed to apply the Federal Rule, and can refuse to do so only if the Advisory Committee, this Court, and Congress erred in their *prima facie judgment* that the Rule in question transgresses neither the terms of the Enabling Act nor constitutional restrictions.

We are reminded by the *Erie* opinion that neither Congress nor the federal courts can, under the guise of formulating rules of decision for federal courts, fashion rules which are not supported by a grant of federal authority contained in Article I or some other section of the Constitution; in such areas state law must govern because there can be no other law. But the opinion in *Erie,* which involved no Federal Rule and dealt with a question which was "substantive" in every traditional sense (whether the railroad owed a duty of care to Tompkins as a trespasser or a licensee), surely neither said nor implied that measures like Rule 4(d)(1) are unconstitutional. For the constitutional provision for a federal court system (augmented by the Necessary and Proper Clause) carries with it congressional power to make rules governing the practice and pleading in those courts, which in turn includes a power to regulate matters which, though falling with the uncertain area between substance and procedure, are rationally capable of classification as either.... Although this Court has never before been confronted with a case where the applicable Federal Rule is in direct collision with the law of the relevant State, courts of appeals faced with such clashes have rightly discerned the implications of our decisions.

> "One of the shaping purposes of the Federal Rules is to bring about uniformity in the federal courts by getting away from local rules. This is especially true of matters which relate to the administration of legal proceedings, an area in which federal courts have traditionally exerted strong inherent power, completely aside from the powers Congress expressly conferred in the Rules. The purpose of the *Erie* doctrine...was never to bottle up federal courts with 'outcome determinative' and 'integral relations' stoppers—when there are 'affirmative countervailing

> [federal] considerations' and when there is a Congressional mandate (the Rules) supported by constitutional authority." *Lumbermen's Mutual Casualty Co. v. Wright,* 322 F.2d 759, 764 (C.A.5th Cir. 1963).

Erie and its offspring cast no doubt on the long-recognized power of Congress to prescribe housekeeping rules for federal courts even though some of those rules will inevitably differ from comparable state rules.

... [T]hough a court, in measuring a Federal Rule against the standards contained in the Enabling Act and the Constitution, need not wholly blind itself to the degree to which the Rule makes the character and result of the federal litigation stray from the course it would follow in state courts, it cannot be forgotten that the *Erie* rule,... [was] created to serve another purpose altogether. To hold that a Federal Rule of Civil Procedure must cease to function whenever it alters the mode of enforcing state-created rights would be to disembowel either the Constitution's grant of power over federal procedure or Congress' attempt to exercise that power in the Enabling Act. Rule 4(d)(1) is valid, and controls the instant case.

Reversed.

Mr. Justice BLACK concurs in the result.

Mr. Justice HARLAN, concurring. [Omitted.]

Notes

1. What did Rule 4(d)(1) permit that Massachusetts § 9 did not? How did this difference have the potential to affect the outcome in the case?
2. The Court again struggled with what to do with the substance-procedure dichotomy to which *Erie* alluded. Why did the Court conclude that Rule 4 is procedural? What role did the Rules Enabling Act play in the Court's conclusion?
3. The Court concluded Rule 4(d)(1) is constitutional. Think back to *Erie*; in what way could a rule not be constitutional?
4. What does outcome-determinative mean after *Hanna*? How does *Hanna* tie the outcome-determinative consideration back to *Erie*?
5. The Court offered two reasons for its conclusion. First, it applied the *Erie* doctrine and concluded that Rule 4(d)(1) should apply, not the Massachu-

setts rule. Second, it concluded that the *Erie* doctrine should not be used to determine the constitutionality of a Federal Rule of Civil Procedure. Are both parts of the Court's analysis necessary to reach its result? If not, why not? If so, why? Does it make any difference if both parts are not required?

6. In the U.S. common-law system, many aspects of the law develop through judicial opinions. As new sets of facts are presented, the courts revisit, refine, and clarify the law as it had been previously stated. Notice that important features of earlier cases become irrelevant. For example, section 34 of the Federal Judiciary Act, mentioned in *Erie*, is no longer mentioned or relevant by the time the Court comes to its decision in *Hanna*. Likewise, that statutory section is no longer useful or relevant for your outline of the course materials.

— ★ —

SIX

THE ANATOMY OF A LAWSUIT: TRIAL COURT

A. RESPONDING TO THE COMPLAINT

1. Overview

After a plaintiff decides in which court to file her lawsuit, she must initiate the lawsuit by filing a pleading, typically called a "complaint," and serve a copy of that complaint on the defendant. *See* Fed. R. Civ. P. 3 & 4. When the defendant receives a copy of the plaintiff's complaint, he will review the complaint to see if he believes it meets certain minimum requirements for the action to proceed. For complaints filed in federal court, the Federal Rules of Civil Procedure prescribe those requirements. For state court pleadings, similar requirements are created by state rules or statutes.

For the federal courts, Rule 8 of the Federal Rules of Civil Procedure provides that a complaint must state the basis for the court's jurisdiction. Does the plaintiff contend that the case presents a federal question? That the parties are diverse? Exactly why does the plaintiff believe that the federal court has authority to consider this case?

Rule 8 also requires that the complaint contain "a short and plain statement of the claim showing that the pleader is entitled to relief." This phrase is shorthand for the events and mental states that a plaintiff must ultimately prove in order to prevail and obtain relief. The nature of the allegations necessary to meet this requirement is the subject of the cases that follow.

Lastly, Rule 8 requires that the complaint provide the defendant with some notice of the remedies that the plaintiff seeks. Does she seek damages? Or an order directing the defendant to do or not do something (known as an injunction)? Or does she maybe seek a declaration of the parties' rights?

If the defendant accepts that the plaintiff's complaint meets all three of these requirements, the defendant will file an "answer," a pleading that admits or denies each of the allegations — the jurisdictional allegations and the substantive allegations — in the plaintiff's complaint. The defendant's answer could also add claims (called counterclaims) against the plaintiff (Fed. R. Civ. P. 13) or claims against third-parties, thus bringing more parties into the litigation (Fed. R. Civ. P. 14). If the defendant contends that there are relevant affirmative defenses, the defendant must include them in the answer as well. Fed. R. Civ. P. 8(c). After the defendant files an answer, the litigation will move into its next phase — discovery — described in section B of this Chapter.

The defendant could, however, file a motion, rather than an answer, in response to the complaint. For example, the defendant could file a motion for a more definite statement (Fed. R. Civ. P. 12(e)), a motion for judgment on the pleadings (Fed. R. Civ. P. 12(c)), or a motion to strike a portion of the complaint (Fed. R. Civ. P. 12(f)). The defendant might even choose not to file any response to the complaint. The court, however, would thereafter enter judgment, called a default judgment, for the plaintiff, so this is not a wise choice for the defendant.

But the most commonly filed motion in response to a complaint is the motion to dismiss. A defendant can move to dismiss on many grounds, such as for lack of subject-matter jurisdiction (Fed. R. Civ. P. 12(b)(1)); lack of personal jurisdiction (Fed. R. Civ. P. 12(b)(2)); or failure to join a required party (Fed. R. Civ. P. 12(b)(7)), among other reasons (see Fed. R. Civ. P. 12(b)(1)-(b)(7)). But the motion examined in the next subsection is a motion to dismiss for failure to state a claim, often called a Rule 12(b)(6) motion.

2. Motion to Dismiss

If a defendant believes the complaint does not meet the second requirement of Rule 8 — "a short and plain statement of the claim showing that the pleader is entitled to relief" — the defendant will file a motion to dismiss for failure to state a claim. This motion is called a demurrer in some state courts. If the trial court grants this motion, the court will dismiss the complaint, which may or may not end the litigation. The court may believe that the plaintiff can remedy the complaint's deficiencies. If so, the court would dismiss the complaint but grant the plaintiff permission to file an amended complaint. The defendant would then have another opportunity to respond, possibly by filing another motion to dismiss.

Federal Rule of Civil Procedure 12(b)(6) provides the basis for a motion seeking dismissal due to the complaint's "failure to state a claim upon which relief can be granted." As with all motions, the non-moving party (here, the plaintiff) will have an opportunity to respond. And typically, the moving party (here, the defendant) would have an opportunity to file a brief reply. The court would thereafter rule on the motion, either with or without providing the parties an opportunity to argue the motion in a hearing before the court.

The basis of a motion under Rule 12(b)(6) is the contention that the complaint does not state a claim. The cases below will provide more detail as to the meaning of that standard, but a little background is helpful. A legal theory can be broken down into elements. For example, negligence has four elements:

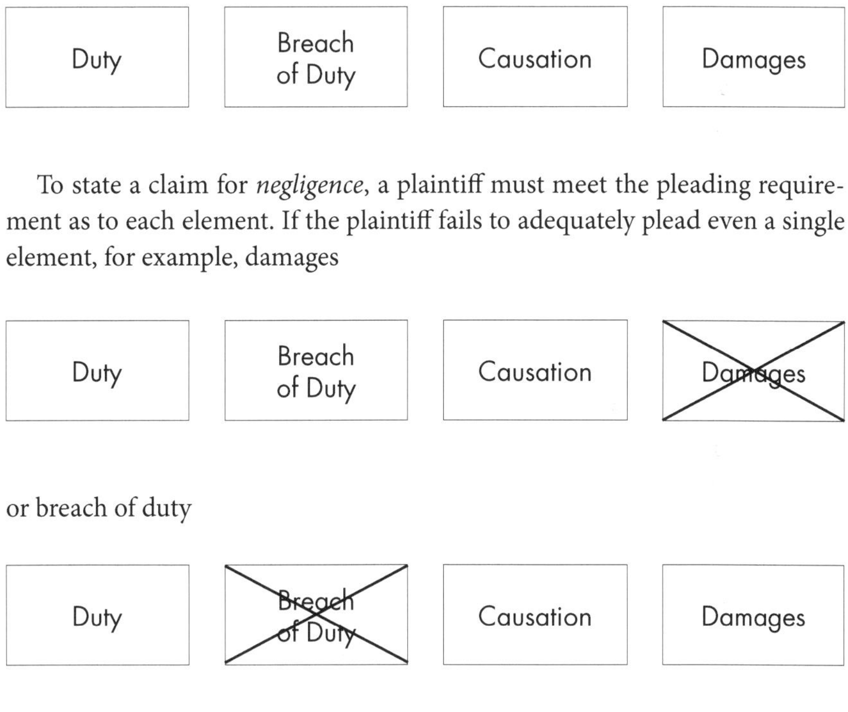

To state a claim for *negligence*, a plaintiff must meet the pleading requirement as to each element. If the plaintiff fails to adequately plead even a single element, for example, damages

or breach of duty

the plaintiff has failed to state a claim.

If the plaintiff's legal theory is something different from negligence, however, as it is in the cases below, the complaint must have sufficient allegations to support the requirements for *that* legal theory. Thus, the precise allegation requirements will vary from legal theory to legal theory, but the general test or standard will remain the same.

To bring you closer to the actual motion process and the trial court's decision-making, you will read orders written by two different district courts. Like the vast majority of district court orders, they are not published in any printed volumes, although they are available from on-line resources. In each case below, the plaintiff alleged that the defendant had violated federal law by discriminating on the basis of the plaintiff's age, and the defendant moved to dismiss under Rule 12(b)(6). In one case, the court granted the defendant's motion. In the other case, the court denied the motion. Why was it proper to grant the motion in one case, but not in the other?

Waters v. Durango Fire & Rescue Authority

United States District Court, D. Colorado

2009 U.S. Dist. LEXIS 122235, 2009 WL 4906684, No. 09-cv-00272-PAB-MJW (Dec. 16, 2009)

PHILIP A. BRIMMER, District Judge.

This matter is before the Court on defendant Durango Fire and Rescue Authority's motion to dismiss [plaintiff's amended complaint]....

The case arises out of an investigation defendant initiated regarding allegations against plaintiff by fellow employees of Durango Fire and Rescue Authority. During the investigation, defendant placed plaintiff on leave. After the investigation concluded, plaintiff did not return to work, contending that the emotional toll of the investigation rendered him disabled. Defendant then terminated plaintiff.

Plaintiff alleges that defendant, on account of conducting an investigation contrary to the terms of its personnel manual and terminating him for failing to return to work, has... discriminated against him on account of age.... Defendant now seeks dismissal of plaintiff's claims... for failure to state a claim pursuant to Federal Rule of Civil Procedure 12(b)(6).

I. STANDARD OF REVIEW

1. Rule 12(b)(6)

Dismissal of a claim under Rule 12(b)(6) is appropriate where the plaintiff fails to state a claim upon which relief can be granted. For a complaint to state a claim it must contain "a short and plain statement of the claim showing that the pleader is entitled to relief." Fed. R. Civ. P. (8)(a)(2). Rule 8(a)'s "short and plain statement" mandate requires that a plaintiff allege enough factual matter that, taken as true, makes his "claim to relief... plausible on its face." *Bryson v. Gonzales*, 534 F.3d 1282, 1286 (10th Cir. 2008).

"The court's function on a Rule 12(b)(6) motion is not to weigh potential evidence that the parties might present at trial, but to assess whether the plaintiff's Complaint alone is legally sufficient to state a claim for which relief may be granted." *Dubbs v. Head Start, Inc.*, 336 F.3d 1194, 1201 (10th Cir. 2003). In doing so, the Court "must accept all the well-pleaded allegations of the complaint as true and must construe them in the light most favorable to the plaintiff." *Alvarado v. KOB-TV, LLC*, 493 F.3d 1210, 1215 (10th Cir. 2007). At the same time, however, a court need not accept conclusory allegations.

Generally, "[s]pecific facts are not necessary; the statement need only 'give the defendant fair notice of what the claim is and the grounds upon which it rests.'" *Erikson v. Pardus*, 551 U.S. 89, 93 (2007) (per curiam). The "plausibility" standard requires that relief must plausibly follow from the facts alleged, not that the facts themselves be plausible.

However, "where the well-pleaded facts do not permit the court to infer more than the mere possibility of misconduct, the complaint has alleged-but it has not shown-that the pleader is entitled to relief." *Ashcroft v. Iqbal*, 129 S. Ct. 1937, 1950 (2009). Thus, even though modern rules of pleading are somewhat forgiving, "a complaint still must contain either direct or inferential allegations respecting all the material elements necessary to sustain a recovery under some viable legal theory." *Bryson*, 534 F.3d at 1286.

...

III. DISCUSSION

...

3. Age... Discrimination

Plaintiff fails to state a claim of discrimination on the basis of... age.... Pursuant to the Age Discrimination in Employment Act ("ADEA"), "[i]t shall be unlawful for an employer to fail or refuse to hire or to discharge any individual or otherwise discriminate against any individual with respect to his compensation, terms, conditions, or privileges of employment, because of such individual's age." 29 U.S.C. § 623(a)(1). To ultimately succeed on such a claim, plaintiff "must prove by a preponderance of the evidence... that age was the 'but for' cause of the challenged employer decision." *Gross v. FBL Fin. Servs., Inc.*, 129 S. Ct. 2343, 2351 (2009).

Here, plaintiff pleads nothing more than that he was terminated and was in the protected age group. Adding the conclusory allegation that he was terminated because of his age does not save his claim. Such skeletal allegations "do not permit the court to infer more than the mere possibility of misconduct." *Iqbal*, 129 S. Ct. at 1950. Because the complaint does not "contain either direct or inferential allegations respecting all the material elements necessary to sustain a recovery under some viable legal theory," the claim for discrimination on the basis of age must be dismissed. *Bryson*, 534 F.3d at 1286.

...

IV. CONCLUSION

For the foregoing reasons, it is

ORDERED that defendant Durango Fire and Rescue Authority's motion to dismiss... is GRANTED. It is further

ORDERED that the clerk shall forthwith enter judgment in favor of defendant and against plaintiff....

Pinkney v. Maverick Condominium Association, Inc.

United States District Court, M.D. Florida

2011 U.S. Dist. LEXIS 62801, 2011 WL 2433505,
No. 6:11-cv-241-Orl-19DAB (June 14, 2011)

ORDER

PATRICIA C. FAWSETT, District Judge.

...

I. Plaintiff's Allegations

In this employment discrimination case, Plaintiff Ollie Pinkney asserts that she was unlawfully terminated from her position as a porter for Defendant Maverick Condominium Association, Inc. ("Maverick") on April 30, 2009.

Pinkney claims that she was terminated upon returning to work after two personal days off that Maverick had previously approved. According to Plaintiff, Maverick gave no reason for her termination, and she was the oldest and only female porter employed by Maverick at the time she was terminated. Plaintiff asserts that she was 48 years old and had worked for Maverick for approximately five years at the time she was terminated.

Pinkney further contends that "Defendant's other full-time porters, who were an estimated ten (10) to fifteen (15) years younger than Plaintiff, were not terminated from employment." ... According to Pinkney, she performed her job duties for Maverick in a successful and satisfactory manner, and she suffered various forms of damages as a result of her termination.

II. Procedural History

...

On May 19, 2011, Pinkney filed a Second Amended Complaint asserting [that she was terminated on the basis of age in violation of the Age Discrimination in Employment Act ("ADEA")]. Maverick has moved to dismiss the Second Amended Complaint for failure to state a claim upon which relief can be granted, and Pinkney has filed a Response in opposition to Maverick's Motion to Dismiss.

III. Standard of Review

When ruling on a motion to dismiss for failure to state a claim upon which relief may be granted under Federal Rule of Civil Procedure 12(b)(6), a court must limit its consideration to the complaint [and] the written instruments attached to it as exhibits.... In determining the merits of the motion, a court must "accept all factual allegations in the complaint as true." *Tellabs,* [*Inc. v. Makor Issues & Rights, Ltd.*,] 551 U.S. [308,] 323 [(2007)]. However, "the tenet that a court must accept as true all of the allegations contained in a complaint is inapplicable to legal conclusions." *Ashcroft v. Iqbal*, 129 S.Ct. 1937, 1949 (2009). Thus, "[t]hreadbare recitals of the elements of a cause of action, supported by mere conclusory statements, do not suffice." *Id.*

Once a court "identif[ies] pleadings that, because they are no more than conclusions, are not entitled to the assumption of truth," the court must next determine whether the well-pled facts "'state a claim to relief that is plausible on its face.'" *Id.* at 1949–50. "A claim has facial plausibility when the plaintiff pleads factual content that allows the court to draw the reasonable inference that the defendant is liable for the misconduct alleged." *Id.* at 1949. "Determining whether a complaint states a plausible claim for relief will...be a context-specific task that requires the reviewing court to draw on its judicial experience and common sense." *Id.* at 1950. As the United States Supreme Court explained:

> The plausibility standard is not akin to a probability requirement, but it asks for more than a sheer possibility that a defendant has acted unlawfully. Where a complaint pleads facts that are merely consistent with a defendant's liability, it stops short of the line between possibility and plausibility of entitlement to relief.

Id. at 1949. On a Rule 12(b)(6) motion to dismiss, when a court considers the range of possible interpretations of the defendant's alleged conduct, if the "more likely explanations" involve lawful, non-actionable behavior, the court should find that the plaintiff's claim is not plausible. *Id.* at 1950–51.

IV. Analysis

Maverick argues that Plaintiff's ADEA...claim[] should be dismissed because Plaintiff fails to allege sufficient facts in support of her claims. The Court disagrees. As discussed below, the factual allegations of the Second Amended Complaint, presumed to be true for purposes of this Motion, permit a plausible inference that Pinkney was terminated on the basis of her age...in violation of the ADEA....

...

The ADEA makes it unlawful for an employer to terminate an employee "because of [her] age." 29 U.S.C. § 623(a). To sufficiently plead an ADEA claim, Plaintiff must allege facts plausibly establishing that her age was a "but-for" cause of her termination, and it is unnecessary to allege facts directed to every element of a...case of discrimination.... The requisite causal connection between age and termination may be sufficiently pled by, *inter alia*, factual allegations indicating that the plaintiff was replaced by a substantially younger individual or that the plaintiff was treated differently than a similarly situated, substantially younger employee.

Plaintiff contends that she was terminated upon returning to work after two authorized days of leave without any explanation from Maverick. Maverick's alleged failure to provide Plaintiff an explanation for her termination, by itself, does not permit an inference of age discrimination because an employer may lawfully terminate an employee for any non-discriminatory reason or no reason at all. However, Plaintiff further alleges that she "was the oldest porter employed by Defendant," that she performed her job duties in "a successful and satisfactory manner," and that "Defendant's other full-time porters, who were an estimated ten (10) to fifteen (15) years younger than Plaintiff, were not terminated from employment." These allegations suggest that Plaintiff was terminated in lieu of similarly situated, substantially younger porters, and thus, that Plaintiff was terminated because of her age. Accordingly, Pinkney's age discrimination claim against Maverick is well pled.

. . .

Conclusion

Based on the foregoing, it is ORDERED that the Motion to Dismiss Second Amended Complaint by Defendant Maverick Condominium Association, Inc. is DENIED.

Notes

1. The "but-for" standard mentioned in both cases is met in the context of these cases if "but for" the plaintiff's age, the plaintiff would not have been terminated. In other words, if the plaintiff were not of an older age, the plaintiff would not have been terminated. Put yet another way, if the plaintiff were sufficiently younger, the plaintiff would not have been terminated.
2. List the allegations that were contained in the complaint in each case. Which allegations are factual? Which allegations are conclusions? Which allegations in *Pinkney* caused that court to deny the motion to dismiss? NOTE: The answer is NOT that the plaintiff in *Pinkney* returned to work and the plaintiff in *Waters* did not.
3. What is the basic standard for a motion to dismiss? What role does the legal theory for the plaintiff's claim play in deciding a motion to dismiss?
4. Consider Federal Rule of Civil Procedure 11(b), which provides in part:

   By presenting to the court a pleading, written motion, or other paper — whether by signing, filing, submitting, or later advocating it — an attorney or unrepresented party certifies that to the best of the person's knowledge, information, and belief, formed after an inquiry reasonable under the circumstances:

> ...
>
> (3) the factual contentions have evidentiary support or, if specifically so identified, will likely have evidentiary support after a reasonable opportunity for further investigation or discovery....

What concerns might have motivated this rule?

5. In *Waters*, the court granted the motion to dismiss. What did the court order to happen next in the litigation? Reflect back on the earlier reading in this Chapter. Did the court have another option as to what it could have ordered to happen next in the litigation? Why might it have chosen the result that it did over that other option?
6. Consider the following:

   Hypo 1: If in *Pinkney*, the plaintiff had instead alleged a legal claim based on race discrimination and the allegations were only as described in the above decision, would that change the district court's conclusion? Would the court have granted or denied the motion?

   Hypo 2: Assume that in the motion to dismiss in *Pinkney*, the defendant had disputed the plaintiff's contention that the plaintiff was the oldest employee. Would that have changed the court's ruling?

   Hypo 3: Assume that in *Waters*, the plaintiff, in his opposition to the defendant's motion to dismiss, had stated that he was the oldest employee, and he was the only employee subject to the improper investigation and subsequent firing. Could the court now deny the motion to dismiss? If so, why? If not, why not?

   Hypo 4: Assume now that the complaint in *Waters* included the following additional allegation:

   > Waters' supervisor, Caroline Jones, knew that Waters was on permissible disability leave, but she nevertheless decided to fire Waters. When Jones called Waters to tell him he was fired, she said, "I am firing you because you are too old. I know this is illegal. And if anyone asks me, I'll tell them that I fired you because you are too old. Looking at your old face makes me depressed. I have a pathological hatred of old people. As soon as anyone turns 50 around here, I fire them. So you have to go."

   Do you think that the court would have granted or denied the motion to dismiss if these allegations were in the plaintiff's complaint?

7. Sometimes, an exam question might ask you to consider whether a motion to dismiss would be successful against a set of allegations provided in the exam question. What do you think the professor is asking you to do with such a question?

Notes on Legal Ethics

1. Federal Rule of Civil Procedure 11 is not the only limit on an attorney's representations to the court. Every state has a code of conduct with which attorneys who are members of its bar must comply. The Model Rules of Professional Conduct (formerly known as the Model Code of Professional Responsibility) is a set of rules on which many states have modeled their actual rules of conduct.
2. Rule 3.3(a) of the Model Rules of Professional Conduct addresses representations in court. This rule requires that lawyers "not knowingly: (1) make a false statement of fact or law to a tribunal or fail to correct a false statement of material fact or law previously made to the tribunal by the lawyer; (2) fail to disclose to the tribunal legal authority in the controlling jurisdiction known to the lawyer to be directly adverse to the position of the client and not disclosed by opposing counsel; or (3) offer evidence that the lawyer knows to be false." The Rule further requires that even if a lawyer does not initially know that a client or witness has offered false material evidence but later learns of its falsity, "the lawyer shall take reasonable remedial measures, including, if necessary, disclosure to the tribunal." *Model Rules of Prof'l Conduct* R. 3.3(a)(3); *see also Model Rules of Prof'l Conduct* R. 3.3(a)(1).
3. There are many other rules governing attorney conduct. For example, there is a duty of competence. *See Model Rules of Prof'l Conduct*, R. 1.1. Lawyers also have a duty of confidentiality to their clients, and a responsibility not to undertake representation of a party with an interest adverse to an existing client. *See Model Rules of Prof'l Conduct*, R. 1.6-1.8. There are rules concerning lawyer communication with third parties and represented parties, to name a few more. *See Model Rules of Prof'l Conduct*, R. 4.1 & 4.2. Violation of any of these rules can cause an attorney to be brought before the bar's disciplinary committee and face punishment up to disbarment. This punishment would be in addition to any consequence that a court might impose for a violation of Rule 11 of the Federal Rules of Civil Procedure, such as monetary sanctions or adverse rulings in the case.

—★—

Now that you understand how the motion to dismiss operates in the trial court, the two cases that follow illustrate how appellate courts review the trial court's dismissal rulings. If you take Securities Regulations, you might read a case like the first one. The second case is a classic corporate law case that is included in many corporate-law textbooks. Textbooks include cases such as these not because they concern motions to dismiss but for what the cases tell us about the relevant substantive law, such as securities regulations and corporate law. Nevertheless, it will be easier to understand these cases if you do not have the added distraction of trying to understand the procedural posture of the case. Indeed, a good grasp of the procedural posture will help you better understand the substantive points should you encounter such cases in future law courses.

Ryan v. Ryan

United States Court of Appeals for the Eighth Circuit

889 F.3d 499 (2018)

LOKEN, Circuit Judge.

Streck, Inc. ("Streck") is a successful, closely held Nebraska corporation founded by Dr. Wayne Ryan in 1982. In 1985, Dr. Ryan and his wife Eileen gifted equal amounts of voting and nonvoting Streck stock to their five children.... In August 2015, [daughter] Stacy filed this action against Streck and [her sister] Connie, alleging violations of § 10(b) of the Securities and Exchange Act of 1934, 15 U.S.C. § 78j(b); Securities and Exchange Commission Rule 10b-5, 17 C.F.R. § 240.10b-5; and multiple violations of Nebraska law.... The district court granted Defendants' motions to dismiss.... Stacy appeals.... We affirm the order dismissing the Complaint....

I. Background

The following facts are alleged in Stacy's 124-paragraph Complaint and are taken as true for the purposes of ruling on Defendants' motions to dismiss under Rule 12(b)(6) of the Federal Rules of Civil Procedure.... [T]he Ryans gifted each of their children 5,500 voting shares and 2,789,470 nonvoting shares of Streck stock. All five children executed stock redemption agreements in 1989 and 2003 providing that each would receive book value if he or she redeemed shares with Streck. In mid-2007, without Stacy's knowledge, Streck and Connie revoked Connie's stock redemption agreement, and Connie purchased 154,000 Streck voting shares, without Board approval, in exchange for her promissory note.

In December 2007, Connie sent Stacy the proposed [revised Redemption Agreement ("RRA")], which significantly revised the prior agreement. Paragraph 7 of the RRA provided that Streck "shall have the right to repurchase the stock, in whole or in part, owned by Stockholder at any time." Paragraph 9 provided that the stock "shall be purchased at the fair market value of the stock... as set forth in the most recent valuation prepared by Juris Valuation Advisors [JVA]... immediately preceding the date of the written notification of the option exercised by Stockholder or the Corporation."... Though initially hesitant, Stacy signed the RRA.... Unbeknownst to Stacy, while her other siblings signed RRAs, Connie did not.

In March 2012, Dr. Ryan notified the Ryan siblings he planned to buy all outstanding Streck stock and remain CEO with new management, and that the most recent stock valuation was $3.32 per nonvoting share and $3.49 per voting share, giving them each a total valuation of almost $9.3 million. In April, he emailed the siblings asking if they wanted to retain ownership of their shares. Stacy replied that she was concerned about Connie's involvement in Streck and wanted more information before deciding whether to sell her shares. She received no response.

On June 19, Dr. Ryan wrote Stacy that Streck had decided to redeem her shares for $9,280,235 and she was required to sign the enclosed Stock Purchase Agreement (SPA) to complete the transaction. Stacy refused to sign the SPA. Streck wired payment for her shares to her bank account.... The notes of a June 11 meeting between Connie, Dr. Ryan, and his estate-planning lawyer reflect that redemption of the shares of siblings other than Connie would be completed by the end of Streck's fiscal year, after which Streck would distribute $10 million to each of the remaining shareholders—Dr. Ryan, Eileen, and Connie. On July 13, Dr. Ryan sent a memo to the siblings other than Stacy and Connie offering to purchase their stock for $3.49 per voting share and $3.32 per nonvoting share if they agreed to sell before July 27, 2012.

Streck's attorneys continued to urge Stacy to sign the SPA, advising that her siblings—including Connie—had signed SPAs and would be receiving the same price as Stacy for their voting and nonvoting shares. On August 22, Stacy signed the SPA, crossing out a mutual release of claims provision, a change that Streck accepted. The SPA provided that Stacy's $9,280,235 payment was "determined according to paragraph 9 of the [RRA]." Unbeknownst to Stacy, Connie did not execute an SPA and retained her shares. When Eileen died in 2013, Connie inherited 159,500 voting shares pursuant to a 2007 change to Eileen's trust, giving Connie two-thirds voting control of Streck. Stacy alleged that a professional appraisal completed in 2014 determined that the fair market value of outstanding Streck stock on March 7, 2013, with applicable discounts, was $8.33 per voting share and $8.09 per nonvoting share.

...Stacy filed this action in federal court, alleging that a series of wrongful acts by Connie and Streck caused her to execute the SPA and complete the redemption of her shares in Streck "for substantially less than fair market value under the terms of the [RRA]." In addition to claims under Section 10(b) of the Exchange Act and SEC Rule 10b-5, she alleged violations of the Securities Act of Nebraska, breach of fiduciary duty, [and] shareholder oppression.... [Section 10(b) of the Securities and Exchange Act of 1934, 15 U.S.C. § 78j(b), makes it unlawful "[t]o use or employ, in connection with the purchase or sale of any security...any manipulative or deceptive device or contrivance in contravention of such rules and regulations as the Commission may prescribe as necessary or appropriate in the public interest or for the protection of investors."] For relief, Stacy sought to invalidate Connie's 2007 purchase of 154,000 voting shares, rescind the SPA, set aside the redemption of Stacy's shares, and "damages to which Plaintiff is entitled."

In the February 2016 order granting Defendants' motions to dismiss, the district court took judicial notice of an October 2011 JVA valuation determining that Streck stock was worth $3.49 per voting share and $3.32 per nonvoting share, the prices at which Streck redeemed Stacy's shares. The district court dismissed Stacy's claims under federal and Nebraska securities laws, and her claims of fraud, breach of fiduciary duty and shareholder oppression, because Stacy did not plausibly allege that wrongful acts caused her loss—she had "consented to Streck's repurchase of the stock at Streck's sole election" in the RRA and did not plead "sufficient facts to raise an inference that Defendants somehow manipulated the 2011 Valuation itself."...

...

II. The Order Dismissing the Complaint

...

B. Dismissal of Stacy's Claims. On appeal, we review a Rule 12(b)(6) dismissal for failure to state a claim de novo, "taking all facts alleged in the complaint as true, and making reasonable inferences in favor of the nonmoving party." To avoid dismissal, a complaint must plead "enough facts to state a claim to relief that is plausible on its face." *Bell Atlantic Corp. v. Twombly*, 550 U.S. 544, 570 (2007). "A claim has facial plausibility when the plaintiff pleads factual content that allows the court to draw the reasonable inference that the defendant is liable for the misconduct alleged." *Ashcroft v. Iqbal*, 556 U.S. 662, 678 (2009).

A.... Stacy [asserts] that the Complaint alleged sufficient facts to raise an inference that Defendants manipulated the 2011 JVA Valuation. As the district court recognized, that assertion, if plausibly pleaded, might support claims requiring proof that wrongful acts caused Stacy's alleged loss. However, the district court concluded, "[a]lthough she alleges a host of transgressions in her Complaint, immaterial to her claims, she has not pled sufficient facts to raise an inference that Defendants somehow manipulated the 2011 Valuation itself." On appeal, Stacy argues the allegation that a 2014 appraisal valuing Streck shares as of March 2013 at substantially more than what Stacy was paid plausibly pleaded that Defendants manipulated the 2011 Valuation. However, that Streck shares had a greater value in March 2013 is not evidence that Defendants "manipulated" the valuation determined by JVA in October 2011. "[W]here the well-pleaded facts do not permit the court to infer more than the mere possibility of misconduct, the complaint has alleged—but it has not 'show[n]'—'that the pleader is entitled to relief.' " *Iqbal*, 556 U.S. at 679, quoting Fed. R. Civ. P. 8(a)(2). Stacy's Complaint did not plead facts plausibly showing that Defendants manipulated the 2011 JVA Valuation in a manner that caused her alleged loss.

B. Finally reaching the merits of the critical issue, Stacy argues the district court erred in concluding that she did not sufficiently plead that Defendants' alleged misconduct caused her to execute the SPA and sell her shares when she otherwise would not have done so. It is undisputed that, in a private action under SEC Rule 10(b)-5 or under the substantially identical provision in the Securities Act of Nebraska, the plaintiff must prove "loss causation." Plaintiff must prove a "nexus between the defendant's fraudulent conduct and the plaintiff's pecuniary loss." Thus, to defeat a motion to dismiss, the plaintiff must plead facts that plausibly allege that defendant's misconduct caused the plaintiff's loss.

The district court concluded that Stacy did not plausibly plead loss causation because the Complaint alleged that the RRA gave Streck the right to purchase her stock at its election, and therefore, "the Defendants' alleged misconduct could not have caused Stacy Ryan to sell her stock." The court noted that our decision in *St. Louis Union Trust Co. v. Merrill Lynch, Pierce, Fenner & Smith, Inc.*, 562 F.2d 1040, 1043-44 (8th Cir. 1977), "compels this conclusion." In *St. Louis Union*, plaintiffs alleged that the defendant redeemed shares without disclosing that it planned to make a public offering. Because the shares were purchased pursuant to a stock restriction giving the firm the absolute right to purchase, what the selling shareholders knew or did not know about a future public offering "was wholly irrelevant to their decision to sell the stock."

Stacy argues that her case is more like *Ayres v. Merrill Lynch, Pierce, Fenner & Smith, Inc.*, 538 F.2d 532, 533-34 (3d Cir.), than *St. Louis Union*. In *Ayres*, a retired former employee and stockholder alleged that the defendant violated federal and state securities laws when it exercised an option to redeem his shares on retirement without informing him that it planned to make a public offering.... [A] divided panel of the Third Circuit concluded that the defendant's nondisclosures were not immaterial because they may have affected the plaintiff's voluntary decision to retire and sell his stock. We conclude that *Ayres*, even if correct, is distinguishable. Like the plaintiffs in *St. Louis Union*, Stacy was obligated to redeem her shares when Streck exercised its right to repurchase under Paragraph 7 of the RRA. As we said in distinguishing *Ayers* in *St. Louis Union*, "[Stacy was] powerless to prevent the contingency which gave [Streck] its absolute right to purchase." Thus, the district court correctly concluded that Defendants' alleged misconduct could not have caused Stacy to sell her stock.

...

For these reasons, we conclude the district court correctly dismissed the claims requiring proof of loss causation that was not plausibly pleaded — the federal and state securities law claims and state law claims of fraudulent misrepresentation and inducement, breach of fiduciary duty, and shareholder oppression....

...

Notes

1. Notice that the decision does not necessarily mention every element of the plaintiff's legal theory, but it does not need to do so. Why?
2. How did the manipulation of share prices relate to the plaintiff's legal theory? In other words, based on the nature of the plaintiff's claim, why was

price manipulation an essential fact such that the absence of allegations to support it caused her claim to fail?

3. In analyzing the manipulation issue, the court seemed not to consider the much higher estimate of stock prices as of March 7, 2013. Why were those estimates not sufficient to state a claim for price manipulation? The court stated there were not enough allegations to "raise an inference that Defendants manipulated the 2011 JVA Valuation." Can you imagine a set of factual allegations that might make stock prices in 2013 sufficient to create an inference of manipulation with respect to the 2011 valuation?
4. The claims also included a causation requirement. Given the alleged facts, why was it not possible that potential wrongdoing by the defendants caused the plaintiff's alleged losses? In answering that question, consider whether the plaintiff had any choice but to sell her shares.
5. The motion-to-dismiss standard articulated by the court is identical, as it should be, to the standard applied by trial courts. The only addition is a standard of review. The appellate court explained that it was conducting a "de novo" review of the district court's decision. This book discusses standards for review of trial court decisions more fully in Chapter 7, but, for now, it will be helpful to know that "de novo" is a standard that allows the appellate court to look at the existing record and make an independent assessment without any deference to the decision of the trial court.

In the next case, *Shlensky v. Wrigley*, the court did not use the words "plausible" or "plausibility," but did it nevertheless use the equivalent of that standard? Or did it use a different standard?

Shlensky v. Wrigley

Appellate Court of Illinois, First District

237 N.E.2d 776 (1968)

MR. JUSTICE SULLIVAN delivered the opinion of the court.

This is an appeal from a dismissal of plaintiff's amended complaint on motion of the defendants. The action was a stockholders' derivative suit against the directors for negligence and mismanagement. The corporation was also made a defendant. Plaintiff sought damages and an order that defendants cause the installation of lights in Wrigley Field and the scheduling of night baseball games.

Plaintiff is a minority stockholder of defendant corporation, Chicago National League Ball Club (Inc.), a Delaware corporation with its principal place of business in Chicago, Illinois. Defendant corporation owns and operates the major league professional baseball team known as the Chicago Cubs. The corporation also engages in the operation of Wrigley Field, the Cubs' home park, the concessionaire sales during Cubs' home games, television and radio broadcasts of Cubs' home games, the leasing of the field for football games and other events and receives its share, as visiting team, of admission moneys from games played in other National League stadia. The individual defendants are directors of the Cubs and have served for varying periods of years. Defendant Philip K. Wrigley is also president of the corporation and owner of approximately 80% of the stock therein.

Plaintiff alleges that since night baseball was first played in 1935 nineteen of the twenty major league teams have scheduled night games. In 1966, out of a total of 1,620 games in the major leagues, 932 were played at night. Plaintiff alleges that every member of the major leagues, other than the Cubs, scheduled substantially all of its home games in 1966 at night, exclusive of opening days, Saturdays, Sundays, holidays and days prohibited by league rules. Allegedly this has been done for the specific purpose of maximizing attendance and thereby maximizing revenue and income.

The Cubs, in the years 1961–65, sustained operating losses from its direct baseball operations. Plaintiff attributes those losses to inadequate attendance at Cubs' home games. He concludes that if the directors continue to refuse to install lights at Wrigley Field and schedule night baseball games, the Cubs will continue to sustain comparable losses and its financial condition will continue to deteriorate.

Plaintiff alleges that, except for the year 1963, attendance at Cubs' home games has been substantially below that at their road games, many of which were played at night.

Plaintiff compares attendance at Cubs' games with that of the Chicago White Sox, an American League club, whose weekday games were generally played at night. The weekend attendance figures for the two teams were similar; however, the White Sox week-night games drew many more patrons than did the Cubs' weekday games.

Plaintiff alleges that the funds for the installation of lights can be readily obtained through financing[,] and the cost of installation would be far more than offset and recaptured by increased revenues and incomes resulting from the increased attendance.

Plaintiff further alleges that defendant Wrigley has refused to install lights, not because of interest in the welfare of the corporation but because of his personal opinions "that baseball is a 'daytime sport' and that the installation of lights and night baseball games will have a deteriorating effect upon the surrounding neighborhood." It is alleged that he has admitted that he is not interested in whether the Cubs would benefit financially from such action because of his concern for the neighborhood, and that he would be willing for the team to play night games if a new stadium were built in Chicago.

Plaintiff alleges that the other defendant directors, with full knowledge of the foregoing matters, have acquiesced in the policy laid down by Wrigley and have permitted him to dominate the board of directors in matters involving the installation of lights and scheduling of night games, even though they knew he was not motivated by a good faith concern as to the best interests of defendant corporation, but solely by his personal views set forth above. It is charged that the directors are acting for a reason or reasons contrary and wholly unrelated to the business interests of the corporation; that such arbitrary and capricious acts constitute mismanagement and waste of corporate assets, and that the directors have been negligent in failing to exercise reasonable care and prudence in the management of the corporate affairs.

The question on appeal is whether plaintiff's amended complaint states a cause of action. It is plaintiff's position that fraud, illegality and conflict of interest are not the only bases for a stockholder's derivative action against the directors. Contrariwise, defendants argue that the courts will not step in and interfere with honest business judgment of the directors unless there is a showing of fraud, illegality or conflict of interest.

...

Plaintiff in the instant case argues that the directors are acting for reasons unrelated to the financial interest and welfare of the Cubs. However, we are not satisfied that the motives assigned to Philip K. Wrigley, and through him to the other directors, are contrary to the best interests of the corporation and the stockholders. For example, it appears to us that the effect on the surrounding neighborhood might well be considered by a director who was considering the patrons who would or would not attend the games if the park were in a poor neighborhood. Furthermore, the long run interest of the corporation in its property value at Wrigley Field might demand all efforts to keep the neighborhood from deteriorating. By these thoughts we do not mean to say that we have decided that the decision of the directors was a correct one. That is beyond our jurisdiction and ability. We are merely saying that the decision is one properly before directors and the motives alleged in the amended complaint showed no fraud, illegality or conflict of interest in their making of that decision.

While all the courts do not insist that one or more of the three elements must be present for a stockholder's derivative action to lie, nevertheless we feel that unless the conduct of the defendants at least borders on one of the elements, the courts should not interfere. The trial court in the instant case acted properly in dismissing plaintiff's amended complaint.

We feel that plaintiff's amended complaint was also defective in failing to allege damage to the corporation. The well pleaded facts must be taken as true for the purpose of judging the sufficiency of the amended complaint. However, one need not accept conclusions drawn by the pleader. Furthermore, pleadings will be construed most strongly against the pleader prior to a verdict or judgment on the merits.

There is no allegation that the night games played by the other nineteen teams enhanced their financial position or that the profits, if any, of those teams were directly related to the number of night games scheduled. There is an allegation that the installation of lights and scheduling of night games in Wrigley Field would have resulted in large amounts of additional revenues and incomes from increased attendance and related sources of income. Further, the cost of installation of lights, funds for which are allegedly readily available by financing, would be more than offset and recaptured by increased revenues. However, no allegation is made that there will be a net benefit to the corporation from such action, considering all increased costs.

Plaintiff claims that the losses of defendant corporation are due to poor attendance at home games. However, it appears from the amended complaint, taken as a whole, that factors other than attendance affect the net earnings or losses. For example, in 1962, attendance at home and road games decreased appreciably as compared with 1961, and yet the loss from direct baseball operation and of the whole corporation was considerably less.

The record shows that plaintiff did not feel he could allege that the increased revenues would be sufficient to cure the corporate deficit. The only cost plaintiff was at all concerned with was that of installation of lights. No mention was made of operation and maintenance of the lights or other possible increases in operating costs of night games and we cannot speculate as to what other factors might influence the increase or decrease of profits if the Cubs were to play night home games.

...

Finally, we do not agree with plaintiff's contention that failure to follow the example of the other major league clubs in scheduling night games constituted negligence. Plaintiff made no allegation that these teams' night schedules were profitable or that the purpose for which night baseball had been undertaken was fulfilled. Furthermore, it cannot be said that directors, even those of corporations that are losing money, must follow the lead of the other corporations in the field. Directors are elected for their business capabilities and judgment and the courts cannot require them to forego their judgment because of the decisions of directors of other companies. Courts may not decide these questions in the absence of a clear showing of dereliction of duty on the part of the specific directors and mere failure to "follow the crowd" is not such a dereliction.

For the foregoing reasons the order of dismissal entered by the trial court is affirmed.

Affirmed.

DEMPSEY, P.J. and SCHWARTZ, J., concur.

Notes

1. First, a little background on the Chicago Cubs: Until 2016, the team was often referred to as the "loveable losers." Prior to 2016, the team's last World Series victory (the highest baseball honor in the United States) was in 1908. No other team had such a long losing record. In 2016, the Cubs won the World Series, breaking its 108-year drought. *Shlensky*, however, was decided in 1968 — 60 years into the drought and long before the Cubs would again be World Series champions.
2. *Shlensky* is included in this book, not for its corporate law teachings, but because it is a concrete example of a case that arises from a dismissal in the trial court that you will likely read if you take a corporate law course. The case is included to illustrate how the procedural devices that you are learning in this course will appear throughout your other courses.

3. The appellate court in *Shlensky* affirmed the dismissal, finding the complaint's allegations did not state a cause of action. The opinion describes numerous factual allegations, and yet the court concluded those allegations were not enough. What was the legal theory in *Shlensky*, and why were the allegations in the complaint insufficient to state a claim on those theories?

B. CONDUCTING DISCOVERY

Discovery in the United States is the step in the litigation process during which parties formally obtain information relevant to the case. Lawyers, not judges, lead the discovery; and the parties, not the government, finance the work. This approach of delegating responsibility to the parties is seen as both necessary and superior to other alternatives. It is necessary, because the United States does not discourage litigation. Litigation is considered an overall positive process because it provides a vehicle for remedying wrongs no matter how powerless the plaintiff and how powerful the defendant. Putting the courts in charge of discovery in the many cases filed each year would either limit the number of cases that could be filed or slow down the process considerably, delaying justice for everyone including those seriously harmed. Placing the responsibility for litigation in the hands of the parties distributes the responsibility among those involved in the litigation.

This approach is also considered to be superior to having the court or government drive litigation. The parties involved in the dispute have the greatest motivation to investigate thoroughly. And parties do just that. Litigation attorneys spend most of their hours on discovery: crafting requests for discovery, opposing or responding to requests for discovery, overseeing the gathering of information and documents responsive to discovery requests, reviewing discovery responses, and more. By assigning the discovery responsibility to the parties, the United States judicial system provides the parties every opportunity and incentive to perform the task thoroughly.

As this discussion illustrates, the most obvious purpose of discovery is the identification and preservation of evidence that can directly aid a party's case at trial. Discovery also facilitates settlement by helping parties identify their points of agreement and disagreement, as well as their case's strengths and weaknesses. If settlement fails, discovery fosters fairness in the trial, by ensuring that both parties, regardless of their financial ability to conduct expensive private investigations, have relatively equal access to relevant information.

The actual forms of formal discovery are fairly uniform throughout the legal systems in the United States. One regularly recognized form of discovery, called interrogatories, consists of written requests for information directed to an opposing party in the litigation. For example, in an employment discrimination case, the plaintiff might send the following two interrogatories (along with others) to the defendant (plaintiff's former employer):

1. Please state all reasons for Plaintiff's termination.
2. Please state all policies and procedures that you contend Plaintiff violated while employed by you.

The party to whom the interrogatories are directed (in this hypothetical, the defendant) must answer under oath or object if the party believes a proper ground exists for not responding. Fed. R. Civ. P. 33(b). There is also a third possible response: If, to respond, the party would have to examine or summarize business records, and "if the burden of deriving or ascertaining the answer will be substantially the same for either party, the responding party may answer by" identifying and providing access to the relevant records. Fed. R. Civ. P. 33(d).

Parties may also request the production of documents or other things from an opposing party; may request "entry onto designated land or other property possessed or controlled by the responding party, so that the requesting party may inspect, measure, survey, photograph, test, or sample the property," Fed. R. Civ. P. 34(a)(2); and may obtain a court order requiring "a party whose mental or physical condition . . . is in controversy to submit to a physical or mental examination by a suitably licensed or certified examiner," Fed. R. Civ. P. 35(a)(1).

Yet another form of discovery is designed to identify the precise points of controversy between the parties. In this form of discovery, a party may serve a written request to the opposing party to admit certain facts, the application of law to fact, or opinions about either. Fed. R. Civ. P. 36(a)(1). If the party does not respond to the requests for admissions in the prescribed time limit, the court will deem each item admitted for purposes of the litigation. Fed. R. Civ. P. 36(a)(3).

For example, if the plaintiff in an employment discrimination case contends that she began employment with the employer on May 1, 1996, she might send the following request for admission to the defendant, her former employer: "Admit that plaintiff began employment with defendant on May 1, 1996."

A final, frequently-utilized form of discovery is a deposition. *See* Fed. R. Civ. P. 30. At a deposition, one party asks questions of the deponent, who must answer under oath. A court reporter creates a verbatim written transcript of the questions and answers. The deposition may also be videotaped. Unlike many other forms of discovery, which one party can only direct to another party, a party can take the deposition of a non-party, for example a coworker.

In addition to all of these forms of permissive discovery, the federal rules require the disclosure of certain information to the opposing party. This part of discovery is described as "mandatory disclosures."

Discovery in the United States is quite broad compared to the systems in many other countries, but, even in the United States, there are limits. For example, courts can limit the number of interrogatories that can be sent or depositions that can be taken. And some types of information are completely protected from discovery by a doctrine called "privilege." There are various forms of privilege. For example, attorney-client privilege protects conversations between an attorney and client about matters related to the client's legal representation. Another common example is work-product privilege (also called work-product doctrine), which protects attorney work product created in anticipation of litigation (a concept that courts have interpreted fairly expansively).

There are other limits as well that are discussed in the next case. What do those limits tell you about the ideals underlying discovery in the United States?

Securities & Exchange Commission v. Rajaratnam

United States Court of Appeals for the Second Circuit

622 F.3d 159 (2010)

GERARD E. LYNCH, Circuit Judge:

Defendants-Appellants Raj Rajaratnam and Danielle Chiesi (hereinafter, "Appellants") appeal from a district court (Jed S. Rakoff, Judge) discovery order compelling Appellants to disclose thousands of wiretapped conversations, originally provided to Appellants by the United States Attorney's Office ("USAO") in parallel criminal proceedings, to Plaintiff–Appellee Securities and Exchange Commission ("SEC") for use in this civil enforcement action against Appellants.... [I]n deciding whether and how much to disclose, a district court must balance the agency's right of access to these materials in civil discovery against the privacy interests at stake. In the instant case, we conclude that... the district court clearly exceeded its discretion in ordering disclosure of thousands of conversations involving hundreds of parties, prior to any ruling on the legality of the wiretaps and without limiting the disclosure to relevant conversations.

... [In a separate proceeding,] Appellants were [criminally] indicted for insider trading and conspiracy. [Also, the SEC filed a civil complaint against Appellants and others, charging them with insider trading and conspiracy based on the same conduct at issue in the criminal case.] ...

While the Appellants' civil and criminal cases are proceeding before different judges, both cases revolve around the same allegations: that Appellants engaged in widespread and repeated insider trading at several hedge funds.... According to the SEC, the scheme, which allegedly generated over $52 million in illegal profits, involved tips from insiders concerning "market moving events such as quarterly earnings announcements, takeovers, and material contracts," that spurred the defendants to trade shares of numerous public companies illegally.

The criminal investigation into these allegations included court-ordered wiretapping of communications between [Appellants] and others. According to Appellants, the wiretapped conversations, which spanned sixteen months, included 18,150 communications involving 550 separate individuals, which were intercepted from ten separate telephones—including Appellants' home, office and mobile phones. As part of criminal discovery, the USAO provided to Appellants copies of these wiretapped communications, the orders authorizing the wiretaps, and the government's applications for those orders. The USAO did not, however, share those materials with the SEC.

The SEC instead sought access to the wiretap recordings by demanding them from Appellants in discovery in the civil case.... Appellants opposed the demand on the grounds that the materials were not relevant.... The SEC then moved to compel disclosure.

The district court... ordered Appellants to produce the wiretapped conversations to the SEC and to any other party to the civil action that demanded them. The court noted that while the USAO had not shared the wiretap materials with the SEC, the Appellants possessed these materials, they apparently asserted the right to share them with other defendants pursuant to a joint defense agreement, and no protective order had been issued in the criminal case barring Appellants from using the wiretap materials in the civil case, or from disclosing them to the SEC. It found that "the notion that only one party to a litigation should have access to some of the most important non-privileged evidence bearing directly on the case runs counter to basic principles of civil discovery in an adversary system and therefore should not readily be inferred, at least not when the party otherwise left in ignorance is a government agency charged with civilly enforcing the very same provisions that are the subject of the parallel criminal cases arising from the same transactions."

...

DISCUSSION

...

IV. Did the District Court Exceed its Discretion in Entering the Instant Order?

...

A. The SEC's Right of Access

Under the circumstances of this case, where the civil defendant has properly received the... materials at issue from the government, the SEC has a presumptive right to discovery of these materials from its adversary based on the civil discovery principle of equal information.

The Supreme Court has acknowledged the "fundamental maxim of discovery that '[m]utual knowledge of all the relevant facts gathered by both parties is essential to proper litigation.'" *Société Nationale Industrielle Aérospatiale v. U.S. Dist. Court for the S. Dist. of Iowa*, 482 U.S. 522, 540 n. 25 (1987), quoting *Hickman v. Taylor*, 329 U.S. 495, 507 (1947). "To that end, either party may compel the other to disgorge whatever facts he [or she] has in his [or her] possession." *Hickman*, 329 U.S. at 507.

Federal Rule of Civil Procedure 26(b)(1) embodies this principle by permitting parties to "obtain discovery regarding any nonprivileged matter that is relevant to any party's claim or defense." Fed. R. Civ. P. 26(b)(1); see also *id.* ("Relevant information need not be admissible at the trial if the discovery appears reasonably calculated to lead to the discovery of admissible evidence."). However, while the SEC has a right of access to the materials possessed by Appellants, that right of access does not outweigh any and all privacy interests at issue. A balancing is required for a district court reasonably to exercise its discretion.

The right of access to discovery materials is frequently qualified in the interest of protecting legitimate interests. For example, a district court may permit the withholding of evidence that would otherwise be subject to discovery in order to avoid disclosing privileged information, Fed. R. Civ. P. 26(b)(5)(A) (accounting for a party "withhold[ing] information otherwise discoverable by claiming that the information is privileged"); or trial preparation materials, Fed. R. Civ. P. 26(b)(3) (setting limitations on when and what kind of attorney work-product "documents and tangible things" may be disclosed, but noting that court "must protect against disclosure of the mental impressions, conclusions, opinions, or legal theories of a party's attorney or other representative concerning the litigation"). A district court must also limit "the frequency or extent of discovery" if it determines that it is "unreasonably cumulative or duplicative, or can be obtained from some other source that is more convenient, less burdensome, or less expensive... [or where] the burden or expense of the proposed discovery outweighs its likely benefit." Fed. R. Civ. P. 26(b)(2)(C). And a district court may issue protective orders "for good cause... to protect a party or person from annoyance, embarrassment, oppression, or undue burden or expense." Fed. R. Civ. P. 26(c)(1). In short, as is true generally in the discovery context, the SEC has a discovery right to the information in question, but that right is not absolute.

We first examine the weight of the SEC's interest. Appellants' unilateral access to this information in preparing for trial would surely be prejudicial to the SEC, because, even if Appellants do not use any of the recordings at the civil trial, they could still use the materials in preparation for trial — for example, by preparing to cross-examine witnesses at deposition or at trial, by attacking the credibility of witnesses, or by deciding how to structure their defense. Placing the parties on a level playing field with respect to such functions is the very purpose for which civil discovery exists. For this reason, we find that the SEC's right of access is significant.

Appellants make several arguments that there is no relevant informational imbalance.... They argue that... the SEC could simply depose Appellants if it wished to learn about their telephone conversations. Moreover, they argue that they do not intend to use these materials in their civil defense. Appellants also argue that informational equality is not always guaranteed, pointing to differential rules of access for civil and criminal litigants with regards to sensitive information involved in grand jury proceedings and materials protected by executive privilege. Finally, Appellants argue that there is no informational harm because the wiretapped conversations at issue here are not relevant. While these arguments demonstrate that the SEC's rights to discovery cannot be absolute, and some of them bear on the balance to be struck, they do not convince us that the SEC does not have a significant interest in access to these materials that, if it outweighs the privacy interests at stake, could permit a district court to order disclosure.

...

Appellants' deposition is not a perfect substitute for access to the wiretapped conversations... given the likelihood that Appellants would not remember the contents of many potentially relevant conversations to which their attorneys, in possession of recordings of those conversations, would still have access. In any event, parties to litigation are not limited in discovery to their adversaries' recollection as to matters reduced to writing, recorded, or otherwise memorialized....

[Also], while Appellants state that they do not intend to use the materials in preparation for their civil trial, that intention does not eliminate the unfair advantage they might have against the SEC, given that the team of lawyers defending the criminal case substantially overlaps with that defending the civil case. It would be nearly impossible to stop the attorneys from, at the very least subconsciously, using information from these materials in preparation for the civil trial. At any rate, Appellants do not maintain that they are legally precluded from using the wiretap materials at their civil trial should it become tactically advisable to do so. It therefore cannot be said that this imbalance would be insignificant.

...

[W]hile a civil discovery interest in material may weigh less heavily than a criminal discovery interest, it does not follow that the SEC's right to informational equality is outweighed by Appellants' privacy interests in the instant case.

Finally, since the district court did not evaluate the materials to determine their relevance, we are not in a position to evaluate Appellants' claim that the wiretap conversations are not relevant. If they are relevant, see Fed. R. Civ. P. 26(b)(1) ("Unless otherwise limited by court order... [p]arties may obtain discovery regarding any nonprivileged matter that is relevant to any party's claim or defense...."), then Appellants' possession of the conversations would put the SEC at a disadvantage, and the SEC has a presumptive right to discover them. And, as we conclude below, any disclosure of wiretap conversations should be limited to relevant conversations in any event.

In sum, despite Appellants' arguments to the contrary, the SEC clearly has an interest in access to these wiretap conversations insofar as they create an informational imbalance prejudicing its preparation for the civil trial.

B. The Privacy Interests at Stake

While the SEC has a right of access to the wiretap materials, that right must be balanced against the strong privacy interests at stake in connection with the fruits of electronic surveillance. The privacy interests in the instant case merit particular attention given that the disclosure order implicated thousands of conversations of hundreds of innocent parties, and that the district court ordered disclosure prior to any ruling on the legality of the interceptions and without limiting the disclosure to relevant conversations.

...The fact that [the law] does not impose an absolute ban on civil discovery orders of the kind at issue here does not mean that the concerns for privacy that underlie [the laws governing wiretaps] are irrelevant or can be disregarded. To the contrary, we conclude that those concerns, and the evident desire of Congress to limit disclosures of the fruits even of lawful wiretapping, must be carefully weighed before discovery is ordered.

C. The District Court Could Not Properly Balance the Interests at Stake on the Record Before It

At the present stage of this litigation, a definitive balancing of the interests at stake in this case is impossible, because the record is not adequately developed to support the broad order appealed from. Nevertheless, it is clear that the order appealed from, for those very reasons, cannot be sustained. The district court exceeded its discretion in failing to balance properly the relevant privacy interests against the SEC's right of access in two major ways: (1) by ordering the disclosure of the conversations prior to a ruling on the legality of the interceptions, and (2) by failing to limit the disclosure order to relevant conversations.

1. The Suppression Motions Have Not Been Decided

The sheer number of conversations and parties at interest in this case evince a strong privacy interest that would require an equally strong right of access to support disclosure. Even absent such numbers, a district court could not effectively balance these competing interests while the legality of the wiretaps is at issue. If the legality of the wiretaps is upheld, any privacy rights against interception would have been infringed lawfully and with good purpose. On the other hand, if the wiretaps are found to have been unlawful, the privacy rights at issue would already have been grievously infringed, and further dissemination of conversations that had been illegally intercepted would only compound the injury.... Conversely, a determination that the wiretaps were legal would reduce the privacy concerns, and would make it all but inevitable that some or all of the most relevant conversations would be publicly played at the criminal trial.

At a minimum, [] ordering discovery of the wiretap materials before any determination of the legality of the surveillance involved exceeded the district court's discretion. A primary reason for the pretrial disclosure of the material to Appellants in the criminal case in the first place was to enable them to make motions addressing their legality before the judges presiding over the related criminal cases. Appellants and the defendants in the related cases have indeed made, or indicated they will make, such motions before Judges Holwell and Sullivan, and proceedings to resolve them are under way. A district court has a legitimate interest in maintaining control over its docket and enjoys considerable discretion in setting schedules for discovery, motions, and trial, but that interest is insufficient to support an order directing the further dissemination of wiretap materials pending a decision on the legality of their acquisition.

Given that there were so many reasons to wait until a court had ruled on the legality of the interceptions, and no persuasive reasons to proceed without waiting, the district court's decision to order disclosure of the wiretap communications prior to any ruling on their legality clearly "cannot be located within the range of permissible decisions." *In re Sims*, 534 F.3d 117, 132 (2d Cir. 2008). The privacy interests at stake prior to a ruling on the legality of interceptions clearly outweigh the SEC's interest in discovery.

2. The Court's Failure to Limit the Disclosure to Relevant Conversations

The district court also clearly exceeded its discretion by failing to limit the disclosure of the wiretapped conversations to relevant conversations. The SEC does not have a right of access to irrelevant conversations, even if lawfully intercepted, because Appellants' possession of these conversations would not benefit them in preparing for the civil trial. Indeed, both the SEC and USAO agree that the order should be limited to relevant disclosures. The point assumes particular significance here where ordering the disclosure of all the conversations without limiting discovery to relevant material could infringe the privacy rights of hundreds of individuals, whose irrelevant, and potentially highly personal, conversations with the Appellants would needlessly be disclosed to the SEC and other parties, without furthering any legitimate countervailing interest. The district court clearly exceeded its discretion by this failure to limit the disclosure.

While the district court was correct that the SEC had a legitimate right of access to the wiretap materials, it could not properly balance that interest against the privacy interests at stake while the legality of the wiretaps was still unresolved. In any event, the district court exceeded its discretion in ordering disclosure of wiretap materials without regard to relevancy, particularly in a case involving a large number of recordings intercepting conversations of innocent parties. In sum, because the challenged order was thus "clearly outside the range of permissible decisions," we conclude that Appellants have shown a "clear and indisputable right" to the writ of mandamus to vacate that order.

CONCLUSION

For the foregoing reasons, we... VACATE the district court's discovery order, and REMAND the cause to the district court for further proceedings not inconsistent with this opinion.

Notes

1. Did the decision that you read above arise from the civil or criminal proceeding involving appellants? Note: Two months after this decision, the trial court in the criminal case denied appellants' motion to suppress the results of the wiretap, finding, among other things, that the wiretaps had been legal. *United States v. Rajaratnam*, No. 09 Cr. 1184 (RJH), Nov. 24, 2010. On remand from the Second Circuit in the civil case, the district court entered a ruling very similar to its earlier one. *See SEC v. Galleon Management, LP*, 274 F.R.D. 120 (S.D.N.Y. 2011).

2. In 2011, a jury in Rajaratnam's criminal case found him guilty of 14 counts of securities fraud and conspiracy. Chiesi had earlier plead guilty to three counts of conspiracy to commit securities fraud. Rajaratnam's punishment in the criminal case included an 11-year sentence, a $10 million fine, and an order of forfeiture of $53.8 million, each of which were upheld on appeal.

   In 2011, the trial court in the civil action ordered Rajaratnam to pay a financial penalty of $92.8 million for his insider trading. In 2019, the appellate court affirmed this financial penalty as well.

3. What evidence was the SEC attempting to obtain from appellants? How had appellants acquired this evidence?

4. Review the introductory materials on discovery in this Chapter. Of the discovery options discussed in the materials preceding this case, which

one do you think the SEC must have used to attempt to force appellants to provide this evidence during discovery? How do you think appellants responded to that request?

5. The introductory materials to this case explained that discovery is conducted and controlled by the parties. This case illustrates that when that process breaks down between the parties, there is a role for the court. A party can file a motion to compel discovery, as the SEC did here. Most courts, though, require extensive efforts by the parties to resolve their dispute before they can file a motion to compel. *See, e.g.*, C.D. Cal. Local Rule 37-1 ("Before filing any motion relating to discovery... counsel for the parties must confer in a good-faith effort to eliminate the necessity for hearing the motion or to eliminate as many of the disputes as possible.... If both counsel are located in the same county, the conference must take place in person at the office of the moving party's counsel unless the parties agree to meet someplace else."); C.D. Cal. Local Rule 37-2 (requiring that "[i]f counsel are unable to settle their differences, they must formulate a written stipulation unless otherwise ordered by the Court").
6. What were the trial court's reasons for requiring the production of the disputed evidence?
7. According to the appellate court, how had the trial court erred? What factor or consideration about this evidence made the appellate court concerned about compelling appellants to share the evidence with the SEC?
8. What arguments did appellants make to oppose discovery of the evidence? What was the court's response to those arguments?
9. What was to happen when the case was returned to the trial court? If the trial court were again to rule that appellants had to produce this evidence, would that decision necessarily be erroneous? Are there any circumstances under which that decision could be correct? What are those circumstances?
10. What limits on discovery does the court discuss in its opinion? What do you learn about the theory underlying discovery in the United States? At the beginning of the appellate court's decision it says: "[I]n deciding whether and how much to disclose, a district court must balance the agency's right of access to these materials in civil discovery against the privacy interests at stake." Do you think the court viewed those two considerations as equally balanced? Is one more important than the other?

Notes on Agency Enforcement of Laws

1. *Rajaratnam* illustrates another role of administrative agencies—enforcement. In *Ryan*, the plaintiff, a private citizen, was suing under a regulation promulgated by the SEC. In contrast, in *Rajaratnam*, the SEC, through its Enforcement Division, brought the lawsuit.

2. The SEC claimed that Rajaratnam had committed insider trading, which is the use of confidential information to trade on the stock exchange. Possession of confidential (or "inside") information can provide a trader with an unfair advantage over others trading on the market who are unaware of the information. With respect to insider trading, Congress has authorized the SEC to bring a civil action in district court to recover civil penalties. *See* 15 U.S.C. § 78u-1(a)(1). However, Congress has not granted the SEC any criminal enforcement authority. Notice in *Rajaratnam* that the United States Attorney's Office, which is a part of the Department of Justice rather than the SEC, had brought the criminal charges against Rajaratnam.

3. Congress prescribes the remedies that an agency can obtain in civil litigation or agency enforcement action. For insider-trading cases, Congress has authorized the SEC to obtain civil penalties. Prior to 2002, these penalties, if awarded, were added to the U.S. treasury. In 2002, though, Congress expanded the potential use of the civil penalties received by the SEC by permitting the SEC to add the penalties to a fund created for the benefit of victims of the defendant's insider trading. *See* 15 U.S.C. § 7246. The SEC can also seek injunctions, which, in this context, are typically orders that prohibit future violations, and may also seek to bar or suspend individuals from acting as corporate officers or directors. *See* 15 U.S.C. §§ 77t(b); 78u(d)(1).

4. Many agencies, like the SEC, are also authorized to hold administrative proceedings. "Administrative proceedings differ from civil court actions in that they are heard by an administrative law judge (ALJ), who is independent of the Commission. Both the Division staff and the defendant may appeal all or any portion of the initial decision to the Commission.... The Commission may affirm the decision of the ALJ, reverse the decision, or remand it for additional hearings. Administrative sanctions include cease and desist orders, suspension or revocation of broker-dealer and investment advisor registrations, censures, bars from association with the securities industry, civil monetary penalties, and disgorgement." https://www.sec.gov/enforce/how-investigations-work.html

5. Did you notice that the previous paragraph describes an adjudicatory proceeding within an executive-branch agency? Typically, the Executive Branch is charged with prosecuting violations of law enacted by the Legislative Branch, and the Judicial Branch is responsible for adjudication. Nevertheless, administrative agencies often have some sort of semi-adjudicative authority, in that the exclusive job of the Administrative Law Judge (ALJ), who is technically independent from the agency, is to adjudicate proceedings for one agency, for example, the SEC. But unlike federal district court judges, federal appellate judges, and Justices of the Supreme Court of the United States, ALJs do not have lifetime tenure. How might that difference be important in this setting?

6. This structure might lead you to the question: why would an agency ever file suit in district court if the agency can have the frequent-player advantage of proceeding before an ALJ? In 2015, the Wall Street Journal reported that in the previous five years, the SEC had won 90% of its cases brought before its own administrative law judges but had won only 69% of its cases brought in federal court. *See* https://www.wsj.com/articles/sec-wins-with-in-house-judges-1430965803. Not surprisingly, the SEC was more and more frequently choosing to proceed before an ALJ, rather than in district court, a practice that has been subject to criticism but is lawful.

C. MOTION FOR SUMMARY JUDGMENT

Like the motion to dismiss, the motion for summary judgment provides a means for one party to ask the court to resolve the case prior to trial. Unlike a motion to dismiss, which only a defendant can file (because such a motion responds to the plaintiff's complaint), any party or even all parties can move for summary judgment. If the plaintiff and the defendant each file a motion for summary judgment, the motions are often referred to as cross-motions for summary judgment. For reasons that will be discussed in the notes following the next case, it is most common for only the defendant to move for summary judgment. We will therefore focus on cases in which the defendant moved for summary judgment.

As you learned in section A of this Chapter, when a court rules on a motion to dismiss, it may only consider the allegations in the complaint. The court is not similarly limited when ruling on a motion for summary judgment. At this stage, the court will consider the evidence presented by the parties both for and against summary judgment. For this reason, parties often wait to file a motion for summary judgment until after discovery is completed. If a party moves for summary judgment while discovery is still ongoing, the federal rules (and the rules in many state jurisdictions as well) permit the court to defer ruling on the motion for summary judgment while the non-moving party completes discovery. *See* Fed. R. Civ. P. 56(d) ("If a nonmovant shows by affidavit or declaration that, for specified reasons, it cannot present facts essential to justify its opposition, the court may: (1) defer considering the motion or deny it; (2) allow time to obtain affidavits or declarations or to take discovery; or (3) issue any other appropriate order.").

If the defendant moves for summary judgment and the court grants the motion, the case ends without a trial, and the court enters a judgment in favor of the defendant. In other words, the plaintiff loses. If the court denies the defendant's motion for summary judgment in any respect, the case will not end at that time, because the claims on which the court denied summary judgment will continue to proceed to trial. In other words, no one has yet won or lost the case.

As you read the next case, pay close attention to the standard for summary judgment. This standard references the parties' "burdens." The plaintiff bears the burden of proving his or her claims at trial. To prove that claim, the plaintiff must offer evidence supporting every element of the claim. The claim in the case below is based on the legal theory of negligence. As the case explains, the elements of a negligence claim are: duty, breach, causation, and damages. Thus, to prevail, the plaintiff must, at a minimum, offer evidence to support each element. Suppose that the gray in the boxes below indicates that the plaintiff offered some evidence on that element. The boxes in gray below would then illustrate that the plaintiff offered evidence to support each element.

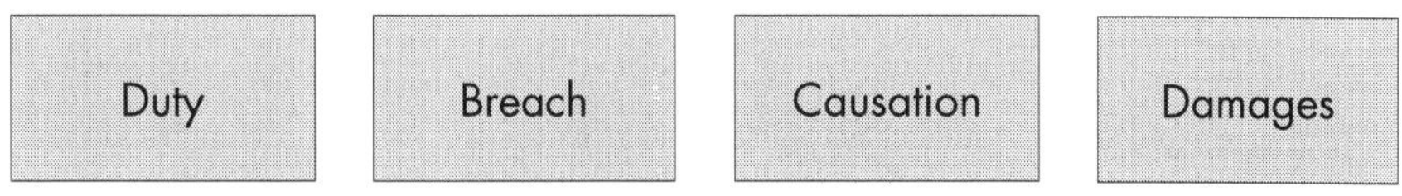

But now assume that the plaintiff fails at trial to offer any evidence on the element of breach of duty.

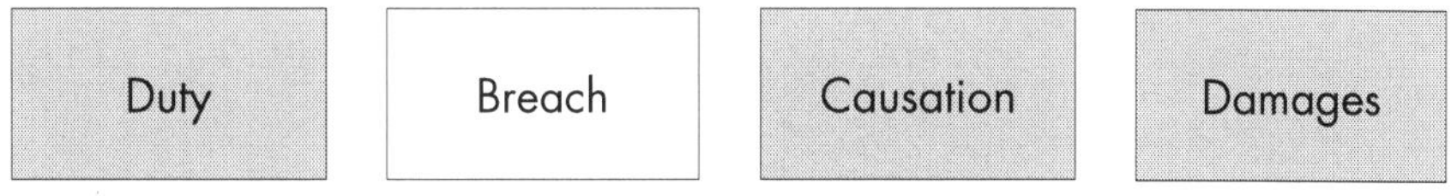

The court would not allow the jury to render a verdict for the plaintiff.

Understanding this aspect of trial is helpful to understanding summary judgment. To prevail on summary judgment, a defendant must only show that the plaintiff has no evidence to support one of the elements of the plaintiff's claim. Thus, the defendant would be entitled to summary judgment if the plaintiff had no evidence to support the duty element of the claim:

Duty	Breach	Causation	Damages

Or no evidence to support the breach element:

Duty	Breach	Causation	Damages

Or no evidence to support the causation element:

Duty	Breach	Causation	Damages

Or no evidence to support the damages element:

Duty	Breach	Causation	Damages

Or no evidence to support any combination of elements:

Duty	Breach	Causation	Damages

Brewer v. Toney

United States District Court, W.D. Louisiana
No. 11-0185, 2012 WL 1491919 (Apr. 27, 2012)

ROBERT G. JAMES, District Judge.

Pending before the Court is a Motion for Summary Judgment filed by Defendants Royce Toney, Sheriff of Ouachita Parish; Sergeant Connie Miller; Deputy Joshua Foster; and Deputy Kyle Walker (collectively "Defendants").... For the following reasons, Defendants' Motion for Summary Judgment is GRANTED.

I. FACTUAL AND PROCEDURAL HISTORY

On February 1, 2010, Defendants Miller, Foster, and Walker ("the deputy Defendants") responded to a domestic disturbance complaint at Plaintiff Tina Brewer's ("Mrs. Brewer") mobile home. The third-party complainant stated that Mrs. Brewer was involved in a dispute and "has weapons in residence and makes threats often but not today." After arriving, the deputy Defendants spoke with Mrs. Brewer's father, James Dyer ("Dyer"), who advised them that Mrs. Brewer and her husband, Plaintiff Charles Brewer ("Mr. Brewer"), had been fighting. Dyer did not advise the deputy Defendants that he believed Mrs. Brewer intended to hurt herself.

The deputy Defendants approached Mrs. Brewer on the front porch of her mobile home. Foster observed dried blood on the fingers and knuckles of Mrs. Brewer's right hand and that the pinky finger on her left hand appeared to be broken. Mrs. Brewer told the deputy Defendants that she and Mr. Brewer had been driving down Louisiana Highway 139 when they began to argue over Mrs. Brewer's belief that Mr. Brewer had taken their income tax refund and spent it on drugs. The argument escalated into a physical altercation, and Mrs. Brewer claimed that Mr. Brewer had grabbed her hands, breaking her left pinky finger; punched her in the back of the head; and slapped her face. The fight then ended, and the couple drove home. Mrs. Brewer stayed in the vehicle for approximately two hours, waiting for Mr. Brewer to take her to the hospital. She stated that Mr. Brewer walked down the road near their home at some point earlier, and she had not seen him return.

After talking with Mrs. Brewer, the deputy Defendants learned that there was an outstanding felony warrant for Mrs. Brewer's arrest on drug-related charges. Around this time, Walker left the scene to another call.

Miller, Foster, and Mrs. Brewer entered her residence, and the deputies advised Mrs. Brewer that she was being placed under arrest. Miller and Foster permitted Mrs. Brewer to enter her bedroom, so that she could put on shoes. Both Miller and Foster went into the bedroom with her. Foster observed that the bedroom was in complete disarray with clothes everywhere. Miller noted that clothes were piled at the foot of the bed almost as high as the bed itself and that they were also piled on the bed. Additionally, there were objects or articles piled on a dresser to the left side of the bed and on the floor between the dresser and a night stand. Neither Miller nor Foster observed any firearms in Mrs. Brewer's home.

After Mrs. Brewer put on her shoes, Foster walked her to the patrol unit, where she was secured in the back seat. He told her that they would take her to LSU Health Sciences Center/EA Conway Medical Center for treatment prior to transporting her to Ouachita Correctional Center ("OCC"). Foster did not handcuff Mrs. Brewer because of the injuries to her hands. Miller was attempting to document Mrs. Brewer's injuries by taking photographs of her hands when Mrs. Brewer said that she was going to be sick and needed to use the bathroom.

Miller escorted Mrs. Brewer to the bathroom in her mobile home, which was connected to the bedroom that Miller and Foster had previously observed. Miller asked Mrs. Brewer if she had any medications that she needed to take with her, and Mrs. Brewer replied that she wore contact lenses and needed them to see. Mrs. Brewer found her contact lens solution, but stated that she needed some other eye drops for an eye infection. Miller saw a small, white bottle that looked like a dropper bottle, on a stand located against a wall, which was a few feet from the bedroom in the entrance to the kitchen area. Because Mrs. Brewer had repeatedly requested the eye drops, Miller stepped out of the bedroom and walked towards the stand to look at the bottle. Miller was outside the bedroom for five to ten seconds when she heard a noise in the bedroom. Miller immediately returned, and Mrs. Brewer said she had shot herself. Miller saw a dark stain in the abdomen area of Mrs. Brewer's shirt. She lifted the shirt and saw a bullet hole in Mrs. Brewer's abdomen. Foster returned to the bedroom, and he and Miller looked for the weapon, but could not find it because the bedroom was in such disarray.

Emergency medical assistance was contacted and arrived on the scene. After their arrival, the weapon was located.

Prior to shooting herself, Mrs. Brewer did not advise or indicate to any of the deputy Defendants that she wished to or intended to harm herself.

On January 28, 2012,... Mrs. Brewer filed suit against Defendants alleging [certain federal claims and] negligence.

...

II. LAW AND ANALYSIS

A. Summary Judgment Standard

Summary judgment "should be rendered if the pleadings, the discovery and disclosure materials on file, and any affidavits show that there is no genuine issue as to any material fact and that the movant is entitled to judgment as a matter of law." Fed. R. Civ. P. 56(c)(2). The moving party bears the initial burden of informing the court of the basis for its motion by identifying portions of the record which highlight the absence of genuine issues of material fact. A fact is "material" if proof of its existence or nonexistence would affect the outcome of the lawsuit under applicable law in the case. A dispute about a material fact is "genuine" if the evidence is such that a reasonable fact finder could render a verdict for the nonmoving party.

If the moving party can meet the initial burden, the burden then shifts to the nonmoving party to establish the existence of a genuine issue of material fact for trial. The nonmoving party must show more than "some metaphysical doubt as to the material facts." *Matsushita Elec. Indus. Co., Ltd. v. Zenith Radio Corp.*, 475 U.S. 574, 586 (1986). In evaluating the evidence tendered by the parties, the Court must accept the evidence of the nonmovant as credible and draw all justifiable inferences in its favor.

...

C. Negligence

In their Complaint, Plaintiffs also allege state law claims of negligence against the deputy Defendants. Defendants argue that the Court should grant summary judgment on the negligence claims in their favor because Mrs. Brewer's intention to harm herself was not foreseeable. Plaintiffs argue that Mrs. Brewer's self-inflicted injury was foreseeable to the deputy Defendants because they knew there were firearms in the residence and Mrs. Brewer had recently been in a violent confrontation with her husband.

In Louisiana, to recover on a negligence claim, a plaintiff must demonstrate that

> (1) the defendant had a duty to conform his or her conduct to a specific standard of care (the duty element); (2) the defendant failed to conform

> his or her conduct to the appropriate standard (the breach of duty element); (3) the defendant's substandard conduct was a cause-in-fact of the plaintiff's injuries (the cause-in-fact element); (4) the defendant's substandard conduct was a legal cause of the plaintiff's injuries (the scope of liability or scope of protection element); and, (5) actual damages (the damages element).

Mathieu v. Imperial Toy Corp., 646 So. 2d 318, 322 (citations omitted).

The Louisiana Supreme Court has held, "Generally, a police officer has a duty to perform his function with due regard for the safety of all citizens who will be affected by his action. His authority must at all times be exercised in a reasonable fashion and he must act as a reasonably prudent man under the circumstances." *Hardy v. Bowie*, 98-CC-2821 (La.9/8/99); 744 So.2d 606, 614 (quotations and citations omitted).

Although the deputy Defendants owed Mrs. Brewer a duty of reasonable care during her arrest, their conduct in this case did not breach that duty. Even if the officers were aware that Mrs. Brewer made threats in the past, the nature of those threats is unclear, and Mrs. Brewer did not give the officers any indication during the arrest that she intended to harm herself. The deputy Defendants increased the risk of harm by choosing not to handcuff Mrs. Brewer, but they did so out of a concern for her recent injury. Furthermore, the attending deputy left Mrs. Brewer alone for only a few moments because the deputy was trying to retrieve Mrs. Brewer's eye drops. In light of these undisputed facts, the Court finds that Plaintiffs have failed to demonstrate the presence of a material issue of fact that the deputy Defendants breached their duty of reasonable care toward Mrs. Brewer. Therefore, Defendants' Motion for Summary Judgment with regard to the negligence claims is GRANTED.

CONCLUSION

For the foregoing reasons, Defendants' Motion for Summary Judgment is GRANTED, and Plaintiffs' claims are DISMISSED WITH PREJUDICE.

Notes

1. Who was the "movant" in this case? Who was the "nonmoving party"?
2. The four basic elements of negligence are duty, breach, causation, and damages. (*Brewer* breaks causation into two parts: cause-in-fact and legal

cause.) For which of these elements did Plaintiff fail to create a genuine issue of material fact? How did the evidence eliminate any genuine issue of material fact as to that element? What type of evidence would the plaintiff had to have submitted to create a genuine issue of material fact?

3. How many elements of negligence involved a genuine issue of material fact? Did the court answer that question? Was it necessary for the court to answer that question?
4. The court quoted from a Louisiana Supreme Court decision requiring that a police officer act as a "reasonably prudent man under the circumstances." To what element did this requirement relate? To help you answer this question, compare the two sentences quoted from the Louisiana Supreme Court decision to the first sentence of the next paragraph in *Brewer*. Can you see any parallelism between the two sentences of the Louisiana Supreme Court decision and the first sentence of the next paragraph in *Brewer*?
5. Consider the following scenarios. What if, in opposition to the motion for summary judgment, the plaintiff had submitted a declaration or affidavit stating:

   Hypo 1: "The officer left me alone in the bedroom for 20 minutes while he sat on the sofa and smoked a cigarette."

   Hypo 2: "When the officers arrived, I told them that I wanted to kill myself."

   Hypo 3: "When the officers first went into my bedroom with me, I told them that I had a gun in my room."

   Hypo 4: "The gun was plainly visible in my bedroom."

Mantooth v. Cleveland County

United States District Court, W.D. Oklahoma

No. CIV-09-159-HE, 2009 WL 5216916 (Dec. 30, 2009)

JOE HEATON, District Judge.

In this case, plaintiff asserts claims under 42 U.S.C. § 1983 for alleged violations of his Fourth Amendment rights arising out of his detention and arrest by Cleveland County sheriff's deputies and from excessive force allegedly employed by one of them. He... also asserts claims for negligence and assault and battery under Oklahoma state law. Defendants are Cleveland County Deputy Sheriff Rick Abbott, one of the deputies involved in the underlying incident, and Cleveland County, Oklahoma. [This excerpt will focus solely on the claims against Deputy Sheriff Abbott.]

Defendants have moved for summary judgment as to all of plaintiff's claims....

FACTUAL BACKGROUND

The [initial] circumstances out of which this case arose are undisputed. During the afternoon of June 1, 2008, Kim Willis called 911 to report a domestic disturbance between her and plaintiff as to their son. Cleveland County sheriff's deputies responded, with defendant Rick Abbott arriving first at the home.... Two other deputies... arrived soon thereafter. Willis and plaintiff were sitting in a pickup at their residence when the officers arrived. Willis got out of the pickup and confirmed that she had made the 911 call, but indicated the situation was resolved. Defendant Abbott moved Ms. Willis aside and moved toward plaintiff in the pickup. Roughly at this point, the parties' versions of events begin to differ markedly.

Defendants' evidence supports the following version of events. Abbott, concerned with plaintiff possibly having a weapon, ordered plaintiff to show his hands and get out of the pickup. Plaintiff refused to show his hands, was very slow in eventually getting out of the pickup, acted aggressive in manner as he stepped away from the pickup and toward the officers, and was abusive and profane in his language. Plaintiff was ordered to "get on the ground," which, after repeated commands, he eventually did. The two additional deputies arrived at approximately this time. By this time, at least Abbott (and perhaps all the deputies) had their guns drawn. [One of the other deputies] began attempting to handcuff plaintiff, who was resisting by rearing up and rolling over. Defendant Abbott put his knee between plaintiff's shoulder and back area to prevent him from rolling over while [the other officer] handcuffed [plaintiff]. The deputies then began moving plaintiff toward one of the officer's cars. He began resisting physically and was abusing Abbott verbally. Plaintiff attempted to head-butt defendant, at which point Abbott took him to the ground again. By that point, plaintiff had suffered injuries, including a bleeding scrape on his head. Plaintiff then started shaking his head and told [a] deputy... that he had a sexually transmitted disease and hoped she got his blood on her.

Plaintiff's evidence, principally his own testimony and that of family members who were present, paints a different picture. That evidence, viewed most favorably to plaintiff, indicates he promptly showed his hands (while sitting in the pickup) upon the deputy's command, [and] he promptly got out of the pickup, and did not unduly resist. Plaintiff admits a profane challenge to the deputy being on his property, but states his language was equal to or better than that used by the deputy. Plaintiff got on the ground as ordered and was not physically resisting the effort to handcuff him. He told the deputies he would not resist, as his five-year-old son was watching the events. Nonetheless, deputy Abbott unnecessarily put his boot on the back of plaintiff's head, driving his head down into the gravel. At approximately the same time, Abbott threatened Willis with arrest if she did not "shut up." Following the handcuffing, the deputies then got plaintiff up and walked him toward one of the officers' cars. Plaintiff acknowledges that, on the way, he said to Abbott "did it make you feel like a man to do that in front of my family?" but denied head-butting or otherwise physically resisting. According to plaintiff's evidence, Abbott responded by deliberately tripping plaintiff and knocking him to the ground face-first, knowing that plaintiff could not protect himself from the fall due to the handcuffs. Plaintiff acknowledges he was bleeding, but denies trying to get the blood on Sites or making any statements about disease.

It is undisputed that plaintiff was eventually arrested for obstructing an officer and for throwing human waste on an officer and threatening harm to an officer. The charges were later dismissed. Defendant Abbott was suspended by the then-sheriff of Cleveland County after plaintiff complained about Abbott's conduct. After an internal review, Abbott was terminated as a deputy based on the department's review of this incident. Following the election of a new sheriff some months later, Abbott was reinstated as a deputy.

...

DISCUSSION

Summary judgment should be granted where—in light of the pleadings, discovery materials, and any affidavits—there is no "genuine issue" as to any "material fact" and the movant is entitled to judgment as a matter of law. Fed. R. Civ. Pro. 56(c)(2). The court must review the evidence, and draw all reasonable inferences therefrom, in the light most favorable to the nonmoving party. The court may not make determinations of credibility nor weigh evidence, and must disregard all evidence favorable to the movant that the trier of fact[1] would not be required to believe. Mere conclusory allegations, without evidentiary support, do not create a genuine issue of fact.

Summary judgment "necessarily implicates the substantive evidentiary standard of proof that would apply at the trial...." *Anderson v. Liberty Lobby, Inc.*, 477 U.S. 242, 252 (1986). Where the nonmoving party bears the burden of proof at trial, as the plaintiff does in this case, he cannot rely on his pleadings to defeat summary judgment; instead, he must put forth evidence sufficient to create a genuine issue of material fact. Nevertheless, the moving party must demonstrate its entitlement to judgment as a matter of law.

Constitutional Claims

Applying these standards to plaintiff's constitutional claims against deputy Rick Abbott, the court concludes the motion for summary judgment must be denied. A police officer violates a person's Fourth Amendment right to be free from unreasonable seizures if the officer makes a warrantless arrest without probable cause or an investigatory stop without a reasonable suspicion that the individual was engaged in criminal activity. An officer violates a person's Fourth Amendment right to be free from excessive force during a seizure if the officer's conduct was not "objectively reasonable in light of the facts and circumstances... from the perspective of a reasonable officer on the scene." *Olsen v. Layton Hills Mall*, 312 F.3d 1304, 1313-14 (10th Cir.2002).

The above description of the differing evidence offered by the parties makes it apparent there are multiple material factual disputes, including the question of how deputy Abbott approached plaintiff, how plaintiff reacted to that approach (whether he responded appropriately to the officer's instructions, etc.), what level of force was used, and the extent to which plaintiff's conduct provoked or justified the force used by Abbott or others. This precludes summary judgment on the issues of whether defendant's seizure of plaintiff or the force used to do it was reasonable. Viewing the evidence in the light most favorable to plaintiff, justiciable questions exist as to whether Abbott's conduct constitut-

1. [Sometimes, the judge, not a jury, will hear and decide the facts in a case. This may occur because there does not exist a right to jury trial for the particular claims that the plaintiff brings or because the parties, for whatever reason, choose to waive their right to jury trial, thus permitting the judge to render the verdict on the claims. The phrase "trier of fact" and the word "factfinder" are used to encompass both situations — whether the judge or a jury is acting as the factfinder. — Ed.]

ed a violation of plaintiff's Fourth Amendment rights, hence summary judgment for Abbott is unwarranted.

. . .

State Statutory or Common Law Claims

Plaintiff asserts claims for negligence and assault and battery. Plaintiff argues that a jury might conclude from the above-described circumstances that Abbott was negligent in his treatment of plaintiff. The court can discern nothing in plaintiff's pleadings or in the evidentiary materials submitted with his response that would support a finding of negligence on the part of Abbott. Every action he allegedly took was intentional. [In contrast, negligence results from a failure to exercise due care required by the circumstances. *Ply v. Nat'l Union Fire Ins. Co.*, 81 P.3d 643, 648 (Okla. 2003).] Plaintiff may or may not be able to prove what he has alleged, but, in the circumstances of this case, there is no apparent basis for a determination of negligence. Summary judgment is appropriate for the defendants as to plaintiff's negligence claims.

Whether Abbott's contact with plaintiff involves the tort of assault and battery depends on whether Abbott's actions were justified under the circumstances. [Both assault and battery require the intent to cause a harmful or offensive contact with another.] In attempting to effect the arrest of the plaintiff, Abbott was authorized [by Oklahoma law] to use reasonable force, free from liability for assault or battery, when met with forcible resistance. As discussed above, a justiciable question remains as to whether Abbott's actions were reasonable under the circumstances....

CONCLUSION

For the foregoing reasons, defendants' motion for summary judgment is GRANTED IN PART and DENIED IN PART. The motion is granted with respect to plaintiff's negligence claims. The motion is otherwise denied....

Notes

1. Who was the "movant" in this case"? Who was the "nonmoving party"?
2. What ruling did the trial court make on the motion for summary judgment? Was the case over after the trial court ruled on the motion for summary judgment? What else was left to occur in the trial court? In other

words, what do you suppose would occur next in the trial court before this case would be completed?

3. Why did the court grant summary judgment on some claims but not others? Can you articulate the standard for summary judgment? What information can the court consider? In what ways does summary judgment differ from a motion to dismiss?

4. Assume for purposes of discussion, that the plaintiff agreed completely with the defendant's version of events. In that situation, should the court grant or deny summary judgment on the constitutional claims? What if, instead, the plaintiff agreed with everything in the defendants' version of events *except* he contended that the plaintiff had a scrape on his arm, not on his head, as the defendants contended. Would the dispute as to this fact require denial of summary judgment on the plaintiff's constitutional claim? What if the plaintiff had a reputation for being a liar?

5. The case above discusses the standard the court should apply when the defendant moves for summary judgment. When a plaintiff moves for summary judgment, the standard is slightly different. A plaintiff is entitled to summary judgment only when evidence shows that the jury *must* find for that plaintiff, a very challenging standard to meet. In other words, the plaintiff must demonstrate that there is only one conclusion that a jury could reach on *each* of the elements of the claim. This makes the standard for summary judgment more difficult for the plaintiff than for the defendant. Does it help to know that in a civil case, the plaintiff generally has the burden of proving the elements of his or her claim at trial? (In contrast, the defendant typically bears the burden of proving any defenses.)

Notes on Constitutional Law and Sovereign Immunity

1. The state and federal governments enjoy sovereign immunity, which means that individuals cannot sue state or federal governments unless they consent to the action. The government can, however, waive sovereign immunity. In the Federal Tort Claims Act, for example, Congress waived sovereign immunity for certain tort claims against the United States. *See* 28 U.S.C. § 1346. The Tucker Act creates a limited waiver for certain contract claims. *See* 28 U.S.C. § 1491.

2. The plaintiff in *Mantooth* brought a claim under 42 U.S.C. § 1983, which creates a private cause of action against local governments (but not state governments or the federal government), and state and local officials for violations of federal constitutional rights. Specifically, Mantooth alleged violations of his Fourth Amendment rights against unlawful arrest and excessive force. He sued a sheriff's deputy. He also sued a local government—a county in Oklahoma. Sovereign immunity does not apply to local governments, and so they are subject to suit under § 1983, although it is extremely difficult to establish their liability. *See, e.g., Monell v. Dep't of Soc. Servs.*, 436 U.S. 658, 691 (1978).
3. The counterpart to § 1983 for lawsuits against federal officials is a "*Bivens* action," named after the Supreme Court decision in *Bivens v. Six Unknown Named Agents*, 403 U.S. 388 (1971), in which the Supreme Court held that a violation of an individual's Fourth Amendment rights by federal officers can give rise to a cause of action for damages.
4. Although governmental employees are not protected by sovereign immunity, they are entitled to *qualified* immunity. This immunity protects government officials from civil suits challenging the official's performance of discretionary functions unless the plaintiff shows that the official violated "clearly established statutory or constitutional rights of which a reasonable person would have known." *Harlow v. Fitzgerald*, 457 U.S. 800, 818 (1982). As this book goes to press, the wisdom of the continued existence of qualified immunity is a matter of considerable debate. *See, e.g.*, https://www.nytimes.com/2021/03/08/us/supreme-court-qualified-immunity.html; Joanna C. Schwartz, *The Case Against Qualified Immunity*, 93 Notre Dame Law Rev. 1797 (2018).
5. After reading the four prior notes you might conclude that enforcing constitutional rights through civil lawsuits can be rather difficult, and some scholars would agree. *See* Richard H. Fallon, *Bidding Farewell to Constitutional Torts*, 107 Cal. L. Rev. 933 (2019).

In the next case, the appellate court reversed the trial court's grant of summary judgment. With which court would you agree if you were ruling on the motion for summary judgment?

Small v. WellDyne, Inc.

United States Court of Appeals for the Fourth Circuit

927 F.3d 169 (2019)

QUATTLEBAUM, Circuit Judge:

On November 19, 2013, Bertha Small ingested prescription medications that were sent to her by mistake. Ms. Small was accustomed to receiving medications in the mail. On the day she ingested the pills, Ms. Small received a package addressed to her home in North Carolina that contained six prescription medications. The package was similar in size and color to the packages containing the medications she normally received.

WellDyneRx, Inc. and WellDyne, Inc. (collectively referred to as "WellDyne"), operate in the growing mail-order pharmacy industry by filling prescriptions for health care plans and other pharmacies. Relevant to this case, WellDyne was under a contract with Exactus Pharmacy Solutions, Inc. ("Exactus") to fill and ship prescription medication to Exactus' customers. Exactus placed an order with WellDyne to fill and ship a package of prescription medication to an Exactus customer in California. However, WellDyne mistakenly shipped that package of prescription medication to Ms. Small. The package contained the pills Ms. Small ingested.

Although the outside of the package contained Ms. Small's name and address, the label on each bottle listed the California patient's name, the California patient's prescribing doctor and the name of the medication. However, Ms. Small, elderly and barely literate, did not read the labels of the bottles before taking the pills.

After ingesting the pills, Ms. Small began to experience confusion and hallucinations. A few days later, she fell and fractured her leg. She was admitted to the hospital for her leg, but stayed for almost a month. During that time, Ms. Small was treated for several other medical problems that arose during her stay. She died on January 2, 2014, approximately ten days after being discharged.

I.

On behalf of Ms. Small's estate, her son Michael Small (we refer to the plaintiff and the decedent interchangeably as "Ms. Small") sued WellDyne and Exactus asserting claims for negligence, negligence per se and breach of the implied warranty of fitness for a particular purpose against both defendants. Ms. Small also alleged Exactus was vicariously liable for the actions of Well-Dyne under agency and joint venture theories.

After the close of discovery and the filing of a series of motions by the parties, the district court granted summary judgment in favor of WellDyne and Exactus as to all counts. The district court first held that Ms. Small was contributorily negligent as a matter of law which completely barred her recovery in North Carolina. The district court reasoned Ms. Small acted unreasonably by neither reading the labels on the medications nor heeding the warnings of her adult daughter, Shirley....

Small timely appealed the district court's order. We have jurisdiction over this appeal pursuant to 28 U.S.C. § 1291.

II.

We begin with a de novo review of the district court's decision to grant summary judgment in favor of Exactus and WellDyne on the issue of contributory negligence. Summary judgment is appropriate if the evidence shows that there is no genuine issue as to any material fact and that the moving party is entitled to judgment as a matter of law. Fed. R. Civ. P. 56(a); *Anderson v. Liberty Lobby, Inc.*, 477 U.S. 242, 247 (1986). The judge is not to weigh the evidence, but rather to determine if there is a genuine issue of fact for trial. *Anderson*, 477 U.S. at 249, 106 S. Ct. 2505. All evidence should be viewed in the light most favorable to the non-moving party. *Id.* at 261, 106 S. Ct. 2505 n.2.

Utilizing this standard, we first look to the law of North Carolina on contributory negligence. Under North Carolina law, "if an issue of contributory negligence is raised as an affirmative defense, and proved, it completely bars plaintiff's recovery for injuries resulting from defendant's negligence." A "'plaintiff is contributorily negligent when [s]he fails to exercise such care as an ordinarily prudent person would exercise *under the circumstances* in order to avoid injury.'" "[T]he existence of contributory negligence does not depend on plaintiff's subjective appreciation of danger; rather, contributory negligence consists of conduct which fails to conform to an objective standard of behavior...."

Summary judgment is rarely appropriate for issues of contributory negligence because "the standard used in contributory negligence cases, that of reasonable care, usually requires a jury determination." Summary judgment is appropriate where the evidence is uncontroverted that the plaintiff failed to use ordinary or reasonable care and that failure was at least one of the proximate causes of the injury. But in "'borderline cases,' fairness and judicial economy suggest that courts should decide in favor of submitting issues to the jury."

WellDyne and Exactus argue that the evidence establishes, as a matter of law, Ms. Small failed to use ordinary care when she took the misdelivered medication without reading the labels on the medication. The defendants contend the misdelivered package arrived after Ms. Small had already received her normal medications package from WellDyne. They note the medications were delivered in an unusual way — without a phone call in advance. The pill bottles, the defendants point out, were labeled for Exactus' customer in California, contained no identifying information as to Ms. Small or her doctors and the bottles in the second package were different in size and number to those Ms. Small normally received. Finally, according to defendants, there was no evidence that Ms. Small's doctors had prescribed or discussed any new medications. Accordingly, WellDyne and Exactus argue that there is no genuine issue of material fact as to whether Ms. Small failed to use ordinary care and thus was contributorily negligent as a matter of law.

In response, Ms. Small argues that a reasonable jury could find that she acted reasonably under the circumstances of this case. Ms. Small was a barely literate, geriatric patient who received a familiar looking package of medications from a familiar pharmacy, addressed to her. Also, Ms. Small points out that she had been prescribed some of the misdelivered medications in the past and the pills appeared similar in size and shape to her regular medications. Finally, Ms. Small argues that the testimony from her experts, that she acted reasonably, created a genuine issue of material fact.

North Carolina courts have not addressed a case like this one where a plaintiff ingested misdelivered prescription medications without reading the label. Indeed, there is scarce caselaw nationwide addressing this situation. However, *Champs Convenience Stores, Inc. v. United Chemical Co., Inc.*, 329 N.C. 446 (1991) involves an analogous situation. There, a store employee called the defendant chemical company asking for a cleaning product to control the dust on the grocery store's wood floors. *Id.* at 858. The defendant recommended a product and instructed the employee on how to use it. *Id.* Thirty minutes later, the defendant delivered a chemical product, but it was the wrong one. *Id.* The invoice listed the product recommended on the phone, but the label and instructions listed the actual chemical inside the container. *Id.* at 456. The employee admitted that if she had read the instructions, she would not have used the product. *Id.* But she neglected to read the instructions or the label and applied the misdelivered chemicals to the store floor. *Id.* at 858. The toxicity from the chemical rendered the groceries inedible, and the North Carolina Department of Agriculture issued an embargo for contents of the store, causing the store to close. *Id.* at 859. The store remained closed until it was sold approximately one year later. *Id.* When the store owner sued the chemical product seller seeking to recover its losses, the seller claimed the store was contributorily negligent in using the chemicals without reading the labels or the instructions. *Id.* Ultimately, the North Carolina Supreme Court held that "the evidence was insufficient to require the court to find contributory negligence as a matter of law." *Id.* at 862. The court, relying on the defendant's delivery of the wrong product and the invoice listing the correct product, concluded contributory negligence was proper for the jury to decide. *Id.* at 862. In light of the similarities of *Champs* to our case, we, sitting in diversity, cannot say that as a matter of law that Ms. Small was contributorily negligent for failing to read the labels on the medications.

We also note that part of the district court's reasoning for finding that Ms. Small was contributorily negligent was its factual finding that Ms. Small took the medications after being instructed not to by her adult daughter Shirley. But Shirley testified that she warned Ms. Small not to take the medicine the day after the package arrived. On the other hand, Michael David, Shirley's fiancé who lived at Ms. Small's residence, testified by affidavit that he saw Ms. Small take the misdelivered medications the same day the medications were delivered. Viewing the evidence in the light most favorable to Ms. Small, the non-moving party, a jury could reasonably conclude that Ms. Small ingested the misdelivered medications before being warned by her daughter Shirley.

For the reasons set forth above, we reverse the district court on the issue of contributory negligence....

Notes

1. What is an "affirmative defense"? An affirmative defense, if established, prevents the plaintiffs from prevailing on their claims even if the plain-

tiffs have established all of the elements of their claim. In other words, a successful negligence claim requires evidence of duty, breach of duty, causation, and damages. Normally, if the plaintiff establishes each of these elements, the plaintiff can prevail, but if the defendants can establish an affirmative defense, the plaintiff will nevertheless lose despite having established the elements of the claim.

2. In *Small*, the affirmative defense was contributory negligence. The word "contributory" reflects the notion that the plaintiff's own negligence contributed in some manner to the harmful event. Under North Carolina law, contributory negligence, if it exists, precludes the defendant's liability.

3. North Carolina is one of only a few states that still treats negligence by the plaintiff as a complete bar to recovery regardless of how much or how little that negligence contributed to the events. *Swain v. Preston Falls East, L.L.C.*, 156 N.C. App. 357, 361 (2003). Even if the plaintiff's negligence is only 1% responsible for the event and the defendant's conduct is 99% responsible, under North Carolina law, the plaintiff cannot prevail. The harshness of this rule has prompted most states to move to a comparative negligence defense. This approach allocates a percentage of responsibility to the plaintiff and to the defendant based on their respective negligence, rather than completely foreclosing liability whenever the plaintiff's negligence played any contributory role, no matter how slight, in the plaintiff's injury. The plaintiff's percentage of responsibility is then used to reduce the total sum of damages.

4. What factual disputes did the court rely on to conclude summary judgment should not have been granted? Did the appellate court rely on *disputes* in the facts to conclude summary judgment was not appropriate?

5. Do you think WellDyne could have instead successfully argued that it was entitled to summary judgment because there was no question of material fact with respect to the claim of negligence and that Welldyne, as a matter of law, was not negligent? Do there appear to be any factual disputes as to WellDyne's conduct?

6. Even though the case was filed in federal court, the appellate court looked to North Carolina court decisions to decide whether or not to grant summary judgment. Why did the court consider North Carolina judicial decisions relevant?

D. TRIAL

1. Overview

If the plaintiff's claims survive a motion for summary judgment and the parties do not settle,[1] trial is the next step. In the American system, only a small percentage of civil cases are actually resolved by trial.[2] Despite the declining occurrence of civil trials, they remain a significant part of the American legal system. In contrast to the civil law practice of discontinuous trials, the common law practice is a trial that runs from weekday to weekday until it is completed.

The entire civil system of motions and procedures is built on the awareness that a trial may potentially be the final stage at this level of the proceedings. Look back at the motion to dismiss, discovery, and the motion for summary judgment: each procedure is guided by what could happen at trial. Thus, even though these procedures precede trial, it is the possibility of trial that dictates their standards, rules, and outcomes.

And the same is generally true for the parties: their focus is on trial long before a trial date may have been set because knowing what may or may not be permissible at trial will best determine the strength of their case. For example, it ultimately does not matter that a truly reliable witness would have testified favorably to the defense if that witness has died and the witness's statement is not preserved in some manner that is admissible at trial, because the factfinder will never hear about those statements.

2. Evidence

The rules governing the admissibility of evidence are crucial at trial. Those rules control what evidence the factfinder can consider when rendering a verdict. In federal courts, the Federal Rules of Evidence contain the relevant rules. Most states also have evidentiary rules, and they are often similar in substance to the Federal Rules of Evidence. The rules are far too complex for an overview

---

1. A settlement is an agreement reached by the parties outside of court wherein the parties agree to do certain things (often the defendant agrees to pay the plaintiff a certain sum of money) in exchange for the plaintiff voluntarily dismissing the complaint. The courts are generally not involved in this process other than to grant the requested dismissal.

2. A study in conducted in 2010 concluded that only 1.1% of civil cases filed in federal court were resolved by trial. Judicial Business of the United States Courts: 2010 Annual Report of the Director 168 tbl. C-4 (Administrative Office of the U.S. Courts, 2010), available at http://www.uscourts.gov/uscourts/Statistics/JudicialBusiness/2010/JudicialBusinespdfversion.pdf. Most cases are resolved by settlement.

course, such as this one, to cover them in any detail. But what is helpful to understand at this point are the methods for enforcing the evidentiary rules. Parties can request a pre-trial ruling that certain evidence will or will not be admissible at trial. Such requests are generally called motions in limine. However, parties will often not know in advance the exact nature of a witness's testimony, and as a result, much of the enforcement of the evidentiary rules occurs during trial. The trial procedure for raising an evidentiary challenge is the objection, which can be made to an attorney's question to a witness or to a witness's answer.

The first two cases that follow illustrate the two ways in which a party can seek to enforce the rules of evidence: by motion in limine or by objection during trial. The cases also discuss some of the basic principles of evidentiary law. Can you identify those principles?

Anderson v. City of Chicago

United States District Court, N.D. Illinois

No. 09 C 2311, 2010 U.S. Dist. LEXIS 123033,
2010 WL 4811937 (Nov. 19, 2010)

AMY J. ST. EVE, District Judge.

[Plaintiffs sued defendant police officers for false arrest in violation of 42 U.S.C. § 1983.] Before the Court is Plaintiffs' motion in limine # 1, which seeks to bar Defendants from introducing any evidence of, or referring to, Plaintiff Christopher Monroe's alleged and witness Mario Anderson's admitted gang membership at trial. [NOTE: The witness Anderson is different from the individual named Anderson who is listed in the case name.] For the following reasons, the Court, in its discretion, grants Plaintiffs' motion without prejudice.

ANALYSIS

"There is [] always the possibility that a jury will attach a propensity for committing crimes to defendants who are affiliated with gangs or that a jury's negative feelings towards gangs will influence its verdict." *United States v. Irvin*, 87 F.3d 860, 865-66 (7th Cir.1996). Accordingly, the Seventh Circuit has repeatedly warned that evidence of a party's gang membership is highly prejudicial, especially when the gang evidence is not relevant to a central issue in a case. The Seventh Circuit has found gang affiliation evidence admissible under certain circumstances—primarily in cases involving charges of a criminal conspiracy. "Assessing the probative value of [evidence], and weighing any factors counseling against admissibility is a matter [] for the district court's sound judgment under [Federal Rules of Evidence] 401 and 403." *Sprint v. Mendelsohn*, 552 U.S. 379, 387 (2008). [Rule 401 defines "relevant evidence" as "evidence having any tendency to make the existence of any fact that is of consequence to the determination of the action more probable or less probable than it would be without the evidence." Rule 403 authorizes the court to exclude relevant evidence "if its probative value is substantially outweighed by the danger of unfair prejudice, confusion of the issues, or misleading the jury, or by considerations of undue delay, waste of time, or needless presentation of cumulative evidence."]

The specific "gang evidence" at issue in this motion in limine concerns Plaintiff Christopher Monroe and witness Mario Anderson. Plaintiff Monroe has denied any gang affiliation or membership. Mr. Anderson admitted to being in a gang, and testified that Plaintiff Monroe was also in a gang. Plaintiffs argue that any evidence, or reference to, Plaintiff Monroe's alleged and Mr. Anderson's admitted membership in or affiliation with gangs is not relevant, is inadmissible character evidence, and—to the extent it may be relevant and probative, which Plaintiffs argue it is not—is unfairly prejudicial under Federal Rule of Evidence 403. Defendants argue that this evidence goes to the heart of their theory of the case, and that it is both relevant and probative. Specifically, Defendants argue that this gang evidence is admissible for three reasons: (1) to show that the Defendants acted reasonably under the circumstances; (2) to demonstrate Monroe and Anderson's "motive" and "bias"; and (3) to impeach Plaintiff Monroe. Defendants' arguments fail.

1. This Alleged Gang Evidence Is Not Admissible to Inform the Jury's Decision on the Reasonableness of Defendants' Actions

Plaintiffs' motion in limine seeks to bar evidence of, or reference to, Plaintiff Monroe's alleged and Mr. Anderson's admitted gang membership. Defendants argue that the evidence is relevant to demonstrate the reasonableness of the Defendants' actions and the circumstances under which they took place. Since probable cause to arrest provides an absolute defense to any claim brought under § 1983 for false arrest, the circumstances leading up to Plaintiffs' arrests are relevant to this case. Probable cause exists "when the facts and circumstances that are known to [an officer] reasonably support a belief that the individual has committed, is committing, or is about to commit a crime." *Holmes v. Vill. of Hoffman Estates*, 511 F.3d 673, 679 (7th Cir.2007). To the extent that gang affiliation would have given the Defendants probable cause to arrest Plaintiffs on the night in question—and the Court does not make a finding on that issue here—nowhere in Defendants' pleadings does it indicate that the Defendant Officers knew anything about these two individuals' alleged gang affiliations before they [went to the home where Plaintiffs were arrested], before they arrested Plaintiffs, before the allegations of excessive force, or even before Plaintiff Monroe and Mr. Anderson's depositions. Because of this, and in light of the substantial prejudice that accompanies gang affiliation, the Court bars Defendants from introducing evidence of Plaintiff Monroe's alleged and Mr. Anderson's admitted gang membership for this purpose.

2. The Alleged Gang Evidence Fails to Show "Motive" or "Bias"

Defendants argue that Plaintiff Monroe's alleged and Mr. Anderson's admitted gang membership is "relevant to show a motive for the otherwise inexplicable act of attacking a police officer when he was entering an apartment." Defendants allege that Plaintiff Monroe "threw punches at [Defendant Thurman] when [Thurman] entered the second floor," and that Mr. Anderson "admitted to throwing objects at [Defendant] Thurman when he entered the second floor." A review of the deposition transcripts that Defendants submitted, however, undermines Defendants' argument. Mr. Anderson's testimony reads:

> A. The police kicked down the upstairs door, because it's a door before you come upstairs. Then they came up the back way, they kicked down that door. Then when they opened the door, there was this man holding my mama and he was choking her. And I didn't know who he was, so I started throwing stuff at him.
>
> He was in regular clothes, like a plain hoodie and jeans with some boots on. I didn't know he was police, so I was throwing stuff at him.
>
> ...
>
> Q. What did you throw?
>
> A. Everything, like bowls, spoons, cups, and all that, anything I could see or find.
>
> Q. Did anything break?
>
> A. No. It was plastic cups.
>
> Q. What about the bowls or spoons?
>
> A. It was plastic. Oh, no, ain't no spoons or nothing break.

Q. Were the bowls plastic?

A. Yes.

Nothing about this "attack" suggests that Mr. Anderson knew that Defendant Thurman was a police officer. In fact, Mr. Anderson explicitly denies that knowledge. The alleged motive for the "attack" seems to be that an unidentified stranger had burst into his home and was "holding and choking" his mother. Evidence of gang membership in connection with this incident is not relevant, is unfairly prejudicial, and the Court bars Defendants from admitting it for this purpose.

Defendants further argue that Plaintiff Monroe's alleged and Mr. Anderson's admitted gang membership is admissible to show Mr. Anderson's bias in testifying in favor of Plaintiff Monroe. Given the highly prejudicial nature of gang evidence, the Court bars Defendants from introducing or referring to gang membership for this purpose. If they wish to demonstrate bias, Defendants may introduce evidence of Mr. Anderson's friendship with Plaintiff Monroe.

3. Gang Evidence Does Not Impeach Plaintiff Monroe

Defendants next argue that the Court should permit them to introduce evidence of Plaintiff Monroe's alleged gang membership for impeachment purposes under Rule 608. [Rule 608 provides that "[t]he credibility of a witness may be attacked or supported by evidence in the form of opinion or reputation, but subject to these limitations: (1) the evidence may refer only to character for truthfulness or untruthfulness, and (2) evidence of truthful character is admissible only after the character of the witness for truthfulness has been attacked by opinion or reputation evidence or otherwise."]

Defendants contend that Mr. Anderson's identification of Plaintiff Monroe as a gang member, and Plaintiff Monroe's denial of the same, "is highly probative of Monroe's credibility, or lack thereof." The Court disagrees. Mr. Anderson is not the authority on Plaintiff Monroe's affiliation-or lack thereof-with a gang. Unlike the cases Defendants cited to support their argument, in this case, there is no reliable evidence that Plaintiff Monroe lied about his gang affiliation. The Court rejects Defendants' suggestion that Plaintiff Monroe's denial of a gang affiliation may be admitted under Rule 608 as probative of his truthfulness or untruthfulness. Defendants are barred from using any alleged gang evidence for this purpose.

Imm v. Chaney

Court of Appeals of Georgia

651 S.E.2d 855 (2007)

PHIBBS, Judge.

Patrick Imm was assisting Michael Chaney in erecting a wooden fence in Chaney's yard when Chaney accidentally injected a nail into Imm's foot. Imm sued Chaney for negligence, seeking compensatory damages for a disabling injury. Chaney answered the complaint, asserting that negligence attributable to Imm was greater than or equal to any negligence by Chaney. Imm later amended his complaint to seek punitive damages based on the claim that Chaney's actions had showed a want of care which would raise the presumption of conscious indifference to consequences.FN1 The jury returned a verdict in favor of Chaney. After entering judgment on the verdict, the court denied Imm's motion for judgment notwithstanding the verdict or new trial. Imm appeals. We affirm.

Evidence at trial showed that at the time of the accident, Chaney was operating a nail gun to erect fence posts. Imm decided to use his foot to secure one of the posts. Chaney repeatedly told Imm that he needed to move his foot. After Imm assured Chaney that he did not need to do so, Chaney injected one nail into the post without incident. But the second nail injected by Chaney went through the post into Imm's foot. As a result, Imm was taken to a hospital emergency room and underwent surgery.

...

8. Imm contends that the court erred in allowing Chaney's attorney to cross-examine him concerning his use of a morphine pump.

While testifying on direct examination, Imm acknowledged that he had been given morphine at the time of his surgery and that usage of the drug adversely affects one's mental state. On cross-examination, Chaney's attorney asked Imm if he had been taking morphine on the day of the trial. After Imm said no, counsel asked him if he had had a morphine pump installed in recent years. Imm's attorney thereupon objected on the ground of relevance. After the court overruled the objection, Imm testified that he had forgotten that he did have a morphine pump installed for an injury unrelated to the one in this case and that, in fact, he was taking morphine at the time of the trial. Because Imm's use of the morphine at the time of trial could have affected his credibility as a witness, the court did not abuse its discretion in overruling Imm's relevance objection.

...

Notes

1. These decisions reflect some fundamental evidentiary considerations. The first consideration is whether the evidence is relevant. How is relevance defined? Why did the defendants contend that gang membership was relevant? What issues did they contend the evidence was relevant to? Why did the court reject those arguments? In other words, for what reasons was that evidence not relevant? Do you agree that the evidence is not relevant?

2. At issue in *Anderson,* is a second foundational consideration. Even if the evidence is relevant, it may not be admissible. Why may a court properly exclude relevant evidence? How does prejudice factor into the decision to exclude relevant evidence? But isn't all evidence adverse to a party's case "prejudicial"? What do you think the court means when it describes the evidence as "prejudicial"?

3. The court concluded that evidence of possible gang membership was not relevant on the issue of bias. In that portion of the court's discussion, there is a passing reference to another factor that courts will consider. What other fact supported the court's conclusion that it was not necessary to allow evidence of gang membership in order to demonstrate potential bias? How might that information factor into the analysis when the evidence sought to be introduced has significant potential for unfairly prejudicing the jury?

4. The court in *Anderson* also did not find the gang-membership evidence to have any bearing on credibility. Why? Is it not fairly common for gang members to lie? Did Defendants rely on the propensity of gang members to lie as the reason for arguing that the evidence undercut Plaintiff's credibility? If not, why did the Defendants contend this evidence was relevant to the issue of credibility? Why did the court reject this argument?

5. In *Imm*, the evidentiary issue was brought to the court's attention by way of an objection. Notice that the party's objection was followed by a very summary reference to the basis for the objection. This is a standard requirement for objections. It is generally considered inadequate to simply say "objection." The party must give some brief—sometimes just a single word—basis for the objection. What was the basis for the objection in *Imm*? What was the trial court's ruling on that basis for the objection? What reasoning did the appellate court give for affirming that ruling?

6. Note 3 after *Small v. WellDyne* in section C of this Chapter describes two approaches that states have taken as to the effect of the plaintiff's negligence on the plaintiff's recovery. *Imm* hints at a third approach. Under Georgia law, "the plaintiff shall not be entitled to receive any damages if the plaintiff is 50 percent or more responsible for the injury or damages claimed." Ga. Code § 51-12-33. In other words, if the plaintiff is more responsible than the defendant the plaintiff will recover nothing, regardless of defendant's negligence.

The next case illustrates that evidence will sometimes make its way into evidence *despite* the court having granted a pre-trial in limine motion excluding the evidence.

United States v. Garvey

United States Court of Appeals for the Seventh Circuit

No. 11-3088, 2012 WL 3139943 (Aug. 3, 2012)

KANNE: Circuit Judge

Beginning in 2007, Eric E. Garvey conspired with four others to transport and sell stolen property along the Minnesota–Wisconsin border. At Garvey's trial, all four co-conspirators testified against him. On appeal, ... Garvey also claims that the district court erred in denying his motion for a mistrial after the prosecutor's questioning prompted a witness to declare that he smoked marijuana with Garvey. For the following reasons, we affirm Garvey's conviction.

I. Background

From July 2007 to February 2009, Garvey and four coconspirators engaged in a scheme to steal lawnmowers, tractors, trucks, ATVs, snowmobiles, and trailers along the Minnesota-Wisconsin border and then transport and sell these stolen items to various buyers. Two of Garvey's co-conspirators, Toby Thomas and Jeff Olson, were responsible for stealing the items. On the other end, Chad Wyttenbach and Victor Trejo assisted in storing and selling the stolen property. At various times, Garvey was involved in stealing, transporting, and selling the stolen items. Garvey was charged with one count of conspiring to transport, possess, sell, and dispose of stolen vehicles and goods in interstate commerce, in violation of 18 U.S.C. §§ 2, 371, and eight counts of theft, transportation, or sale of specific stolen vehicles or goods in interstate commerce, in violation of 18 U.S.C. §§ 2312–15.

All four co-conspirators pled guilty and agreed to testify against Garvey at trial, but for purposes of this appeal, we need only discuss the testimony of Wyttenbach and Thomas. Wyttenbach bought stolen John Deere lawnmowers and tractors from Garvey and sold them to four separate buyers. Wyttenbach testified that he gained neither profit nor anything else of value from these transactions. One of his buyers was Justin Hoopman. Wyttenbach arranged for Hoopman to purchase a small lawn tractor from Garvey for $2,000. Wyttenbach transported the tractor to Hoopman's residence and left Hoopman's payment at an arranged place for Garvey to retrieve.

Co-conspirator Thomas testified against Garvey on the second day of trial. Prior to trial, the district court granted a motion in limine preventing the government from introducing any evidence of Garvey's drug use or sales. Thomas was specifically admonished not to mention any drug use or transactions. Despite these instructions, Thomas testified:

Q: In May of 2007, were you associating with Mr. Garvey?

A: Yeah, I believe so.

Q: And what sort of things were you doing with him at that time?

A: Oh, we got together and smoking [sic] weed. [NOTE: Weed is a slang term for marijuana.]

Garvey's counsel objected and the district judge instructed the jury, "any reference to any activities of that kind have no place in this matter and the jury should disregard that last reference." *Id.* Garvey's counsel thereafter moved for a mistrial. The court stated:

> I think it was an unfortunate occurrence. I didn't want to dwell on it. If you want a curative instruction at some point, I will give it.... I am very disappointed that the witness blurted that out. I had hoped it was made abundantly clear to him it was not an appropriate discussion, but this is not the time to address it and so I would ask counsel to step back at this time and we can address it at a break.

At the end of the day, the government informed the court that it had instructed Thomas not to mention drugs and his response was unexpected. The district judge noted that everyone was surprised, but he would not "grant a mistrial based on a single statement unrelated to the activities of this trial." He further explained:

> Frankly, given the amount of testimony of far more heinous conduct, I can't imagine that the fact that at some point this witness smoked marijuana with the defendant would have tainted the jury's ability to listen to the evidence and decide it. It defies credibility that that would be the case, but a record has been made.

Although the court offered to give an additional limiting instruction, Garvey's counsel did not request one.

Over the course of the four-day trial, the government called thirty-one witnesses and presented phone records which demonstrated frequent interaction among Garvey, his co-conspirators, and the buyers during the relevant time periods. The jury convicted Garvey on six of the nine counts. Garvey was sentenced to sixty months' imprisonment on the conspiracy count and ninety months' imprisonment on the remaining counts, to run concurrently with each other. Garvey filed this timely appeal.

II. ANALYSIS

B. Drug Use Testimony

Garvey also challenges the district court's denial of his motion for mistrial after Thomas testified that he smoked marijuana with Garvey. Given the highly prejudicial nature of testimony regarding drug activity, the jury's mixed verdict, and the fact that the case was entirely unrelated to drug charges, Garvey believes the motion should have been granted. We review the denial of a mistrial for an abuse of discretion. A mistrial is appropriate when "an event during trial has a real likelihood of preventing a jury from evaluating the evidence fairly and accurately, so that the defendant has been deprived of a fair trial." *United States v. Powell*, 652 F.3d 702, 709 (7th Cir.2011) (quoting *United States v. Tanner*, 628 F.3d 890, 898 (7th Cir.2010)).

Garvey's request for a mistrial was based on a singular statement made by Thomas, in which he stated "Oh, we got together and smoking [sic] weed." Following this statement, defense counsel immediately objected. The district court sustained the objection, admonished the jurors not to consider Thomas's statement, and offered to provide an additional limiting instruction, which defense counsel declined. "[J]urors are presumed to follow limiting and curative instructions unless the matter improperly before them is so powerfully incriminating that they cannot reasonably be expected to put it out of their minds." *United States v. Smith*, 308 F.3d 726, 739 (7th Cir.2002). Thomas's isolated statement that he smoked marijuana with Garvey was brief, "unadorned with additional details," and not so "powerfully incriminating" as to prevent the jurors from following the district court's instruction, which was prompt and appropriate. See *id.* Accordingly, Garvey cannot overcome the presumption that jurors obey the instructions given to them. The district court did not abuse its discretion in denying Garvey's motion for mistrial.

III. Conclusion

For the foregoing reasons, we AFFIRM the judgment of the district court.

Notes

1. The court excluded any evidence of drug use, and yet the witness testified to "smoking weed" with the defendant. Why do you think that testimony happened?
2. What remedies did the court offer the defendant? Why did the defendant decline some of those remedies?

Notes on Criminal Law

1. *United States v. Garvey* is the only criminal decision in this textbook, and the decision focuses on evidentiary issues, not issues peculiar to criminal law. Nevertheless, a brief overview of criminal law in the United States might prove helpful in your other courses.
2. A core tenet of the United States' criminal justice system is that the government bears the burden of proving the defendant's guilt beyond a reasonable doubt, which is a high standard.
3. In general, crimes contain two components: an "actus reus" and a "mens rea." The "actus reus" is the action part of the crime and generally includes the act, the result, and the causation. The "mens rea" is the required mental state.
4. Mens rea refers to the mental state of the actor. Did the actor plan in advance? Was the conduct intentional, albeit unplanned? Did the actor take

too much risk? Today, most crimes include a "mens rea" component. The laws that do not—the strict liability laws—focus on acts that deserve criminal punishment regardless of intent. Statutory rape laws are one example. These laws punish the act of having sex with a minor even if the perpetrator honestly thought that the minor was over the age of consent (between 16 and 18 in most jurisdictions). But laws such as those are the minority.

5. Just as the civil legal theories you have studied have had required elements, so do crimes. For example, common-law burglary requires (1) breaking and (2) entering (3) the dwelling house (4) of another (5) with intent to commit a felony.
6. Criminal law and criminal procedure are separate courses in law school. Criminal law is defined by the states, but most criminal procedure concerns the rights guaranteed to criminal defendants by the U.S. Constitution. Those rights include the right to a speedy trial, to counsel, and to be free from unreasonable search and seizure, to name a few.

3. Jury Deliberations & Verdicts

a. Overview

After the parties have presented all of their evidence, and the parties have made their closing arguments, the court will read aloud the instructions that will guide the jury's deliberations. The jury then leaves the courtroom to retire to a private room within the courthouse to deliberate.

One of the aspects of the U.S. legal system that often astonishes students from civil law countries is the jury deliberation process. First, the deliberation process is based almost exclusively on trust. No one is present in the deliberation room except the jury—no representative of the court, no representatives of the parties. Thus, while the jurors should only consider the evidence that they heard or saw at trial, there is no one in the deliberation room to guarantee that occurs; no one is present to prevent the jurors from considering, for example, newspaper articles a juror may have read, books on any topic relevant to their analysis, or even a juror's specialized knowledge on a technical topic—each of which the jury should not consider. Nor is there anyone directing the jury to decide the case based on the law as described in the instructions rather than the jurors' personal views of that law. In fact, the primary method of enforcing compliance with the jury's instructions is the jurors reminding each other during deliberations to follow the instructions and limit their consideration to the evidence at trial. Despite the limitations on enforcing these rules, the system most often works as it is intended.

Second, the process of deliberation itself can be unexpected to foreign-trained lawyers. Six to twelve strangers (the typical size of a jury) gather in a room to discuss the evidence and eventually vote on a verdict. In the federal courts, a verdict is only valid if every member of the jury agrees on it, in other words, the jurors reach a unanimous verdict. In state courts, unanimity is not always required in civil cases. In those situations, a majority is usually sufficient. The jurors generally will not reach the requisite unanimity or majority requirement on their first vote. The jurors will then continue to discuss the evidence, debate the issues, and reread the instructions before voting again. The jurors may reach agreement easily or can disagree vehemently during this process. Yet, the process continues until the jurors reach the requisite level of agreement. The jurors will then let the court know that they have reached a verdict. The jury will return to the courtroom where the court will read the jury's verdict to the parties.

Notes

1. You might think there are extensive qualifications — education, age, experience — for serving as a juror. If so, you will be surprised to learn that the requirements are very simple. Generally, any U.S. citizen 18 years or older may qualify to serve as a juror.
2. The jury selection process is called "voir dire." Before a trial begins, a group of potential jurors (the term for these individuals being, "venirepersons") is brought into the courtroom. The court and the parties ask questions of the venirepersons to determine whether they have any impediments to serving as a juror. Will they be available for the full length of the trial? Can they fairly hear and decide the case? Do they have any disqualifying biases? Some venirepersons will be excused "for cause," meaning that those individuals are determined to be not able to properly serve as jurors. The parties are also given a certain number of "strikes" to be used against jurors for any or no reason at all, so long as the reason is not discriminatory against, for example, a particular race or gender.
3. There are situations in which the court can consider juror misconduct, but Rule 606(b) of the Federal Rules of Evidence severely limits the federal

court's ability to do so. That Rule prohibits testimony by jurors as to conduct during deliberations:

> (1) *Prohibited Testimony or Other Evidence.* During an inquiry into the validity of a verdict or indictment, a juror may not testify about any statement made or incident that occurred during the jury's deliberations; the effect of anything on that juror's or another juror's vote; or any juror's mental processes concerning the verdict or indictment. The court may not receive a juror's affidavit or evidence of a juror's statement on these matters.

The Rule then carves out some exceptions to that general rule:

> (2) *Exceptions.* A juror may testify about whether: **(A)** extraneous prejudicial information was improperly brought to the jury's attention; **(B)** an outside influence was improperly brought to bear on any juror; or **(C)** a mistake was made in entering the verdict on the verdict form.

These exceptions would permit a jury to bring to the court's attention that another juror brought a newspaper article about the case into the jury room, for example. But even this misconduct will come to the court's attention only if one of the jurors knows how to raise the issue and does not simply leave for the day after the verdict is rendered, never to think about deliberations again. Importantly, the exceptions do not apply to misunderstandings of the instructions or ignoring the instructions. Thus, that information cannot be considered by the court.

4. What do jury instructions look like? Most jurisdictions have created standard instructions for various causes of action. For example, the following two instructions — identified as 400 and 401 — would be part of the set of instructions given in a negligence case in California. The brackets indicate places where it is intended for the instruction to be personalized to the particular case:

> 400. Negligence — Essential Factual Elements
>
> [Name of plaintiff] claims that [he/she/nonbinary pronoun] was harmed by [name of defendant]'s negligence. To establish this claim, [name of plaintiff] must prove all of the following:
>
> 1. That [name of defendant] was negligent;
> 2. That [name of plaintiff] was harmed; and
> 3. That [name of defendant]'s negligence was a substantial factor in causing [name of plaintiff]'s harm.

401. Basic Standard of Care

Negligence is the failure to use reasonable care to prevent harm to oneself or to others.

A person can be negligent by acting or by failing to act. A person is negligent if that person does something that a reasonably careful person would not do in the same situation or fails to do something that a reasonably careful person would do in the same situation. You must decide how a reasonably careful person would have acted in [name of plaintiff/defendant]'s situation.

5. Verdicts can take various forms. A verdict might simply ask the jury to determine whether or not the jury has concluded the defendant was negligent, and then, if negligent, indicate the amount of damages. Alternatively, the verdict might ask specific questions. An example of such a verdict form follows:

We answer the questions submitted to us as follows:

1. Was [name of defendant] negligent?

Yes No

If your answer to question 1 is yes, then answer question 2. If you answered no, stop here, answer no further questions, and have the presiding juror sign and date this form.

2. Was [name of defendant]'s negligence a substantial factor in causing harm to [name of plaintiff]?

Yes No

If your answer to question 2 is yes, then answer question 3. If you answered no, stop here, answer no further questions, and have the presiding juror sign and date this form.

3. What are [name of plaintiff]'s damages?

a. Past economic loss

[lost earnings $]

[lost profits $]

[medical expenses $]

[other past economic loss $]

[a. Total Past Economic Damages: $]

b. Future economic loss

[lost earnings $]

[lost profits $]

[medical expenses $]

[other future economic loss $]

[b. Total Future Economic Damages: $]

[c. Past noneconomic loss, including [physical pain/mental suffering]: $]

[d. Future noneconomic loss, including [physical pain/mental suffering]: $]

[d. TOTAL $]

b. Province of Judge or Jury? The Law/Fact Distinction

What exactly is the scope of the jury's decision-making process while they are deliberating? Juries are deciding facts, not legal questions. This difference in who decides questions of fact and questions of law exists, in part, because the Seventh Amendment to the United States Constitution preserves the right to a jury trial for resolution of factual, but not legal questions. The Seventh Amendment applies, however, only in federal (not state) courts. Nevertheless, most states have chosen to follow a similar practice of allocating factfinding to the jury and law-finding to the judge.

The line between fact and law is not always clear, though. Some questions are obviously factual: Was the stoplight red? Did the defendant stop at the red light? Was the plaintiff the oldest employee? Did the defendant sign the contract? And some questions are clearly legal: What are the elements of negligence that the jury must find to conclude the defendant is liable? But whether something is factual or legal is not always clear. Like with so many areas of the common law, the answer can be quite uncertain. In fact, the answers to similar questions are sometimes not even consistent with each other. For example, the "reasonableness" of an implied term in a contract is a question of law, but whether a defendant's conduct in a negligence suit was "reasonable" is a question of fact. *See* Emad H. Atiq, *Legal vs. Factual Normative Questions & the True Scope of Ring*, 32 Notre Dame J. L. Ethics & Pub. Pol. 47, 48 (2018).

While you may not be able to predict with perfect accuracy when a question of fact exists for the jury to resolve, the case below — *Sioux City & Pacific Rail-*

road Co. v. Stout—explores that issue. As you read the decision, pay attention to the court's identification of facts that the jury might have found from the evidence. Notice also the latitude that the Court granted the jury in drawing inferences from the facts and that these inferences were also factual findings.

Sioux City & Pacific Railroad Co. v. Stout

Supreme Court of the United States

84 U.S. (17 Wall.) 657 (1873)

MR. JUSTICE HUNT delivered the opinion of the Court.

...The record expressly states that "the counsel for the defendant...rest their defense on the ground that the company was not negligent, and claim that the injury to the plaintiff was accidental or brought upon himself." [The alleged negligence related to the existence and maintenance of a railroad "turntable," a device used to rotate locomotives so that they could be turned around and driven in the direction from which they came. A child playing on the turntable was injured and sued the railroad.]

...

2d. Was there negligence on the part of the railway company in the management or condition of its turntable?

...Unless the defendant was entitled to an order...directing a verdict in its favor, the submission [to the jury] was right. If, upon any construction which the jury was authorized to put upon the evidence, or by any inferences they were authorized to draw from it, the conclusion of negligence can be justified,...the judgment cannot be disturbed. To express it affirmatively, if from the evidence given it might justly be inferred by the jury that the defendant, in the construction, location, management, or condition of its [turntable] had omitted that care and attention to prevent the occurrence of accidents which prudent and careful men ordinarily bestow, the jury was at liberty to find for the plaintiff.

That the turntable was a dangerous machine, which would be likely to cause injury to children who resorted to it, might fairly be inferred from the injury which actually occurred to the plaintiff. There was the same liability to injury to him, and no greater, that existed with reference to all children. When the jury learned from the evidence that he had suffered a serious injury, by his foot being caught between the fixed rail of the roadbed and the turning rail of the table they were justified in believing that there was a probability of the occurrence of such accidents.

So, in looking at the remoteness of the machine from inhabited dwellings, when it was proved to the jury that several boys from the hamlet were at play there on this occasion, and that they had been at play upon the turntable on other occasions, and within the observation and to the knowledge of the employees of the defendant, the jury were justified in believing that children would probably resort to it, and that the defendant should have anticipated that such would be the case.

As it was in fact, on this occasion, so it was to be expected that the amusement of the boys would have been found in turning this table while they were on it or about it. This could certainly have been prevented by locking the turntable when not in use by the company. It was not shown that this would cause any considerable expense or inconvenience to the defendant. It could probably have been prevented by the repair of the broken latch. This was a heavy catch which, by dropping into a socket, prevented the revolution of the table. There had been one on this table weighing some eight or ten pounds, but it had been broken off and had not been replaced. It was proved to have been usual with railroad companies to have upon their turntables a latch or bolt, or some similar instrument. The jury may well have believed that if the defendant had incurred the trifling expense of replacing this latch, and had taken the slight trouble of putting it in its place, these very small boys would not have taken the pains to lift it out, and thus the whole difficulty have been avoided. Thus reasoning, the jury would have reached the conclusion that the defendant had omitted the care and attention it ought to have given, that it was negligent, and that its negligence caused the injury to the plaintiff....

3d. It is true, in many cases, that where the facts are undisputed the effect of them is for the judgment of the court, and not for the decision of the jury. This is true in that class of cases where the existence of such facts come in question rather than where deductions or inferences are to be made from the facts.... In some cases, [] the necessary inference from the proof is so certain that it may be ruled as a question of law. If a sane man voluntarily throws himself in contract with a passing engine, there being nothing to counteract the effect of this action, it may be ruled as a matter of law that the injury to him resulted from his own fault, and that no action can be sustained by him or his representatives. So if a coach driver intentionally drives within a few inches of a precipice, and an accident happens, negligence may be ruled as a question of law. On the other hand, if he had placed a suitable distance between his coach and the precipice, but by the breaking of a rein or an axle, which could not have been anticipated, an injury occurred, it might be ruled as a question of law that there was no negligence and no liability.

But these are extreme cases. The range between them is almost infinite in variety and extent. It is in relation to these intermediate cases that the opposite rule prevails. Upon the facts proven in such cases, it is a matter of judgment and discretion, of sound inference, what is the deduction to be drawn from the undisputed facts. Certain facts we may suppose to be clearly established from which one sensible, impartial man would infer that proper care had not been used, and that negligence existed; another man equally sensible and equally impartial would infer that proper care had been used, and that there was no negligence. It is this class of cases and those akin to it that the law commits to the decision of a jury....

In no class of cases can this practical experience be more wisely applied than in that we are considering. We find, accordingly, although not uniform or harmonious, that the authorities justify us in holding in the case before us, that although the facts are undisputed it is for the jury and not for the judge to determine whether proper care was given, or whether they establish negligence....

It has been already shown that the facts proved justified the jury in finding that the defendant was guilty of negligence, and we are of the opinion that it was properly left to the jury to determine that point.

Upon the whole case, the judgment must be

Affirmed.

Notes

1. In *Sioux City & Pacific Railroad Co. v. Stout*, what facts were the jury inferring? What does the Court even mean by the words "infer" and "inference"? And what facts permitted the jury to make the inference that it did? Did the jury reach the only permissible inference from the evidence?
2. The Court distinguished between situations where there is only one inference a jury could draw from the evidence and the situation where there are multiple inferences. What difference does this distinction make? Can you identify the example the Court gives of when there is just one inference to be drawn?

3. The elements for negligence are often described as duty, breach of duty, causation, and damages. A breach of duty occurs when a defendant fails to exercise reasonable care in fulfilling the duty. In the case above, the Supreme Court explained it is the jury's job to determine "whether proper care was taken."

The previous case was decided in 1873! Issues of what is or is not a factual question have arisen over the years since that 1873 decision. Nearly 150 years after the *Sioux City* decision, the Court addressed whether the size of a punitive damages award is a factual question. Although the majority of the Court concluded the issue was not a pure question of fact, that conclusion was not without dissent, illustrating the challenge in the question.

Cooper Industries, Inc. v. Leatherman Tool Group, Inc.

Supreme Court of the United States

532 U.S. 424 (2001)

JUSTICE STEVENS delivered the opinion of the Court.

A jury found petitioner guilty of unfair competition and awarded respondent $50,000 in compensatory damages and $4.5 million in punitive damages. The District Court held that the punitive damages award did not violate the Federal Constitution. The Court of Appeals concluded that "the district court did not abuse its discretion in declining to reduce the amount of punitive damages."

I

The parties are competing tool manufacturers. In the 1980's, Leatherman Tool Group, Inc. (Leatherman or respondent), introduced its Pocket Survival Tool (PST)....

In 1995, Cooper Industries, Inc. (Cooper or petitioner), decided to design and market a competing multifunction tool. Cooper planned to copy the basic features of the PST, add a few features of its own, and sell the new tool under the name "ToolZall." Cooper hoped to capture about 5% of the multifunction tool market. The first ToolZall was designed to be virtually identical to the PST, but the design was ultimately modified in response to this litigation. The controversy to be resolved in this case involves Cooper's improper advertising of its original ToolZall design.

Cooper introduced the original ToolZall in August 1996 at the National Hardware Show in Chicago. At that show, it used photographs in its posters, packaging, and advertising materials that purported to be of a ToolZall but were actually of a modified PST.... A Cooper employee created a ToolZall "mock-up" by grinding the Leatherman trademark from handles and pliers of a PST and substituting the unique fastenings that were to be used on the ToolZall. At least one of the photographs was retouched to remove a curved indentation where the Leatherman trademark had been. The photographs were used, not only at the trade show, which normally draws an audience of over 70,000 people, but also in the marketing materials and catalogs used by Cooper's sales force throughout the United States. Cooper also distributed a touched-up line drawing of a PST to its international sales representatives.

Shortly after the trade show, Leatherman filed this action asserting claims of trade-dress infringement, unfair competition, and false advertising..., and a common-law claim of unfair competition for advertising and selling an "imitation" of the PST. In December 1996, the District Court entered a preliminary injunction prohibiting Cooper from marketing the ToolZall and from using pictures of the modified PST in its advertising. Cooper withdrew the original ToolZall from the market and developed a new model with plastic coated handles that differed from the PST. In November 1996, it had anticipatorily sent a notice to its sales personnel ordering a recall of all promotional materials containing pictures of the PST, but it did not attempt to retrieve the materials it had sent to its customers until the following April. As a result, the offending promotional materials continued to appear in catalogs and advertisements well into 1997.

After a trial conducted in October 1997, the jury returned a verdict that answered several special interrogatories. [The jury found for Leatherman on all claims. The jury awarded $50,000 in compensatory damages and $4.5 million in punitive damages.]

After the jury returned its verdict, the District Court considered, and rejected, arguments that the punitive damages were "grossly excessive."...

On appeal,... the Court of Appeals affirmed the punitive damages award.... [T]he Court of Appeals concluded, "the district court did not abuse its discretion in declining to reduce the amount of punitive damages." *Ibid.*

...

II

Although compensatory damages and punitive damages are typically awarded at the same time by the same decisionmaker, they serve distinct purposes. The former are intended to redress the concrete loss that the plaintiff has suffered by reason of the defendant's wrongful conduct. The latter, which have been described as "quasi-criminal," ... operate as "private fines" intended to punish the defendant and to deter future wrongdoing. A jury's assessment of the extent of a plaintiff's injury is essentially a factual determination, whereas its imposition of punitive damages is an expression of its moral condemnation.

...

III

"Unlike the measure of actual damages suffered, which presents a question of historical or predictive fact, ... the level of punitive damages is not really a 'fact' 'tried' by the jury." *Gasperini v. Center for Humanities, Inc.*, 518 U. S. 415, 459 (1996) (SCALIA, J., dissenting)....

It might be argued that the deterrent function of punitive damages suggests that the amount of such damages awarded is indeed a "fact" found by the jury.... Some scholars, for example, assert that punitive damages should be used to compensate for the underdeterrence of unlawful behavior that will result from a defendant's evasion of liability.... "The efficient deterrence theory thus regards punitive damages as merely an augmentation of compensatory damages designed to achieve economic efficiency." Galanter & Luban, *Poetic Justice: Punitive Damages and Legal Pluralism*, 42 Am. U. L. Rev. 1393, 1449 (1993).

However attractive such an approach to punitive damages might be as an abstract policy matter, it is clear that juries do not normally engage in such a finely tuned exercise of deterrence calibration when awarding punitive damages. After all, deterrence is not the only purpose served by punitive damages. And there is no dispute that, in this case, deterrence was but one of four concerns the jury was instructed to consider when setting the amount of punitive damages: [(1) "The character of the defendant's conduct that is the subject of Leatherman's unfair competition claims"; (2) "The defendant's motive"; (3) "The sum of money that would be required to discourage the defendant and others from engaging in such conduct in the future"; and (4) "The defendant's income and assets."] Moreover, it is not at all obvious that even the *deterrent* function of punitive damages can be served *only* by economically "optimal deterrence." "[C]itizens and legislators may rightly insist that they are willing to tolerate some loss in economic efficiency in order to deter what they consider morally offensive conduct, albeit cost-beneficial morally offensive conduct; efficiency is just one consideration among many." Galanter & Luban, 42 Am. U. L. Rev., at 1450....

...

The *de* novo standard [which applies to questions of law] should govern its decision. Because the Court of Appeals applied a less demanding standard [that applies to questions of fact] in this case, we vacate the judgment and remand the case for further proceedings consistent with this opinion.

It is so ordered.

THOMAS, J., concurring. [Omitted.]

SCALIA, J., concurring in the judgment. [Omitted.]

GINSBURG, J., dissenting

...

At common law, as our longstanding decisions reiterate, the task of determining the amount of punitive damages "has [always been] left to the discretion of the jury." *Day v. Woodworth,* 13 How. 363, 371 (1852).... The commitment of this function to the jury, we have explained, reflects the historical understanding that "the degree of punishment to be thus inflicted must depend on the peculiar circumstances of each case." *Day,* 13 How., at 371. The relevant factors include "the conduct and motives of the defendant" and whether, "in committing the wrong complained of, he acted recklessly, or wilfully and maliciously, with a design to oppress and injure the plaintiff." Such inquiry, the Court acknowledges, "is a fact-sensitive undertaking."

The Court nevertheless today asserts that a "jury's award of punitive damages does not constitute a finding of 'fact'" within the meaning of the Seventh Amendment. An ultimate award of punitive damages, it is true, involves more than the resolution of matters of historical or predictive fact. But there can be no question that a jury's verdict on punitive damages is fundamentally dependent on determinations we characterize as factfindings, *e.g.*, the extent of harm or potential harm caused by the defendant's misconduct, whether the defendant acted in good faith, whether the misconduct was an individual instance or part of a broader pattern, whether the defendant behaved negligently, recklessly, or maliciously. Punitive damages are thus not "[u]nlike the measure of actual damages suffered," in cases of intangible, noneconomic injury. One million dollars' worth of pain and suffering does not exist as a "fact" in the world any more or less than one million dollars' worth of moral outrage. Both derive their meaning from a set of underlying facts as determined by a jury. If one exercise in quantification is properly regarded as factfinding, it seems to me the other should be so regarded as well.

...

For the Seventh Amendment and practical reasons stated, I would affirm the judgment of the Court of Appeals.

Notes

1. Were there any aspects of the jury's decision as to the amount of punitive damages that were factual? What factual decisions might the jury have made as part of the process of determining the amount of punitive damages to award? Why, then, was the decision as to the amount of punitive damages not also a factual finding?
2. The first step in awarding punitive damages is determining whether punitive damages should even be available in that particular case. The exact requirement for the availability of punitive damages is phrased differently from state to state, but the common factor is that punitive damages are only available in more egregious cases. Thus, the type of conduct that can support punitive damages is often described as wanton, willful, or intentional. A finding of negligence, for example, will not permit a jury to consider awarding punitive damages, because negligence results from lack of care, not from willful conduct. In *Cooper Indus., Inc. v. Leatherman Tool Grp., Inc.*, the availability of punitive damages was not in dispute, merely the amount of those damages. Why do you think that Cooper Industries did not challenge the availability of punitive damages? How would you describe the conduct of Cooper Industries?
3. Typically, the jury is the factfinder, but sometimes, the judge can instead be the factfinder. Parties might agree by contract that their future contract disputes would be decided by a judge, not a jury. Or, in the case of non-contractual disputes, the parties may simply waive their right to a jury trial and agree to have the judge serve as the factfinder. Why would parties make these choices? Juries are unpredictable. There is a risk that the facts of any given case may sway jurors' emotions. The parties may be-

lieve in that situation that the judge, unlike the jury, will accurately follow the law and not be swayed by emotions. Similarly, the parties may fear the topic is too complicated or technical for a jury, which will likely consist of individuals of all levels of education and business experience. Another consideration is cost. Jury trials are lengthier and more expensive. The process of selecting the members of the jury adds length to the trial, and the manner of presentation to the jury can be more performative than a presentation to the court would be.

4. Dispositive Trial Motions

After the trial starts, the parties have one remaining option for asking the court to enter judgment in their favor and that is through a motion for judgment as a matter of law. Fed. R. Civ. P. 50. After the jury has rendered its verdict, the losing party can move for a new trial, but granting this motion would not result in a judgment for any party. The next two cases illustrate the principles that guide these decisions.

a. Judgment as a Matter of Law

The court generally must respect the jury's verdict, even if it is not the result the court would have reached had it been the fact-finder. But when the moving party persuades the court that there is only one verdict that the jury could properly reach, the court can grant judgment as a matter of law for the only party, whether that is the plaintiff or the defendant, who could possibly win given the evidence at trial. *See* Fed. R. Civ. P. 50(a). This motion for judgment as a matter of law was previously called a motion for directed verdict and that terminology will appear in older cases.

The moving party must file the motion for judgment as a matter of law "before the case is submitted to the jury." Fed. R. Civ. P. 50(a)(2). The court can grant the motion at that time, deny the motion, or delay ruling on the motion until after the case is submitted to the jury. Fed. R. Civ. P. 50(a)(2). If the court does not rule on the motion before the jury renders a verdict, the moving party can "renew" the motion. In response to the renewed motion, the court can direct the entry of a judgment different from the one returned by the jury. Fed. R. Civ. P. 50(b). The renewed motion for judgment as a matter of law was previously called a motion for judgment notwithstanding the verdict, and, as with the motion for directed verdict, this terminology will appear in older cases, including *Denman v. Spain*.

The standard for the motion or the renewed motion for judgment as a matter of law is met in only a very narrow set of circumstances, and most of such cases will be disposed of in some way prior to trial, such as through summary judgment. Nevertheless, if such a case proceeds to trial, the court can correct a judgment. *Denman v. Spain* illustrates one set of facts when the court concluded there was no evidence to support the jury's verdict. As you read the case, consider what this decision says about the limit on inferences that a jury may draw.

Denman v. Spain

Supreme Court of Mississippi

135 So. 2d 195 (1961)

LEE, P.J.

Betty Denman, a minor, by her mother and next friend, Joyce H. Denman, sued Mrs. Phina Ross Spain, executrix of the estate of Joseph A. Ross, deceased, to recover damages for personal injuries sustained by her, allegedly resulting from the negligence of the decedent in the operation of an automobile. The issue was submitted to a jury on the evidence of the plaintiff no evidence being offered for the defendant and there was a verdict and judgment for the plaintiff in the sum of $5,000. However, on motion of the defendant, a judgment... notwithstanding the verdict, was sustained and entered. From that action, the plaintiff has appealed.

...

The appellant contends that the evidence offered by her, together with the reasonable inferences therefrom, was sufficient to make an issue for the jury as to whether the alleged negligence of the deceased driver, Ross, proximately caused or contributed to the collision and the consequent damage; and that it was error to set aside the verdict of the jury and enter the judgment for the defendant, notwithstanding that verdict. Hence, she says that such judgment should be reversed, and that the verdict and judgment of the jury should be reinstated.

A careful scrutiny and analysis of the evidence is therefore necessary:

Sunday, March 23, 1958, was a rainy, foggy day. About six o'clock that afternoon, at dusk, Mrs. Eva B. Denman, accompanied by her granddaughter, Betty, the plaintiff, was driving her Ford car southward on U.S. Highway 49E. At that time, Joseph A. Ross, accompanied by Miss Euna Tanner and Mrs. J.L.

Haining, was driving his Plymouth car northward on said highway. Just south of the Town of Sumner, the cars collided. Mrs. Denman, Miss Tanner and Ross were killed. Betty, nearly seven years of age at the time, and Mrs. Haining were injured. Neither had any recollection of what had happened at the time of the collision. Betty, lying in water on her back in a ditch on the east side of the road, cried out and was rescued by some unknown person.

Plaintiff's father, Stuart Denman, who went to the scene shortly after the collision, described the situation substantially as follows: The Ford car was about seven yards off the paved surface on the east side in a bar pit "heading back towards the railroad track, which is in an easterly direction." The engine and transmission were on the opposite side of the road, out of the car and about fifty yards apart. The [P]lymouth was also on the east side, facing west, about fifteen yards north of the Ford.

No proof was offered as to skid marks, or other evidence to show the point of contact between these two vehicles. Eleven photographs of the damaged Plymouth, taken from various positions, and thirteen pictures of the damaged Ford, also taken from various positions, other than being mute evidence of a terrible tragedy, depict no reasonable or plausible explanation as to why this collision occurred, or who was responsible for it. Three other photographs, portraying the topography of this immediate area, afford no excuse whatever for such grievous human error.

Over objection by the defendant, John Barnett testified that he was driving a Dodge pickup north of highway 49E on his way to Tutwiler; that he was traveling at a speed of fifty or fifty-five miles per hour; that the Plymouth, which was in the wreck, passed him about three-fourths of a mile south of where the collision occurred, going at a speed of about seventy miles per hour; that when it passed, it got back in its lane, and neither wavered nor wobbled thereafter; that he followed and observed it for a distance of forty or fifty yards, and that it stayed in its proper lane as long as he saw it. Although another car was on the road ahead of him, he could have seen as far as the place of the accident except for the rain and fog.

Over objection by the defendant, Hal Buckley, ... testified that he was also traveling north on 49E on his way to Tutwiler at a speed of forty to fifty miles per hour. About two hundred yards south of the place where the collision occurred, a light green Plymouth, which he later saw at the scene of the accident, passed him at a speed of seventy-five or eighty miles an hour. He could see its tail lights after it passed, and "he was just steady going; he wasn't doing no slowing up." He saw it until it ran into the other car. On cross-examination, he said that, after this car passed him, it got back on its side of the road, drove straight, and he did not notice that it ever went back over the center. Also on cross-examination, in an effort at impeachment, a part of the transcript [from another] trial, containing this question and answer, was read to him as follows: "What do you estimate the speed of that car was when it passed you the one that was going the same direction that you were?", and the answer was: "Well, I don't have no idea." When he was asked why he made this difference in his testimony, he hesitated and replied, "I didn't give no sorta idea how fast he was going?" He then admitted that, when the car passed him, it got back on its side and drove straight ahead, and that he could see the accident, but he could not tell anything about it or on which side of the road it happened. He also did not notice the other car, which came from the other direction.

...

From this evidence, the plaintiff reasons that the jury could, and did, find that the Ross car was being operated, under inclement weather conditions, at an unlawful and negligent rate of speed, and that, if Ross had had his car under adequate and proper control, in all probability the collision could have been avoided. She voices the opinion that the physical facts, including the pictures of the wrecked vehicles, indicated that the Ford car was probably across the highway at an angle of perhaps forty-five degrees at the time of the collision.

But the testimony of Buckley showed only that the Plymouth was being operated at an excessive and negligent rate of speed. It otherwise showed that the car was in its proper lane. He did not notice it go over the center at any time, but it was driven straight down the road. No eye-witness claimed to have seen what happened. There was no evidence to indicate the place in the road where the vehicles came in contact with each other. There was no showing as to the speed of the Ford, whether fast or slow; or as to whether it was traveling on the right or wrong side of the road; or as to whether it slid or was suddenly driven to the wrong side of the road into the path of the Plymouth. The cars were so badly damaged that the pictures afford no reasonable explanation as to what person or persons were legally responsible for their condition. In other words, just how and why this grievous tragedy occurred is completely shrouded in mystery.

The burden was on the plaintiff to prove, by preponderance of the evidence, not only that the operator of the Plymouth was guilty of negligence but also that such negligence proximately caused or contributed to the collision and consequent damage. By the use of metaphysical learning, speculation and conjecture, one may reach several possible conclusions as to how the accident occurred. However such conclusions could only be classed as possibilities; and this Court has many times held that verdicts cannot be based on possibilities. At all events, there is no sound or reasonable basis upon which a jury or this Court can say that the plaintiff met that burden.

The judgment must be affirmed.

Affirmed.

KYLE, ARRINGTON, ETHRIDGE, and GILLESPIE, JJ., concur.

Notes

1. What evidence do you think the jurors relied on to reach their verdict for the plaintiff? What do you think was their reasoning?
2. What evidence did the defendant put forward that justified the trial court in granting a judgment notwithstanding the verdict in favor of the defendant? If the court's decision was not based on the defendant's evidence, what was it based on?
3. Was there any evidence that showed what happened at the precise moment of the accident? Why are there no eyewitnesses?
4. The court concluded: "By the use of metaphysical learning, speculation and conjecture, one may reach several possible conclusions as to how the accident occurred. However, such conclusions could only be classed as possibilities." Think back on earlier chapters, when else was a mere possibility insufficient?

b. New Trial

The trial court has more latitude when considering whether to grant a new trial. A motion for judgment as a matter of law, if granted, takes away the verdict of the jury that decided the case, and there will be no future jury considering the case. In contrast, the grant of a new trial takes a verdict away from one jury but puts the decision into the hands of another jury that will hear the evidence in the new trial. The standard for granting a new trial, therefore, tends to be more permissive. For example, federal courts can grant a new trial "for any reason for which a new trial has heretofore been granted in an action at law in federal court." Fed. R. Civ. P. 59.

Farrior v. Waterford Board of Education

United States Court of Appeals for the Second Circuit

277 F.3d 633 (2002)

PER CURIAM.

Following her termination as an executive secretary, plaintiff-appellant Peggy Farrior sued the Waterford Board of Education ("the Board") and a group of individual defendants under 42 U.S.C. § 1983, alleging, among other claims, that the Board had violated her First Amendment rights by discharging her for publicly disclosing misfeasance by her supervisor and by ratifying systematic retaliation against her by her supervisors.... Farrior's First Amendment claim was tried to a jury, which found in her favor and awarded $561,474 in damages. The district court then granted the Board's Rule 59 motion for a new trial on the ground that the jury's verdict was against the weight of the evidence. A second jury trial resulted in a verdict in favor of the Board. Farrior now appeals the district court's grant of a new trial.

A district court's grant of a new trial on the ground that the verdict was against the weight of the evidence is reviewed for abuse of discretion. A grant of a new trial on the ground that the verdict was against the weight of the evidence is appropriate if "the jury has reached a seriously erroneous result or... the verdict is a miscarriage of justice." In determining whether the jury's verdict is so "seriously erroneous" as to justify a new trial, the trial judge is free to weigh the evidence and "need not view it in the light most favorable to the verdict winner."

Although the district court's opinion as a whole makes it clear that the right standard was applied and thus we can easily affirm the judgment, we write to clarify one passage. The district court's opinion states that a new trial is appropriate "if the jury's verdict is seriously erroneous or constitutes a miscarriage of justice, or the verdict appears... to be against the weight of evidence." That passage could be interpreted as stating that a new trial is appropriate if a) the verdict is seriously erroneous, b) the verdict is a miscarriage of justice, or c) the verdict is against the weight of the evidence. That understanding of the law would be erroneous because "seriously erroneous" and a "miscarriage of justice" are just descriptions of the standard that courts apply in determining whether a verdict is "against the weight of evidence." However, the district court's formulation could also be read as a restatement: a decision is against the weight of the evidence, for purposes of a Rule 59 motion, if and only if the verdict is seriously erroneous or a miscarriage of justice. Such a reading is correct and follows the reading we place on other prior decisions of this court that have used constructions similar to the district court's formulation. We are confident that the district court in this case applied the correct standard, in light of its correct statement that a "jury's verdict... should rarely be disturbed" and its extensive, careful consideration of the evidence throughout its opinion.

... Because it is clear that the district court applied the correct standard, and that the district court did not abuse its discretion in concluding that the jury's verdict was "seriously erroneous" or a "miscarriage of justice," and thus against the weight of the evidence, we affirm.

Notes

1. Did the appellate court explain the basis in the evidence for the trial court's decision to grant a new trial? Why is there so little information in the opinion about that basis?
2. The Second Circuit's opinion focuses on a potential error in the trial court's formulation of the relevant test. How was the trial court's statement of the test possibly incorrect? Why did the Second Circuit conclude that despite the potential for interpreting the trial court as applying the wrong standard, it would conclude that the trial court had not misapplied the law? If the standard of review is the very deferential abuse-of-discretion standard, why would the application of an incorrect standard even matter?
3. What ruling would the trial court have made if the second jury had also rendered a verdict in favor of the plaintiff and the defendant had again moved for a new trial? How would the situation be different after a second jury returned a verdict for the plaintiff? How might that second verdict factor into the court's analysis of the defendant's second motion for a new trial?

— ★ —

SEVEN

THE ANATOMY OF A LAWSUIT: APPELLATE REVIEW

A. OVERVIEW

After a case ends — whether by involuntary dismissal, summary judgment, trial, or any other means other than settlement — the court will enter judgment for the prevailing party. The losing party has the right, within certain limits, to take an appeal from this final judgment. Although the appeal is technically *from* the judgment, the appellant generally challenges decisions made *before* the judgment. For example, during the course of the litigation, the district court may have permitted the admission of evidence at trial over the losing party's objection. In the appeal, the losing party may argue that the trial court erred in that ruling, and as a result of this error, the judgment is incorrect.

In reviewing the proceedings in the trial court, the appellate court does not retry the case, take evidence, or hear witnesses. It instead focuses its review on the pleadings in the trial court, a transcript of all of the testimony, and the exhibits admitted at trial if one was held. Moreover, even if the appellate court finds that an error occurred in the trial court proceedings, it will not reverse unless it also finds that the error likely affected the outcome of the case. In other words, if the appellate court concludes the error was harmless, the court will affirm the judgment despite the error.

B. AVAILABILITY OF APPEAL

The trial court makes many decisions during the life of a case. The trial court may deny a motion to dismiss, or grant a motion to compel the production of evidence, or overrule an objection at trial, but none of these decisions are immediately appealable. Instead, the parties can challenge these decisions, if at all, only after the final judgment in the case. In other words, as long as the case is still ongoing, a plaintiff or defendant generally has no right to an appeal.

This practice of delaying appellate review until after judgment promotes judicial efficiency. If appeals could be filed while the case were still proceeding in the trial court, the trial proceedings would be delayed while parties waited for an appellate decision. And limiting appeals until after final judgment will eliminate many potential appellate issues, because there will be no point in evaluating rulings made in the trial court that were adverse to the party who ultimately prevailed. Postponing appellate review also allows the appellate court to rule on all of the challenges to the trial court's decisions at the same time — after final judgment in the trial court — rather than piecemeal over the weeks, months, and even years of the life of the case.

The next case — *Liberty Mutual v. Wetzel* — explores what it means to have a final judgment.

Liberty Mutual Insurance Co. v. Wetzel

Supreme Court of the United States

424 U.S. 737 (1976)

MR. JUSTICE REHNQUIST delivered the opinion of the Court.

Respondents filed a complaint in the United States District Court for the Western District of Pennsylvania in which they asserted that petitioner's employee insurance benefits and maternity leave regulations discriminated against women in violation of Title VII of the Civil Rights Act.... The District Court ruled in favor of respondents on the issue of petitioner's liability under that Act, and petitioner appealed to the Court of Appeals for the Third Circuit. That court held that it had jurisdiction of petitioner's appeal under 28 U.S.C. § 1291, and proceeded to affirm on the merits the judgment of the District Court. We granted certiorari, and heard arguments on the merits. Though neither party has questioned the jurisdiction of the Court of Appeals to entertain the appeal, we are obligated to do so on our own motion if a question thereto exists. *Mansfield, Coldwater & Lake Michigan R. Co. v. Swan*, 111 U.S. 379 (1884). Because we conclude that the District Court's order was not appealable to the Court of Appeals, we vacate the judgment of the Court of Appeals with instructions to dismiss petitioner's appeal from the order of the District Court.

Respondents' complaint, after alleging jurisdiction and facts deemed pertinent to their claim, prayed for a judgment against petitioner embodying the following relief:

> "(a) requiring that defendant establish nondiscriminatory hiring, payment, opportunity, and promotional plans and programs;"
>
> "(b) enjoining the continuance by defendant of the illegal acts and practices alleged herein;"
>
> "(c) requiring that defendant pay over to plaintiffs and to the members of the class the damages sustained by plaintiffs and the members of the class by reason of defendant's illegal acts and practices, including adjusted backpay, with interest, and an additional equal amount as liquidated damages, and exemplary damages;"
>
> "(d) requiring that defendant pay to plaintiffs and to the members of the class the costs of this suit and a reasonable attorneys' fee, with interest; and"
>
> "(e) such other and further relief as the Court deems appropriate."

After extensive discovery, respondents moved for partial summary judgment only as to the issue of liability. The District Court, on January 9, 1974, finding no issues of material fact in dispute, entered an order to the effect that petitioner's pregnancy-related policies violated Title VII.... It also ruled that Liberty Mutual's hiring and promotion policies violated Title VII. Petitioner thereafter filed a motion for reconsideration, which was denied by the District Court. Its order of February 20, 1974, denying the motion for reconsideration, contains the following concluding language:

> "In its Order, the court stated it would enjoin the continuance of practices which the court found to be in violation of Title VII. The Plaintiffs were invited to submit the form of the injunction order, and the Defendant has filed Notice of Appeal and asked for stay of any injunctive order. Under these circumstances, the court will withhold the issuance of the injunctive order and amend the Order previously issued under the provisions of Fed. R. Civ. P. 54(b), as follows:"

> "And now this 20th day of February, 1974, it is directed that final judgment be entered in favor of Plaintiffs that Defendant's policy of requiring female employees to return to work within three months of delivery of a child or be terminated is in violation of the provisions of Title VII of the Civil Rights Act of 1964; that Defendant's policy of denying disability income protection plan benefits to female employees for disabilities related to pregnancies or childbirth are [sic] in violation of Title VII of the Civil Rights Act of 1964, and that it is expressly directed that Judgment be entered for the Plaintiffs upon these claims of Plaintiffs' Complaint; there being no just reason for delay."

It is obvious from the District Court's order that respondents, although having received a favorable ruling on the issue of petitioner's liability to them, received none of the relief which they expressly prayed for in the portion of their complaint set forth above. They requested an injunction, but did not get one; they requested damages, but were not awarded any; they requested attorneys' fees, but received none.

...

The District Court and the Court of Appeals apparently took the view that, because the District Court made the recital required by Fed. Rule Civ. Proc. 54(b) that final judgment be entered on the issue of liability, and that there was no just reason for delay, the orders thereby became appealable as a final decision pursuant to 28 U.S.C. § 1291. We cannot agree with this application of the Rule and statute in question.

Rule 54(b) [states:

> "When more than one claim for relief is presented in an action, whether as a claim, counterclaim, cross-claim, or third-party claim, or when multiple parties are involved, the court may direct the entry of a final judgment as to one or more but fewer than all of the claims or parties only upon an express determination that there is no just reason for delay and upon an express direction for the entry of judgment. In the absence of such determination and direction, any order or other form of decision, however designated, which adjudicates fewer than all the claims or the rights and liabilities of fewer than all the parties shall not terminate the action as to any of the claims or parties, and the order or other form of decision is subject to revision at any time before the entry

of judgment adjudicating all the claims and the rights and liabilities of all the parties."

This rule "does not apply to a single claim action.... It is limited expressly to multiple claims actions in which 'one or more but less than all' of the multiple claims have been finally decided and are found otherwise to be ready for appeal."

Here, however, respondents set forth but a single claim: that petitioner's employee insurance benefits and maternity leave regulations discriminated against its women employees in violation of Title VII of the Civil Rights Act of 1964. They prayed for several different types of relief in the event that they sustained the allegations of their complaint, but their complaint advanced a single legal theory which was applied to only one set of facts. Thus, despite the fact that the District Court undoubtedly made the findings required under the Rule, had it been applicable, those findings do not in a case such as this make the order appealable pursuant to 28 U.S.C. § 1291.

...

The judgment of the Court of Appeals is therefore vacated, and the case is remanded with instructions to dismiss the petitioner's appeal.

It is so ordered.

MR. JUSTICE BLACKMUN took no part in the consideration or decision of this case.

Notes

1. The judgment as to liability was not subject to reevaluation in the trial court, so why was that decision not deemed final? What benefit is there in delaying review of the liability decision until after the claim is fully resolved? What might happen at the damages phase?
2. The Court relied on a key statute concerning appeals in federal courts: 12 U.S.C. § 1291. This statute establishes the final judgment requirement. 12 U.S.C. § 1291 ("The courts of appeals (other than the United States Court of Appeals for the Federal Circuit) shall have jurisdiction of appeals from all final decisions of the district courts of the United States...."). Section 1292 creates some exceptions to this final judgment requirement. 28 U.S.C. § 1292(a). Injunctions are immediately appealable, for example, *see id.*, and

the district court can certify for immediate appeal other issues involving "a controlling question of law as to which there is substantial ground for difference of opinion and that an immediate appeal from the order may materially advance the ultimate termination of the litigation," 28 U.S.C. § 1292(b). But even this certification is not sufficient; for an appeal to lie, the Court of Appeals must "in its discretion, permit an appeal to be taken from such order." 28 U.S.C. § 1292(b).

C. STANDARD OF REVIEW

While reviewing the trial court decision, the appellate court will apply one of the various standards of review ranging from the most searching, which is *de novo* review, to the most deferential, which is abuse of discretion. Under *de novo* review, the court essentially performs an independent evaluation of the legal question. Review for abuse of discretion, on the other hand, requires the appellate court to defer to the trial court's decision.

The Supreme Court decision that follows—*Salve Regina College v. Russell*—explains some of the various standards of review and when they should be applied. Notice that some of the concepts that we learned in our earlier classes are mentioned in this case as well.

Salve Regina College v. Russell

Supreme Court of the United States

499 U.S. 225 (1991)

Justice BLACKMUN delivered the opinion of the Court.

...*Erie* mandates that a federal court sitting in diversity apply the substantive law of the forum State, absent a federal statutory or constitutional directive to the contrary. In decisions after *Erie*, this Court made clear that state law is to be determined in the same manner as a federal court resolves an evolving issue of federal law: "with the aid of such light as [is] afforded by the materials for decision at hand, and in accordance with the applicable principles for determining state law."

In this case, we must decide specifically whether a federal court of appeals may review a district court's determination of state law under a standard less probing than that applied to a determination of federal law.

I

The issue presented arises out of a contract dispute between a college and one of its students. Petitioner Salve Regina College is an institution of higher education located in Newport, R.I. Respondent Sharon L. Russell was admitted to the college and began her studies as a freshman in 1982. The following year, respondent sought admission to the college's nursing department in order to pursue a bachelor of science degree in nursing. She was accepted by the department and began her nursing studies in the fall of 1983. [Ultimately the college asked Russell to withdraw from the program, and she did.]

Soon after leaving Salve Regina College, respondent filed this civil action in the United States District Court for the District of Rhode Island. She asserted, among others, claims based on ... nonperformance by the college of its implied agreement to educate respondent. Subject-matter jurisdiction in the District Court was based on diversity of citizenship. *See* 28 U.S.C. § 1332. The parties agree that the law of Rhode Island applies to all substantive aspects of the action. *See Erie R. Co. v. Tompkins, supra.*

At the close of plaintiff-respondent's case in chief, the District Court ... denied the college's motion for a directed verdict on the breach-of-contract claim, reasoning that "a legitimate factual issue" remained concerning whether "there was substantial performance by the plaintiff in her overall contractual relationship at Salve Regina."

At the close of all the evidence, the college renewed its motion for a directed verdict. It argued that under Rhode Island law the strict commercial doctrine of substantial performance did not apply in the general academic context. Therefore, according to petitioner, because respondent admitted she had not fulfilled the terms of the contract, the college was entitled to judgment as a matter of law.

The District Court denied petitioner's motion. Acknowledging that the Supreme Court of Rhode Island, to that point, had limited the application of the substantial-performance doctrine to construction contracts, the District Court nonetheless concluded, as a matter of law, that the Supreme Court of Rhode Island would apply that doctrine to the facts of respondent's case. The Federal District Judge based this conclusion, in part, on his observation that "I was a state trial judge for 18 and 1/2 years, and I have a feel for what the Rhode Island Supreme Court will do or won't do." Accordingly, the District Court submitted the breach-of-contract claim to the jury. The court instructed the jury:

> "The law provides that substantial and not exact performance accompanied by good faith is what is required in a case of a contract of this type. It is not necessary that the plaintiff have fully and completely performed every item specified in the contract between the parties. It is sufficient if there has been substantial performance, not necessarily full performance, so long as the substantial performance was in good faith and in compliance with the contract, except for some minor and relatively unimportant deviation or omission."

The jury returned a verdict for respondent, and determined that the damages were $30,513.40. Judgment was entered. Both respondent and petitioner appealed.

The United States Court of Appeals for the First Circuit affirmed.... Rejecting petitioner's argument that, under Rhode Island law, the doctrine of substantial performance does not apply in the college-student context, the court stated:

> "In this case of first impression, the district court held that the Rhode Island Supreme Court would apply the substantial performance standard to the contract in question. In view of the customary appellate deference accorded to interpretations of state law made by federal judges of that state, we hold that the district court's determination that the Rhode Island Supreme Court would apply standard contract principles is not reversible error."

Petitioner college sought a writ of certiorari from this Court. It alleged that the Court of Appeals erred in deferring to the District Court's determination of state law. A majority of the Courts of Appeals, although varying in their phraseology, embrace a rule of deference similar to that articulated by the Court of Appeals in this case. Two Courts of Appeals, however, have broken ranks recently with their sister Circuits. They have concluded that a district-court determination of state law is subject to plenary review by the appellate court. We granted certiorari to resolve the conflict.

II

We conclude that a court of appeals should review *de novo* a district court's determination of state law.... Independent appellate review of legal issues best serves the dual goals of doctrinal coherence and economy of judicial administration. District judges preside alone over fast-paced trials: Of necessity they devote much of their energy and resources to hearing witnesses and reviewing evidence. Similarly, the logistical burdens of trial advocacy limit the extent to which trial counsel is able to supplement the district judge's legal research with memoranda and briefs. Thus, trial judges often must resolve complicated legal questions without benefit of "extended reflection [or] extensive information."

Courts of appeals, on the other hand, are structurally suited to the collaborative juridical process that promotes decisional accuracy. With the record having been constructed below and settled for purposes of the appeal, appellate judges can devote their primary attention to legal issues. As questions of law become the focus of appellate review, it can be expected that the parties' briefs will be refined to bring to bear on the legal issues more information and more comprehensive analysis than was provided for the district judge. Perhaps most important, courts of appeals employ multi-judge panels that permit reflective dialogue and collective judgment....

Independent appellate review necessarily entails a careful consideration of the district court's legal analysis, and an efficient and sensitive appellate court at least will naturally consider this analysis in undertaking its review. Petitioner readily acknowledges the importance of a district court's reasoning to the appellate court's review. Any expertise possessed by the district court will inform the structure and content of its conclusions of law and thereby become evident to the reviewing court. If the court of appeals finds that the district court's analytical sophistication and research have exhausted the state-law inquiry, little more need be said in the appellate opinion. Independent review, however, does not admit of unreflective reliance on a lower court's inarticulable intuitions. Thus, an appropriately respectful application of *de novo* review should encourage a district court to explicate with care the basis for its legal conclusions. See Fed. Rule Civ. Proc. 52(a) (requiring the district court to "state separately its conclusions of law").

Those circumstances in which Congress or this Court has articulated a standard of deference for appellate review of district-court determinations reflect an accommodation of the respective institutional advantages of trial and appellate courts. In deference to the unchallenged superiority of the district court's factfinding ability, Rule 52(a) commands that a trial court's findings of fact "shall not be set aside unless clearly erroneous, and due regard shall be given to the opportunity of the trial court to judge of the credibility of the witnesses." In addition, it is "especially common" for issues involving supervision of litigation to be reviewed for abuse of discretion. Finally, we have held that deferential review of mixed questions of law and fact is warranted when it appears that the district court is "better positioned" than the appellate court to decide the issue in question or that probing appellate scrutiny will not contribute to the clarity of legal doctrine.

Nothing about the exercise of diversity jurisdiction alters these functional components of decisionmaking or otherwise warrants departure from a rule of independent appellate review. Actually, appellate deference to the district court's determination of state law is inconsistent with the principles underlying this Court's decision in *Erie*. The twin aims of the *Erie* doctrine — "discouragement of forum-shopping and avoidance of inequitable administration of the laws" — are components of the goal of doctrinal coherence advanced by independent appellate review. As respondent has conceded, deferential appellate review invites divergent development of state law among the federal trial courts even within a single State. Moreover, by denying a litigant access to meaningful review of state-law claims, appellate courts that defer to the district courts' state-law determinations create a dual system of enforcement of state-created rights, in which the substantive rule applied to a dispute may depend on the choice of forum. Neither of these results, unavoidable in the absence of independent appellate review, can be reconciled with the commands of *Erie*.

. . .

IV

The obligation of responsible appellate review and the principles of a cooperative judicial federalism underlying *Erie* require that courts of appeals review the state-law determinations of district courts de novo. The Court of Appeals in this case therefore erred in deferring to the local expertise of the District Court.

The judgment of the Court of Appeals is reversed, and the case is remanded for further proceedings consistent with this opinion.

It is so ordered.

Chief Justice REHNQUIST, with whom Justice WHITE and Justice STEVENS join, dissenting. [Opinion omitted.]

Notes

1. What is *de novo* review? What weight is given to the trial court's decision on an issue that is subject to *de novo* review? According to *Salve Regina College*, what is one type of issue that an appellate court reviews *de novo*? Why is that type of issue suited for *de novo* review? The Court described other standards of review and when they apply. What are those standards? To what type of issues do they apply and why?

2. The Supreme Court explained that *de novo* review does not apply to all issues. But why should it not? Would it not be better to have *de novo* review—a fresh look by a second court—of all issues? What harm would be created if every issue were reviewed *de novo*?

3. The *Salve Regina* opinion mentions the review standard for factual findings. In the federal system, if the judge is the factfinder, his or her factual findings will be reviewed under a "clearly erroneous" standard. *See* Fed. R. Civ. P. 52(a)(6). Review under the clearly erroneous standard has been described as requiring a "definite and firm conviction that a mistake has been committed." *See Easley v. Cromartie*, 532 U.S. 234, 242 (2001).

4. When the jury, not the judge, is a factfinder in a civil case, the jury, unlike the judge, does not articulate all of the facts that it found. The review of its decision is therefore by a different standard than for the factual findings made by a judge. The court of appeals reviews the jury's verdict to determine whether it is supported by "substantial evidence." Substantial evidence is such relevant evidence as reasonable minds might accept as adequate to support a conclusion even if it is possible to draw a contrary conclusion from the evidence.

5. Factual findings necessarily include credibility determinations. For example, in order to decide the facts, the factfinder must decide which of two witnesses, who describe an event differently, is more credible. The factfinder may adopt the version of the facts presented by the witness it deems more credible.

The appellate court decision that follows illustrates the application of one of the standards of review—abuse of discretion.

Pugh v. Louisville Ladder, Inc.

United States Court of Appeals for the Fourth Circuit

361 Fed. Appx. 448, 2010 WL 55541 (2010)

DAVIS, District Judge:

In this product liability diversity case, James Paul Pugh, III ("Pugh") alleged that a ladder manufactured by Louisville Ladder, Inc., ("LL") structurally failed during normal use, causing Pugh to fall and suffer injuries. At trial, two engineering experts testified on behalf of Pugh and the jury returned a verdict in Pugh's favor. LL filed the instant appeal arguing that the district court abused its discretion with respect to three evidentiary rulings. [This edited version of the opinion focuses on only one of those rulings.] Finding no abuse of discretion, we affirm.

I.

A.

Excluding the few seconds during which Pugh fell from his ladder, the facts are undisputed. Pugh purchased an eight-foot LL ladder from Home Depot in March of 2003. The ladder was manufactured in Mexico in July of 2002 and had a "load capacity" of 225 pounds. Pugh read all of the warnings on the ladder label and the ladder showed no visible signs of damage at the time of purchase or at the time of use. After purchasing the ladder in March of 2003, Pugh hung it on hooks in his garage where it remained until July 10, 2003, when he used it for the first time.

On July 10, 2003, Pugh placed the ladder on his living room floor in order to install a skylight shade. At the time, Pugh weighed 215 pounds and was carrying less than 10 pounds of tools while using the ladder. Pugh went up and down the ladder twice without incident. On Pugh's third trip up the ladder, he fell while standing on the ladder's sixth step. Pugh has no memory of the actual fall, but recalls later realizing that he was lying on the ground. When Pugh realized that he had fallen, he was dazed and disoriented and felt pain in his head, neck, and shoulders. Pugh was taken to the emergency room and was diagnosed with muscle strain and a concussion.

After Pugh's fall, his ladder evidenced extensive structural damage. The worst damage was located on each of the side rails, between the first and second steps on the left rail and between the second and third steps on the right rail. There were also visible cracks around and through the rivets connecting the first three steps to the side rails. After Pugh's ladder was thoroughly photographed and examined, experts for both parties agreed upon destructive testing to permit more complete examination. Upon microscopic examination at 1000x and 2000x power, Pugh's experts discovered "micro-cracks" at locations throughout the ladder, including at step seven, above the step being used by Pugh when the accident occurred.

The primary issue at trial was the manner in which Pugh's accident occurred. Pugh's theory was that his ladder had a manufacturing defect consisting of microscopic cracks at the ladder's rivets and that, during normal use, such cracks propagated into larger cracks causing catastrophic failure/buckling that resulted in Pugh's fall. In contrast, LL's theory was that the ladder was not defective and did not fail, but that Pugh tipped the ladder during use and the ladder's post-accident severely damaged condition was caused during the accident when Pugh's body fell onto the ladder.

B.

Pugh filed the instant products liability action ... against LL and Home Depot.... Both defendants moved for summary judgment, which was granted with respect to Home Depot but denied with respect to LL....

During LL's presentation of its case, defense counsel attempted to introduce evidence to establish the absence of end-user complaints reporting "cracks" on LL ladders with the same model number as the accident ladder. Pugh objected to such proposed evidence on hearsay grounds and, following a bench conference, the district court excluded such testimony based on its unreliability.

At the conclusion of the case, the jury returned a verdict in Pugh's favor. LL filed the instant appeal challenging: ... the exclusion of testimony regarding the absence of end-user complaints reporting "cracking" of LL ladders with the same model number as Pugh's ladder....

...

II.

...

District courts have broad latitude in determining the admissibility of evidence, and evidentiary rulings, including [expert] rulings, will not be overturned absent an abuse of discretion. *United States v. Delfino*, 510 F.3d 468, 470 (4th Cir.2007). However, even if the district court abuses its discretion, such evidentiary ruling "is reversible only if it affects a party's substantial rights." *Schultz v. Capital Int'l Sec., Inc.*, 466 F.3d 298, 310 (4th Cir.2006); *see* Fed. R. Evid. 103(a).

...

B.

LL [] challenges the district court's ruling excluding testimony regarding the absence of end-user complaints reporting "cracking" of LL ladders with the same model number as Pugh's ladder. At trial, a LL safety engineer testified that LL had a system in place for documenting and tracking incidents/accidents reported to LL by end users. After establishing that LL recorded all customer complaints and criticisms about its ladders, the following exchange occurred:

> LL Counsel: Now, before Mr. Pugh came along with this particular claim in the 85,000 ladders that you sold of this model, did anyone make any kind of claim that the ladder they purchased had cracked and was just unable to hold a user's weight?
>
> Pugh Counsel: Objection.
>
> Court: In that fashion, yes.
>
> LL Counsel: Did anybody claim that their L2211-08S had cracks in it?
>
> Pugh Counsel: Objection.
>
> Court: Approach the bench.

During the bench conference, Pugh immediately indicated that his objection was based on hearsay. LL responded by citing the hearsay exception set forth in FRE 803(7). Such rule states that the following evidence is not excluded by the hearsay rule:

> Evidence that a matter is not included in the memoranda reports, records, or data compilations, in any form, kept in accordance with the provisions of [the business records exception set forth in] paragraph (6), to prove the nonoccurrence or nonexistence of the matter, if the matter was of a kind of which a memorandum, report, record, or data compilation was regularly made and preserved, unless the sources of information or other circumstances indicate lack of trustworthiness.

After hearing from both parties, the district court sustained Pugh's objection to the specific "cracking" question posed, not because LL's business records were deemed to fall outside of FRE 803, but because the court found that the proffered testimony had "no reliability" based on the phrasing of the question asked to the witness. The challenged question asked whether LL received customer complaints about LL ladders that "had cracked." The court concluded that a lay person would simply not identify a structural failure, resulting in a post-accident ladder in a similar condition to Pugh's ladder, as a "cracking" failure.

Applying the deferential abuse of discretion standard, we [] conclude that overturning the district court's ruling would invade the broad discretion afforded the district court and require this court to substitute its judgment for that of the district judge. FRE 803(7) permits the introduction of the absence of a business record to prove the nonoccurrence of an event "unless the sources of information or other circumstances indicate lack of trustworthiness." While the district court used the word "reliability" and not "trustworthiness," the court's rationale for excluding the testimony was not an abuse of discretion as the district court provided adequate justification for finding that "other circumstances" rendered the proffered testimony untrustworthy.

. . .

III.

We conclude that the district court did not abuse its discretion with respect to any of the challenged evidentiary rulings. Finding no abuse of discretion, we reject LL's argument regarding the "cumulative effect" of the alleged errors. Accordingly, we affirm.

AFFIRMED.

Notes

1. *Pugh* illustrates an application of the very deferential, abuse-of-discretion standard of review. What evidence did the trial court exclude in that case? What justification did it give for excluding the evidence? What was the appellate court's reason for affirming the trial court? On what language in Federal Rule of Evidence 803(7) did the appellate court rely? How did this language give the trial court considerable discretion in its determination of an issue under that rule?
2. Assume now that the trial court in *Pugh* had allowed the evidence to be admitted. Assume also that when deciding to admit the evidence, the trial court reasoned that the value of the evidence could be determined by the jury; the plaintiff could raise questions about that value through cross-examination of the witness and could highlight those questions in closing argument, but that ultimately, it was for the jury to decide the significance

of the absence of any reports of "cracking failures." Would the trial court's decision in this hypothetical be reversed on appeal?

3. Now that you have read *Salve Regina* and *Pugh*, consider the following hypotheticals:

   Hypo 1: Plaintiff's witness A was on the witness stand answering questions for 8 hours. At the end of the 8 hours, the trial judge said to Plaintiff's counsel, "I will allow you only one more hour with this witness. You need to wrap up your questions of this witness in the next hour." Plaintiff's counsel objected to this limit on the questioning of the witness, but the trial court overruled the objection. What standard of review would an appellate court likely use to review the trial court's decision to limit the amount of time that the witness would be permitted to testify? Why did you choose that standard of review?

   Hypo 2: Plaintiff wanted to take depositions of 50 employees of the corporate defendant. Defendant objected that this was excessive and sought an order from the trial court limiting the number of depositions. The trial court granted Defendant's request, over Plaintiff's protests, and instructed Plaintiff to identify 15 employees that she would like to depose. Plaintiff thereafter deposed only 15 of Defendant's employees. Plaintiff lost at trial. On appeal, she challenged the trial court's decision to limit the number of employee depositions to 15. What standard of review will the appellate court use? Why did you choose that standard of review?

   Hypo 3: Assume Plaintiff and Defendant disagree about the interpretation of a statute. The trial court accepts Plaintiff's interpretation. What standard of review would an appellate court likely use to review the question of whether that interpretation of the statute was correct? Why did you choose that standard of review?

   Hypo 4: Assume that Defendant wanted to admit evidence at trial of conversations that he had with his neighbor, but that an obscure federal rule required the exclusion of any evidence of conversations between neighbors. (Note: Outside of this hypothetical, no such rule actually exists.) In seeking to have this evidence admitted at trial, Defendant challenged the federal rule as unconstitutional, but the trial court concluded the rule was constitutional. What standard of review would an appellate court likely use to review the trial court's conclusion that the evidentiary rule is constitutional? Why did you choose that standard of review?

D. REVIEW OF THE SUFFICIENCY OF THE EVIDENCE

The standard by which a plaintiff in a civil case must prove her claim is typically by a preponderance of the evidence. Under this standard, for the plaintiff to prevail, the jury must conclude, based on the evidence presented at trial, that the facts required for the plaintiff's claim more likely than not exist and the events more likely than not occurred.

The next case concerns how a reviewing court should review the sufficiency of the evidence after the jury has rendered a verdict. Be warned that the facts of the following case can be difficult to visualize. You are strongly encouraged to draw a model of the railroad tracks and the location of the decedent's body to help you fully understand the arguments of both parties.

Lavender v. Kurn

Supreme Court of the United States

327 U.S. 645 (1946)

Mr. Justice MURPHY delivered the opinion of the Court.

The Federal Employers' Liability Act [(FELA)] permits recovery for personal injuries to an employee of a railroad engaged in interstate commerce if such injuries result in whole or in part from the negligence of any of the officers, agents, or employees of such carrier, or by reason of any defect or insufficiency, due to its negligence, in its cars, engines, appliances, machinery, track, roadbed, works, boats, wharves, or other equipment. 45 U.S.C. § 51.

Petitioner, the administrator of the estate of L.E. Haney, brought this suit under the Act against the respondent... St. Louis-San Francisco Railway Company (Frisco) and the respondent Illinois Central Railroad Company. It was charged that Haney, while employed as a switchtender by the respondents in the switchyard of the Grand Central Station in Memphis, Tennessee, was killed as a result of respondents' negligence. Following a trial in the Circuit Court of the City of St. Louis, Missouri, the jury returned a verdict in favor of petitioner and awarded damages in the amount of $30,000. Judgment was entered accordingly.

On appeal, however, the Supreme Court of Missouri reversed the judgment, holding that there was no substantial evidence of negligence to support the submission of the case to the jury....

...

The Illinois Central tracks run north and south directly past and into the Grand Central Station. About 2700 feet south of the station the Frisco tracks cross at right angles to the Illinois Central tracks. A westbound Frisco train wishing to use the station must stop some 250 feet or more west of this crossing and back into the station over a switch line curving east and north. The events in issue center about the switch several feet north of the main Frisco tracks at the point where the switch line branches off. This switch controls the tracks at this point.

It was very dark on the evening of December 21, 1939. At about 7:30 p.m. a westbound interstate Frisco passenger train stopped on the Frisco main line, its rear some 20 or 30 feet west of the switch. Haney, in the performance of his duties, threw or opened the switch to permit the train to back into the station. The respondents claimed that Haney was then required to cross to the south side of the track before the train passed the switch; and the conductor of the train testified that he saw Haney so cross. But there was also evidence that Haney's duties required him to wait at the switch north of the track until the train had cleared, close the switch, return to his shanty near the crossing and change the signals from red to green to permit trains on the Illinois Central tracks to use the crossing. The Frisco train cleared the switch, backing at the rate of 8 or 10 miles per hour. But the switch remained open and the signals still were red. Upon investigation Haney was found north of the track near the switch lying face down on the ground, unconscious. An ambulance was called, but he was dead upon arrival at the hospital.

Haney had been struck in the back of the head, causing a fractured skull from which he died. There were no known eye-witnesses to the fatal blow. Although it is not clear[,] there is evidence that his body was extended north and south, the head to the south. Apparently he had fallen forward to the south; his face was bruised on the left side from hitting the ground and there were marks indicating that his toes had dragged a few inches southward as he fell. His head was about 5 1/2 feet north of the Frisco tracks. Estimates ranged from 2 feet to 14 feet as to how far west of the switch he lay.

The injury to Haney's head was evidenced by a gash about two inches long from which blood flowed. The back of Haney's white cap had a corresponding black mark about an inch and a half long and an inch wide, running at an angle downward to the right of the center of the back of the head. A spot of blood was later found at a point 3 or 4 feet north of the tracks. The conclusion following an autopsy was that Haney's skull was fractured by some fast moving small round object. One of the examining doctors testified that such an object might have been attached to a train backing at the rate of 8 or 10 miles per hour. But he also admitted that the fracture might have resulted from a blow from a pipe or club or some similar round object in the hands of an individual.

Petitioner's theory is that Haney was struck by the curled end or tip of a mail hook hanging down loosely on the outside of the mail car of the backing train. This curled end was 73 inches above the top of the rail, which was 7 inches high. The overhang of the mail car in relation to the rails was about 2 to 2 1/2 feet. The evidence indicated that when the mail car swayed or moved around a curve the mail hook might pivot, its curled end swinging out as much as 12 to 14 inches. The curled end could thus be swung out to a point 3 to 3 1/2 feet from the rail and about 73 inches above the top of the rail. Both east and west of the switch, however, was an uneven mound of cinders and dirt rising at its highest points 18 to 24 inches above the top of the rails. Witnesses differed as to how close the mound approached the rails, the estimates varying from 3 to 15 feet. But taking the figures most favorable to the petitioner, the mound extended to a point 6 to 12 inches north of the overhanging side of the mail car. If the mail hook end swung out 12 to 14 inches it would be 49 to 55 inches above the highest parts of the mound. Haney was 67 1/2 inches tall. If he had been standing on the mound about a foot from the side of the mail car he could have been hit by the end of the mail hook, the exact point of contact depending upon the height of the mound at the particular point. His wound was about 4 inches below the top of his head, or 63 1/2 inches above the point where he stood on the mound-well within the possible range of the mail hook end.

Respondents' theory is that Haney was murdered. They point to the estimates that the mound was 10 to 15 feet north of the rail, making it impossible for the mail hook end to reach a point of contact with Haney's head. Photographs were placed in the record to support the claim that the ground was level north of the rail for at least 10 feet. Moreover, it appears that the area immediately surrounding the switch was quite dark. Witnesses stated that it was so dark that it was impossible to see a 3-inch pipe 25 feet away. It also appears that many hoboes and tramps frequented the area at night in order to get rides on freight trains. Haney carried a pistol to protect himself. This pistol was found loose under his body by those who came to his rescue. It was testified, however, that the pistol had apparently slipped out of his pocket or scabbard as he fell. Haney's clothes were not disarranged and there was no evidence of a struggle or fight. No rods, pipes or weapons of any kind, except Haney's own pistol, were found near the scene. Moreover, his gold watch and diamond ring were still on him after he was struck. Six days later his unsoiled billfold was found on a high board fence about a block from the place where Haney was struck and near the point where he had been placed in an ambulance. It contained his social security card and other effects, but no money. His wife testified that he never carried much money, not very much more than $10. Such were the facts in relation to respondents' theory of murder.

Finally, one of the Frisco foremen testified that he arrived at the scene shortly after Haney was found injured. He later examined the fireman's side of the train very carefully and found nothing sticking out or in disorder....

The jury was instructed that Frisco [was] liable if it... negligently permitted a rod or other object to extend out from the side of the train as it backed past Haney and that Haney was killed as the direct result of such negligence, if any. The jury was further told that Illinois Central was liable if it was found that the company negligently maintained an unsafe and dangerous place for Haney to work, in that the ground was high and uneven and the light insufficient and inadequate, and that Haney was injured and killed as a direct result of the said place being unsafe and dangerous. This latter instruction as to Illinois Central did not require the jury to find that Haney was killed by something protruding from the train.

The Supreme Court, in upsetting the jury's verdict against both [Frisco] and the Illinois Central, admitted that it could be inferred from the facts that Haney could have been struck by the mail hook knob if he were standing on the south side of the mound and the mail hook extended out as far as 12 or 14 inches. But it held that all reasonable minds would agree that it would be mere speculation and conjecture to say that Haney was struck by the mail hook and that plaintiff failed to make a submissible case on that question. It also ruled that there 'was no substantial evidence that the uneven ground and insufficient light were cause or contributing causes of the death of Haney.'...

We hold, however, that there was sufficient evidence of negligence on the part of both [Frisco] and the Illinois Central to justify the submission of the case to the jury and to require appellate courts to abide by the verdict rendered by the jury.

The evidence we have already detailed demonstrates that there was evidence from which it might be inferred that the end of the mail hook struck Haney in the back of the head, an inference that the Supreme Court admitted could be drawn. That inference is not rendered unreasonable by the fact that Haney apparently fell forward toward the main Frisco track so that his head was 5 1/2 feet north of the rail. He may well have been struck and then wandered in a daze to the point where he fell forward. The testimony as to blood marks some distance away from his head lends credence to that possibility, indicating that he did not fall immediately upon being hit. When that is added to the evidence most favorable to the petitioner as to the height and swing-out of the hook, the height and location of the mound and the nature of Haney's duties, the inference that Haney was killed by the hook cannot be said to be unsupported by probative facts or to be so unreasonable as to warrant taking the case from the jury.

It is true that there is evidence tending to show that it was physically and mathematically impossible for the hook to strike Haney. And there are facts from which it might reasonably be inferred that Haney was murdered.... Under these circumstances it would be an undue invasion of the jury's historic function for an appellate court to weigh the conflicting evidence, judge the credibility of witnesses and arrive at a conclusion opposite from the one reached by the jury.

It is no answer to say that the jury's verdict involved speculation and conjecture. Whenever facts are in dispute or the evidence is such that fair-minded men may draw different inferences, a measure of speculation and conjecture is required on the part of those whose duty it is to settle the dispute by choosing what seems to them to be the most reasonable inference. Only when there is a complete absence of probative facts to support the conclusion reached does a reversible error appear. But where, as here, there is an evidentiary basis for the jury's verdict, the jury is free to discard or disbelieve whatever facts are inconsistent with its conclusion....

We are unable, therefore, to sanction a reversal of the jury's verdict against [Frisco]. Nor can we approve any disturbance in the verdict as to Illinois Central. The evidence was uncontradicted that it was very dark at the place where Haney was working and the surrounding ground was high and uneven. The evidence also showed that this area was entirely within the domination and control of Illinois Central.... It was not unreasonable to conclude that these conditions constituted an unsafe and dangerous working place and that such conditions contributed in part to Haney's death, assuming that it resulted primarily from the mail hook striking his head.

...

The judgment of the Supreme Court of Missouri is reversed and the case is remanded for whatever further proceedings may be necessary not inconsistent with this opinion.

Reversed.

The CHIEF JUSTICE and Mr. Justice FRANKFURTER concur in the result.

Mr. Justice REED dissents.

Mr. Justice JACKSON took no part in the consideration or decision of this case.

Notes

1. What were the theories as to how the plaintiff might have been injured? What evidence supported those theories? What argument did the petitioner make about the sufficiency of the evidence? How did the Supreme Court respond to that argument?
2. Assume you were a member of the jury in the *Lavender* case and had been given both of the following instructions:

   Instruction 1:

   Your verdict depends on whether you find certain facts have been proved by the greater weight of the evidence. In order to find that a fact has been proved by the greater weight of the evidence, you must find that it is more likely true than not true. It is determined by considering all of the evidence and deciding which evidence is more believable.

   Instruction 2:

   Your verdict must be for the plaintiff if all of the following elements have been proved by the greater weight of the evidence:

   First, the decedent was an employee of defendant, and

   Second, defendant failed to provide reasonably safe conditions for work, reasonably safe tools and equipment, or reasonably safe methods of work, and

   Third, defendant in any one or more of the ways described in Paragraph Second was negligent [i.e., that the defendant did not use the care that an ordinarily careful person would use in that situation],

Fourth, such negligence resulted in whole or in part in the death of the decedent.

If any of the above elements has not been proved by the greater weight of the evidence, then your verdict must be for defendant.

Assume also that the facts as suggested by the plaintiff's evidence (if true) would support a finding for the plaintiff on the first three elements of Instruction 2. How would you have decided this case? What would be the focus of your analysis? Would you consider your conclusion based on speculation or, instead, on reasonable inference? If a verdict in this case requires speculation, in what situation would the evidence not require speculation, considering that if we knew exactly what had occurred, the parties would not need a jury to resolve their dispute?

3. How does the role of the jury when deciding a case differ from the role of the judge when ruling on a motion for summary judgment? In what way, are the two — the jury and the judge — allowed to look at evidence differently? How might that difference affect the appellate court's review of the jury's verdict compared to its review of a grant of summary judgment?

4. Employees in most industries receive compensation for their work-related injuries through a workers' compensation system. Under this type of system, an injured worker receives compensation for work-related injuries without proving any fault on the part of the employer, *but* the employee's recovery is usually subject to statutory limits. Congress enacted the FELA (the statute on which the plaintiff based his claims in *Lavender*) in 1908 before this country embraced workers' compensation systems as a means of compensating injured workers. In those early years of the 20th century, "[t]he railroad business was exceptionally hazardous.... [T]he physical dangers of railroading... resulted in the death or maiming of thousands of workers every year," including 281,645 casualties in the year 1908 alone. *CSX Transp., Inc. v. McBride*, 131 S. Ct. 2630, 2636 (2011). Before the FELA was enacted, the "harsh and technical" rules of state common law had "made recovery difficult or even impossible" for injured railroad workers. *Brotherhood of R.R. Trainmen v. Virginia ex rel. Virginia State Bar*, 377 U.S. 1, 3 (1964). Congress responded by enacting the FELA. Under the FELA, the injured worker must prove some fault on the part of the employer in order to recover any compensation. If the injured worker fails in this proof, the worker will receive no compensation

from the employer. However, if the worker succeeds in such proof, there are no limits on the worker's recovery. To this day, railroad workers' exclusive protection still comes from the FELA.

In light of the purpose and role of the FELA, why might the Court have analyzed the adequacy of the evidence as it did in *Lavender*? Indeed, some courts contend that the standard that the Court applied in *Lavender* applies only to FELA cases.

5. The modern practice in most jurisdictions is to preclude review of the sufficiency of the evidence unless the party filed a motion for judgment as a matter of law in the trial court (and in federal court, renewed that motion after the verdict). For these reasons, you will see similarities between the issue presented in *Lavender* and the issue presented in *Denman v. Spain* from Chapter 6.

— ★ —

TABLES OF AUTHORITIES

TABLE OF CASES

Page numbers in **bold** are edited reproductions of cases.

A

B

C

M

O

P

R

S

TABLE OF CONSTITUTIONAL PROVISIONS

—★—

TABLE OF STATUTES

TABLE OF FEDERAL RULES

OTHER AUTHORITIES

Emad H. Atiq, *Legal vs. Factual Normative Questions & the True Scope of Ring*, 32 Notre Dame Journal of Law, Ethics & Public Policy 47 (2018), 188

Joanna C. Schwartz, *The Case Against Qualified Immunity*, 93 Notre Dame Law Rev. 1797 (2018), 167

Lisa S. Bressman & Michael P. Vandenbergh, *Inside the Administrative State: A Critical Look at the Practice of Presidential Control*, 105 Mich. L. Rev. 47 (2006), 30

Richard H. Fallon, *Bidding Farewell to Constitutional Torts*, 107 Cal. L. Rev. 933 (2019), 167

Ruth Ann McKinney, *Reading Like a Lawyer: Time-Saving Strategies for Reading Law Like an Expert* (Carolina Academic Press 2d. ed. 2014), 4

INDEX